The Devil and Commodity Fetishism
in South America

THE DEVIL AND COMMODITY FETISHISM IN SOUTH AMERICA

MICHAEL T. TAUSSIG

The University of North Carolina Press *Chapel Hill*

© 1980 The University of North Carolina Press

All rights reserved

Manufactured in the United States of America

09 08 07 06 05   15 14 13 12 11

Library of Congress Catalog Card Number 79-17685

Library of Congress Cataloging in Publication Data

Taussig, Michael T.
  The devil and commodity fetishism in South America.

  Bibliography: p.
  Includes index.
  1. Economic development—Social aspects—Case studies.
2. Plantations—Colombia—Cauca Valley.   3. Tin mines
and mining—Bolivia.   4. Superstition—Case studies.
I. Title.
HD82.T34   330.9'8'003   79-17685
ISBN 0-8078-1412-1
ISBN 0-8078-4106-4 pbk.

To the plantation workers

and miners of South America

And the Lord said unto Satan, From whence comest thou? And Satan answered the Lord, and said, From going to and fro in the earth, and from walking up and down in it.
     Job 2:2

To articulate the past historically does not mean to recognize it "the way it really was" (Ranke). It means to seize hold of a memory as it flashes up at a moment of danger. Historical materialism wishes to retain that image of the past which unexpectedly appears to man singled out by history at a moment of danger. The danger affects both the content of tradition and its receivers. The same threat hangs over both: that of becoming a tool of the ruling classes. In every era the attempt must be made anew to wrest tradition away from a conformism that is about to overpower it. The Messiah comes not only as the redeemer, he comes as the subduer of the Antichrist. Only that historian will have the gift of fanning the spark of hope in the past who is firmly convinced that even the dead will not be safe from the enemy if he wins. And this enemy has not ceased to be victorious.
     Walter Benjamin, "Theses on the Philosophy of History"

Thus the ancient conception in which man always appears (in however narrowly national, religious or political a definition) as the aim of production, seems very much more exalted than the modern world, in which production is the aim of man and wealth the aim of production.
     Karl Marx, *Pre-Capitalist Economic Formations*

Contents

Preface

My aim in this book is to elicit the social significance of the devil in the folklore of contemporary plantation workers and miners in South America. The devil is a stunningly apt symbol of the alienation experienced by peasants as they enter the ranks of the proletariat, and it is largely in terms of that experience that I have cast my interpretation. The historical and ethnographic context lead me to ask: What is the relationship between the image of the devil and capitalist development? What contradictions in social experience does the fetish of the spirit of evil mediate? Is there a structure of connections between the redeeming power of the antichrist and the analytic power of Marxism?

To answer these questions I have tried to unearth the social history of the devil since the Spanish conquest in two areas of intensive capitalist development: the sugar plantations of western Colombia, and the Bolivian tin mines. One result of this inquiry (emerging more clearly in the mines but equally pertinent to the plantations) is that the devil symbolizes important features of political and economic history. It is virtually impossible to separate the social history of this symbol from the symbolic codification of the history which creates the symbol.

The devil was brought by European imperialism to the New World, where he blended with pagan deities and the metaphysical systems represented by those deities. Yet those systems were as unlike the European as were the indigenous socioeconomic systems. Under these circumstances, the image of the devil and the mythology of redemption came to mediate the dialectical tensions embodied in conquest and the history of imperialism.

In both the plantations and the mines, the role of the devil in the folklore and rituals associated with proletarian production is significantly different from that which exists in the adjoining peasant areas. In both regions, the proletariat has been drawn from the surrounding peasantry, whose experience of commoditization and whose interpretation of proletarianization is heavily influenced by its precapitalist views of the economy. Within the process of proletarianization, the devil emerges as a powerful and complex image, which mediates opposed ways of viewing the human significance of the economy.

There is a vast store of mythology in both Western and South American cultures concerning the man who sets himself apart from the community to sell his soul to the devil for wealth that is not only useless but the harbinger of despair, destruction, and death. What does this contract with the devil symbolize? The age old struggle of good and evil? The innocence of the poor and the evil of wealth? More than this, the fabled devil contract is an indictment of an economic system which forces men to barter their souls for the destructive powers of commodities. Of its plethora of interconnected and often contradictory meanings, the devil contract is outstanding in this regard: man's soul cannot be bought or sold, yet under certain historical conditions mankind is threatened by this mode of exchange as a way of making a livelihood. In recounting this fable of the devil, the righteous man confronts the struggle of good and evil in terms that symbolize some of the most acute contradictions of market economies. The individual is dislocated from the community. Wealth exists alongside crushing poverty. Economic laws triumph over ethical ones. Production, not man, is the aim of the economy, and commodities rule their creators.

The devil has long been banished from Western consciousness, yet the issues symbolized by a contract with him remain as poignant as ever—no matter how much they have been obscured by a new type of fetishism in which commodities are held to be their own source of value. It is against this obfuscation, the fetishism of commodities, that both this book and the devil beliefs are directed. The concept of commodity fetishism, as advanced by Karl Marx in *Capital*, is basic to my deconstruction of the spirit of evil in capitalist relations of production. The fetishization of evil, in the image of the devil, is an image which mediates the conflict between precapitalist and capitalist modes of objectifying the human condition.

Part I of this book concerns the social history of the African slaves and their descendants in the sugar plantations of western Colombia. Together with my *compañera* and coworker Anna Rubbo, I spent almost four years in and around that area. We worked mainly as anthropologists, and were involved in the militant peasant political organization that flourished there in the early 1970s. That experience and the ethnography compiled during that time form the basis for the first half of this book. Without Anna's assistance and the active collaboration of the peasants and day laborers involved in that struggle, this book would not have been written. Most of chapter 3 has appeared previously in *Marxist Perspectives* (Summer, 1979), and chapter 6 contains a great deal of an article I published in *Comparative Studies in Society and History* (April, 1977).

Part II concerns the significance of the devil in the Bolivian tin mines, and here I have had to rely heavily on the writing of others. Especially important to me have been the works of June Nash, Juan Rojas, John Earls, José Maria Arguedas, Joseph Bastien, and Weston LaBarre, as cited in the bibliography. To these authors, and many others referred to in the following pages, I am highly indebted.

I am grateful to the following institutions for their funding of my fieldwork in western Colombia since 1970: the University of London, the Foreign Area Fellowship Program, the Wenner-Gren Foundation, the National Science Foundation, and the Rackham School of Graduate Studies at the University of Michigan, Ann Arbor. I owe special thanks to David Perry of the University of North Carolina Press for his meticulous editing.

PART I

Fetishism: The Master Trope

So that, as rational metaphysics teaches that man becomes all things by understanding them, this imaginative metaphysics shows that man becomes all things by not understanding them; and perhaps the latter proposition is truer than the former, for when man understands he extends his mind and takes in the things, but when he does not understand he makes the things out of himself and becomes them by transforming himself into them.

Giambattista Vico, *The New Science*

CHAPTER I

Fetishism and Dialectical Deconstruction

his book attempts to interpret what are to us in the industrialized world the exotic ideas of some rural people in Colombia and Bolivia concerning the meaning of the capitalist relations of production and exchange into which they are daily being drawn. These peasants represent as vividly unnatural, even as evil, practices that most of us in commodity-based societies have come to accept as natural in the everyday workings of our economy, and therefore of the world in general. This representation occurs only when they are proletarianized and refers only to the way of life that is organized by capitalist relations of production. It neither occurs in nor refers to peasant ways of life.

Any work of interpretation includes elements of uncertainty and intellectual self-effacement. For what truth is being displayed by one's interpretation? Is it nothing more than a mediation between the unfamiliar and the familiar? Assuredly, that is the more honest, if less grandiose, practice of the interpreter; yet, in confronting the implications of this practice we discern that the interpretation of the unfamiliar in terms of the familiar impugns the familiar itself. The truth of interpretation lies in its intellectual structure of contrasts, and its reality is inherently self-critical.

So, although this work focuses on the cultural reactions of peasants to industrial capitalism and attempts to interpret those reactions, it is, inevitably, also an esoteric attempt to critically illuminate the ways by which those of us who are long accustomed to capitalist culture have arrived at the point at which this familiarity persuades us that our cultural form is not historical, not social, not human, but natural—"thing-like" and physical. In other words, it is an attempt forced upon us by confrontation with precapitalist cultures to account for the phantom objectivity with which capitalist culture enshrouds its social creations.

Time, space, matter, cause, relation, human nature, and society itself are social products created by man just as are the different types of tools, farming systems, clothes, houses, monuments, languages, myths, and so on, that mankind has produced since the dawn of human life. But to their participants, all cultures tend to present these categories as if they were not social products but elemental and immutable things. As soon as such categories are defined as natural, rather than as social, products, epistemology itself acts to conceal understanding of the social order. Our experience, our understanding, our explanations—all serve merely to ratify the conventions that sustain our sense of reality unless we appreciate the extent to which the basic "building blocks" of our experience and our sensed reality are not natural but social constructions.

In capitalist culture this blindness to the social basis of essential categories makes a social reading of supposedly natural things deeply perplexing. This is due to the peculiar character of the abstractions associated with the market organization of human affairs: essential qualities of human beings and their products are converted into commodities, into things for buying and selling on the market. Take the example of labor and labor-time. For our system of industrial production to operate, people's productive capacities and nature's resources have to be organized into markets and rationalized in accord with cost accounting: the unity of production and human life is broken into smaller and smaller quantifiable subcomponents. Labor, an activity of life itself, thus becomes something set apart from life and abstracted into the commodity of labor-time, which can be bought and sold on the labor market. This commodity appears to be substantial and real. No longer an abstraction, it appears to be something natural and immutable, even though it is nothing more than a convention or a social construction emerging from a specific way of organizing persons relative to one another and to nature. I take this process as a paradigm of the object-making process in an industrial capitalist society: specifically, concepts such as labor-time are abstracted from the social context and appear to be real things.

Of necessity, a commodity-based society produces such phantom objectivity, and in so doing it obscures its roots—the relations between people. This amounts to a socially instituted paradox with bewildering manifestations, the chief of which is the denial by the society's members of the social construction of reality. Another manifestation is the schizoid attitude with which the members of such a society necessarily confront the phantom objects that have been thus abstracted from social life, an attitude that shows itself to be deeply mystical. On the one hand, these abstractions are cherished as real objects akin to inert things, whereas on the other, they are thought of as animate entities with a life-force of their own akin to spirits or gods. Since these "things" have lost their original connection with social life, they appear, paradoxically, both as inert and as animate entities. If the test of a first-rate intelligence is the ability to hold two opposed ideas at the same time and still retain the ability to function, then the modern mind can truly be said to have proved itself. But this is testimony to culture, not to mind. E. E. Evans-Pritchard gives us an account of the category of time among a people whose society is not organized by commodity production and market exchange, the Nuer of the Upper Nile.

> Though I have spoken of time and units of time the Nuer have no expression equivalent to "time" in our language, and they cannot, therefore, as we can, speak of time as though it were something actual, which passes, can be wasted, can be saved, and so forth. I do not think that they ever experience the same feeling of fighting against time or having to coordinate activities with an abstract passage of time, because their points of reference are mainly the activities themselves, which are generally of a leisurely character. Events follow a logical order, but they are not controlled by an abstract system, there being no autonomous points of reference to which activities have to conform with precision. Nuer are fortunate. [1940:103]

Time for these people is not abstracted from the tissue of life activities, but is embedded in them. It is not clock time but what we could call human time: time is social relations. Yet, as Evans-Pritchard illustrates, we both abstract and actualize time. For us, as E. P. Thompson has vividly displayed using this same example, it is an abstraction, but also a substance, it passes, it can be wasted, it can be saved, and so forth (1967). Moreover, it is animated: so we speak of fighting against it. Time becomes a thing abstracted from social relations because of the specific character of those social relations, and it also becomes an animated substance. This I take to be but a particular illustration of commodity fetishism, whereby the products of the interrelations of persons are no longer seen as such, but as things that stand over, control, and in some vital sense even may produce people. The task before us is to liberate ourselves from the fetishism and phantom objectivity with which society obscures itself, to take issue with the ether of naturalness that confuses and disguises social relations. The "natural" appearance of such things has to be exposed as a social product that can itself determine reality; thus, society may become master of its self-victimization.

In other words, rather than ask the standard anthropological question Why do people in a foreign culture respond in the way they do to, in this case, the development of capitalism? we must ask about the reality associated with our society. For this is the question that their fantastic reactions to our nonfantastic reality force upon us, if only we have the wit to take heed. By turning the question this way we allow the anthropologist's informants the privilege of explicating and publicizing their own criticisms of the forces that are affecting their society—forces which emanate from ours. By this one step we free ourselves of the attitude that defines curious folk wisdom as only fabulation or superstition. At the same time we become sensitive to the superstitions and ideological character of our own culture's central myths and categories, categories that grant meaning as much to our intellectual products as to our everyday life. And it is with the discomfort that such sensitivity breeds that we are forced into awareness of the commonplace and of what we take as natural. We are forced into casting aside the veil of naturalness that we have laid as a pall over the process of social development, obscuring the one feature that distinguishes it from the process of natural development, the involvement of human consciousness. Thus, we are led to challenge the normalcy given to our casting society in the realm of nature. This is our praxis.

My motivation for writing stems both from the effects of four years of fieldwork and involvement in southwestern Colombia in the early 1970s and from my belief that the socially conditioned translation of history and of the human quality of social relations into facts of nature desensitizes society and robs it of all that is inherently critical of its inner form. Yet this translation is ubiquitous in modern society and nowhere more salient than in the "social sciences," in which the natural science model has itself become a natural reflex, institutionally deployed as the guiding strategy for comprehending social life, but which finally only petrifies it. My task, therefore, is to impugn this deployment, to convey something of the "feel" of social experience which the natural science paradigm obscures, and in so doing to construct a criticism that is directed against the petrification of social life by positivist doctrines, which I see as uncritical reflections of society's disguised appearance.

Confronted with this modern mode of comprehension it is all too easy to slip into other forms of idealism, and also into an uncritical nostalgia for times past when human relations were not seen as object-relations beholden to marketing strategies. Because the ethnography with which I am dealing pertains largely to what are sometimes called precapitalist societies, these dangers become pressing problems. For such social formations easily seduce in precisely this problematic way the mind trained and honed by capitalist institutions. Set against the images that capitalist society presents of itself, precapitalist life can appeal (or frighten) on account of its apparent idealism and the enchantment of its universe by spirits and phantoms that display the course of the world and its salvation. Furthermore, precapitalist societies acquire the burden of having to satisfy our alienated longings for a lost Golden Age.

Faced with the unsatisfactory and indeed politically motivated paradigms of explanation that have been insinuated into the mental fiber of modern capitalist society—its mechanical materialism as well as its alienated forms in religion and nostalgia—what counterstrategy is available for the illumination of reality that does not in some subtle way replicate its ruling ideas, its dominant passions, and its enchantment of itself? As I see it, this question is both necessary and utopian. It is essential to pose the challenge, but it is utopian to believe that we can imagine our way out of our culture without acting on it in practical ways that alter its social infrastructure. For this reason, what I call negative criticism is all that is possible, apt, and demanded at the intellectual level. This implies that we adhere to a mode of interpretation that is unremittingly aware of its procedures and categories; thus, our thought is exposed to itself as a process of escalating self-criticism in which self-consciousness finally establishes itself in the realm of the concrete phenomena that initiated our inquiry and led to the first empirical abstractions and distortions of it. But if the mode of comprehension that we espouse is this ever-widening network of self-aware description of the concrete, then it must also be clearly understood, as Fredric Jameson has insisted, that this self-awareness must be acutely sensitive to the social roots and historicity of the abstractions that we employ at any stage of the process (1971).

This self-awareness prefigures the concept of culture and the theory of perception that I employ, as invoked by Sidney Hook's early interpretation of Marxist epistemology. "What is beheld in perception," he writes, "depends just as much upon the perceiver as upon the antecedent causes of perception. And since the mind meets the world with a long historical development behind it, what it sees, its selective reaction, the scope and manner of its attention are to be explained, not merely as physical or biological fact, but as social fact as well" (1933:89). It is, of course, the peculiar and specific character of social relations in market society that has facilitated the insensitivity, if not blindness, to this position, so that the scope and manner of the mind's attention is explained only as physical or biological fact, and not as social fact, as well. In other words, the social fact works in our consciousness to deny itself and to be consumed in the physical and biological.

In Franz Boas's anthropology we find further support for the concept of culture that I wish to use. In highlighting one of Boas's early papers, George W. Stocking, Jr., writes, that this paper "sees cultural phenomena in terms of the imposition of conventional meaning on the flux of experience. It sees them as historically conditioned and transmitted by the learning process. It sees them as determinants of our very perceptions of the external world" (1968 : 159). But Boas's conception is denuded of the tension that is imparted by the meaning of modern history that conditions the learning process. It is not just that our perception is historically conditioned, that the eye becomes here an organ of history, that sensations are a form of activity and not passive carbon copies of externals, but that the history that informs this activity also informs our understanding of seeing and of history itself. And the most forceful and cloying legacy of modern history shaping our experience and therefore our conceptual tools is undoubtedly the alienated relations of person to nature, of subjectivity to its object, and the relations that are formed by social class, by commodity production, and by market exchange. The abstractions we bring to bear on any concrete phenomena will of necessity reflect these alienated relations, but in being aware of this and its implications and in raising it to our consciousness, we can choose whether we will continue to disguise the categories unthinkingly as manifestations of the natural or whether we will reveal them in all their intensity as the evolving product of mutual human relations, albeit concealed by their reified appearance in a society based on commodity production.

The recognition of this choice is the first essential of the historically sensitive dialectician, who must then proceed to work a way out of the socially stamped validation of social facts as physical and autonomous entities akin to immutable and natural things. Marx struggles with this paradox in his analysis of the commodity as both a thing and a social relation, from whence he derives his concept of commodity fetishism as a critique of capitalist culture: the animate appearance of commodities provides testimony to the thing-like appearance of persons, appearances that dissolve once it is pointed out that the definitions of man and of society are market inspired. Similarly, Karl Polanyi berates the market mentality and the market way of seeing the world in his concept of the commodity fiction. It is a fiction, he states, that land and labor are things produced for sale. "Labor is only another name for a human activity that goes with life itself," and "land is only another name for nature, which is not produced by man" (1957:72). Yet in a market organized society this fiction becomes reality, and the system of names that Polanyi draws upon loses its meaning. In its market form society engenders this fictional reality, and it is with these abstractions or symbols that we are forced to operate and comprehend the world.

Yet, to overcome the reifictions imposed on thought by the market organization of reality, it is not enough to realize that the reified appearance of social products is symbolic of social relations. For in such a society symbols acquire peculiar properties, and the social relations signified are far from being transparent. Unless we also realize that the social relations symbolized in things are themselves distorted and self-concealing ideological constructs, all we will have achieved is the substitution of a naive mechanical materialism by an equally naive objective idealism ("symbolic analysis"), which reifies symbols in place of social relations. The social relations that the analyst reads in the symbols, the collective representations, and the objects that fill our daily life are more often than not conventions about social relations and human nature that society parades as its true self. I think this is particularly clear with Emile Durkheim and neo-Durkheimians such as Mary Douglas who analyze symbols and collective representations as emanations of something they call "social structure," reify structure, and in so doing uncritically accept society's distorted projection of itself. The point is that we can abandon mechanical materialism and become aware that facts and things stand in some way as signs for social relations. We then look for the meaning of these signs in this way. But unless we realize that the social relations thus signified are themselves signs and social constructs defined by categories of thought that are also the product of society and history, we remain victims of and apologists for the semiotic that we are seeking to understand. To peel off the disguised and fictional quality of our social reality, the analyst has the far harder task of working through the appearance that phenomena acquire, not so much as symbols, but as the outcome of their interaction with the historically produced categories of thought that have been imposed on them. Karl Marx directs our attention to this where he writes that the signs or "characters that stamp products as commodities, and whose establishment is a necessary preliminary to the circulation of commodities, have already acquired the stability of natural self-understood forms of social life, before man seeks to decipher, not their historical character, for in his eyes they are immutable, but their meaning" (1967, 1:75).

Artfully mediating the self-validating categories of their epoch, the political economists gave voice and force to a symbolic system in the guise of an economic analysis. The meaning of value, symbolized by money, presupposed for them the universal and natural validity of the signs and abstractions engendered by the market mechanism. They presupposed a commoditized world and this presupposition persists today as the natural way of viewing social life. Conditioned by history and society, the human eye assumes its perceptions to be real. It cannot, without great effort, contemplate its perception as a movement of thought that ratifies the signs through which history expresses itself. But to the critic who can stand outside this mutually confirming system of signs the money form of the world of the commodities is the sign that conceals the social relations hidden in the abstractions that society takes to be natural phenomena.

Because the cultures with which this book is concerned are not market organized but market dominated, we are provided with an opportunity to adopt this very same critical stance. Certain human realities become clearer at the periphery of the capitalist system, making it easier for us to brush aside the commoditized apprehension of reality. Marx expressed this potential that lies within the anthropologist's grasp as a source of great power for demotivating the links of meaning that commodity production engendered in the minds of its participants. "The whole mystery of commodities," he wrote in the famous chapter dealing with the fetishism of commodities, wherein he assailed the principal categories of bourgeois thought, "all the magic and necromancy that surrounds the products of labour as long as they take the form of commodities, vanishes therefore, so soon as we come to other forms of production."

With the aid of some of these "other forms of production" this book therefore attempts to interpret capitalist forms of comprehension of social reality. My strategy is to view certain fantastic and magical reactions to our nonfantastic reality as part of a critique of the modern mode of production. It would be a mistake to emphasize the exotic quality of the reactions of these peasants if, by virtue of such an emphasis, we overlook the similar beliefs and ethical condemnations that characterized much economic thought in the history of Western culture down to the end of the Middle Ages, if not beyond. From Aristotle through the teachings of the early Christian Fathers to the Schoolmen a similar hostility toward usury, profiteering, and unjust exchange can be found. However, this hostility was intensified and became associated with the belief in the devil only in the late Middle Ages, the same time that capitalism was on the rise.

Societies on the threshold of capitalist development necessarily interpret that development in terms of precapitalist beliefs and practices. This is nowhere more florid than in the folk beliefs of the peasants, miners, seafarers, and artisans who are involved in the transition process. Their culture, like their work, organically connects soul with hand, and the world of enchanted beings that they create seems as intensely human as the relations that enter into their material products. The new experience of commodity production fragments and challenges that organic interconnection. Yet the meaning of that mode of production and of the contradictions that it now poses is inevitably assimilated into patterns that are preestablished in the group's culture. Those patterns will be changed, to be sure, but not until the commodity economy has created a new epistemology in which the soul itself becomes either a commodity or a deeply alienated spirit and disenchantment sets in. Until the new spirit, the spirit of capitalism, displaces the creations of the imagination that give meaning to life in the precapitalist world, until the new "rules of the game" are assimilated, the fabulations that the commodity engenders will be subject to quite different sorts of fantasy formation. In short, the meaning of capitalism will be subject to precapitalist meanings, and the conflict expressed in such a confrontation will be one in which man is seen as the aim of production, and not production as the aim of man.

Although the insights that are intrinsic to such a reaction seem inevitably to pass away with time and the progressive institutionalization of capitalist structures and common sense eventually accepts the new conditions as natural ones, certain bodies of thought, as well as enormous social movements, have kept them alive and functioning as a critical world force. Marxism and Marxist revolutionary movements in the modern era represent the "rationalization" of the early precapitalist outrage at the expansion of the capitalist system. In this sense Tawney was justified when he referred to Marx as "the last of the Schoolmen." Emphasizing this commonality between Marxism and the precapitalist hostility toward the flowering of the market economy, we must not forget that they also share epistemological features, as well as an anticapitalist moralism and a lauding of the producers' ethic. This common epistemological basis is all too easily overlooked because it is precisely this level of thought and culture that is most taken for granted, although it tenaciously permeates and guides interpretation, including the interpretation of Marxism itself.

Marxism, as it has come to be generally understood in the West, has itself been deeply influenced by that stream of modern thought that is loosely referred to as positivism, and even more loosely but more vividly as vulgar materialism. The mechanistic concepts of ontology and epistemology through which reality is understood as material atoms that interact in accordance with mathematical laws have progressively undermined the critical impetus of Marxism, which was originally based on a synthetic and dialectical understanding of reality in accordance with the Hegelian tradition, albeit sharply qualified by the idea that the content of logic is historical. If we are ever to plumb the full significance of the hostility and the perception of unnaturalness that capitalism can engender among its new work force, we must return to this tradition of the dialectical and historical method, which underscores the role of consciousness in social development, in order to empower the social development of critical consciousness.

If there is an overall aim today that is both intellectually and morally commendable in the mission that is anthropology—the "study of man"—it is not only that the study of other societies reveals the way in which they are influenced by ours but also that such investigations provide us with some critical leverage with which to assess and understand the sacrosanct and unconscious assumptions that are built into and emerge from our social forms. It is with this clearly in mind that the following pages have been written concerning the view of nature and man revealed to us by these rural people in South America who are now undergoing the travail of proletarianization.

CHAPTER 2

The Devil and Commodity Fetishism

I n two widely separated areas of rural South America, as peasant cultivators become landless wage laborers, they invoke the devil as part of the process of maintaining or increasing production. However, as peasants working their own land according to their own customs they do not do this. It is only when they are proletarianized that the devil assumes such an importance, no matter how poor and needy these peasants may be and no matter how desirous they are of increasing production. Whereas the imagery of God or the fertility spirits of nature dominates the ethos of labor in the peasant mode of production, the devil and evil flavor the metaphysics of the capitalist mode of production in these two regions. This book is an attempt to interpret the meaning and implications of this stupendous contrast.

Among the displaced Afro-American peasants who are employed as wage workers by the rapidly expanding sugarcane plantations at the southern end of the tropical Cauca Valley in Colombia are some who are supposed to enter into secret contracts with the devil in order to increase their production and hence their wage. Such a contract is said to have baneful consequences for capital and human life. Moreover, it is believed to be pointless to spend the wage gained through the devil contract on capital goods such as land or livestock because these wages are inherently barren: the land will become sterile, and the animals will not thrive and will die. Likewise, the life-force in the plantation's inventory, the sugarcane, is rendered barren, too: no more cane will sprout from a ratoon cut by a cane cutter who has entered into a devil contract. In addition, it is also said by many persons that the individual who makes the contract, invariably a man, will die prematurely and in pain. Short-term monetary gain under the new conditions of wage labor is more than offset by the supposed long-term effects of sterility and death.

Somewhat similarly, displaced Indian peasants who work as wage-earning tin miners in the Bolivian highlands have created work-group rituals to the devil, whom they regard as the true owner of the mine and the mineral. They do this, it is said, to maintain production, to find rich ore-bearing veins, and to reduce accidents (Nash, 1972; Costas Arguedas, 1961, 2:303–4). Although he is believed to sustain production, the devil is also seen as a gluttonous spirit bent on destruction and death. As he is on the Colombian sugar plantations, the devil is a mainstay of production or of increasing production, but this production is believed to be ultimately destructive of life.

It should be noted that political militancy and left-wing consciousness are high in both of these areas and in both of these industries. Prior to the recent oppression and reorganization of the work force, a large proportion of the Cauca Valley plantation workers belonged to aggressive and skillful trade unions. Strikes and occupations were common. The militancy of the Bolivian mine workers is legendary. Since its inception in 1945 the miners' union has controlled the entire Bolivian labor movement (Klein, 1969:19); for example, June Nash states that as a result of continuous political struggle the workers of the San José mine form one of the most thoroughly politicized segments of the Latin American working class (1972:223).

Interpretations

Is the devil-belief with its associated rite best interpreted as a response to anxiety and thwarted desire? This interpretation of magic and religion is exceedingly popular and has a prestigious pedigree in anthropology. Extending the ideas established by E. B. Tylor and J. G. Frazer, Malinowski argued that magic was a pseudoscience, which was invoked to relieve anxiety and frustration when gaps in knowledge and limitations of reason overcame people in a prescientific culture. In brief, magic is to be explained largely by its purported function or utility.

However, this mode of interpretation is unacceptable because it presupposes most of what needs explaining—the richly detailed motifs and precise configuration of details and meanings that constitute the beliefs and rites in question. Furthermore, it actively diverts attention from the inner meaning of these phenomena. This becomes obvious if we ask this question of the devil-belief and rite: Why is this particular set of ideas, with its pointed meaning and wealth of embedded mythology, chosen in this specific circumstance and time, rather than another set of ideas and practices? Once we raise this question, a different mode of interpretation is suggested. The beliefs of concern to us evolve from a conflict in the world of meaning, from a culture that strives creatively to organize new experiences into a coherent vision that is enlivened by its implications for acting on the world. Magical beliefs are revelatory and fascinating not because they are ill-conceived instruments of utility but because they are poetic echoes of the cadences that guide the innermost course of the world. Magic takes language, symbols, and intelligibility to their outermost limits, to explore life and thereby to change its destination.

Another plausible explanation for the devil-beliefs is that they form part of an egalitarian social ethic that delegitimizes those persons who gain more money and success than the rest of the social group. By imputing to the successful an allegiance to the devil, a restraint is imposed on would-be entrepreneurs. This fits well with the widespread opinion that envy is the motive for sorcery, and it also fits well with the image of the "limited good" ascribed by George Foster to Latin American peasant communities (1960–61; 1965). According to him the world view in these communities regards the good things in life as finite and few; thus, if a person acquires more good things than is customary, that person is in effect taking them away from other people. Now although it appears very plausible to suggest that an egalitarian ideology is associated with the devil-beliefs, this does not go far toward explaining the specific nature of the beliefs in question. Just as an explanation that reduces these beliefs to an emotion such as anxiety is defective, so any explanation that uses function or consequences tells us next to nothing about the metaphors and motifs that the cultures have elaborated in response to their new social condition. To cite some initial problems it could be observed that of the Cauca Valley wage workers only the males are said to make devil contracts for production. What can the image of the "limited good" tell us about this sex difference? Even more important, what critical insight can it bestow on the fact that the devil contracts occur only in conditions of proletarian labor and not in the peasant mode of production? In the Bolivian tin mines the devil rites may well play a role in restraining competition among miners, but that is a deeply complex issue and should not obscure the point that these rites refer to the global political-economic relationship of contested social classes and to the character and meaning of work.

The point cannot withstand too general an application, but it might be noted that the sorts of functionalist interpretations with which I am dissatisfied have an affinity with capitalism and capitalist epistemology—the very cultural form against which the devil-beliefs seem to be pitted. The crucial feature of such modes of interpretation is to reduce a welter of social relationships and intellectual complexes to the one metaphysical abstraction of usefulness. As Marx and Engels argued in *The German Ideology* (1970:109–14), and as many other writers, such as Louis Dumont (1977), have argued since then, this mode of satisfying inquiry by far precedes the utilitarians proper and comes to the fore with the victory of the bourgeoisie in the English revolutions of the seventeenth century. Marx and Engels suggested that interpretations are made with the single criterion of usefulness because in modern bourgeois society all relations are subordinated in practice to the one abstract monetary-commercial relation. Actual relations of people in situations of intercourse like speech and love are supposed not to have the meaning peculiar to them, they wrote, but to be the expression and manifestation of some third relation that is attributed to them—utility. Hence, these relations are seen as disguises of utility. They are interpreted not as themselves but as the profit that they render the individual who disguises his or her interest. This can be seen as an exploitation of intrinsic meaning and as a reduction of relation to individuation that are quite analogous to the bourgeois world view and practical social behavior as Marx critiqued them and as Foster assumes them for Latin American peasants. As Chandra Jayawardena has observed in his critique of Foster's concept, the assertion that all the good things in life, in the mind of the peasant, exist in finite and short supply, is nothing more than the assertion of the principle of scarce resources, incorporated as an axiom in modern economic theory originally developed in and applied to capitalist organization (1968).

It should be added that in the situations of concern here, in Colombia and Bolivia, the workers and the peasants are acutely aware that the economic pie is expandable and is expanding. To their minds it is not the "good" that is limited. What they object to is *how* it is expanding and not the expansion per se. Given the recent concern in developed Western economies with "zero growth" and with "mindless growth," this deserves elaboration, particularly since it is often asserted that peasant and "primitive" economies are based on a zero-growth model. Whether or not this is true, it is as important to draw attention to the character of growth as it is to draw attention to its rate of increase or its stasis. One of our earliest informants on this issue, Aristotle, was clearly of the opinion that the mode, rather than the rate of growth, was crucial to social well-being. As Eric Roll, in his commentary on Aristotle's critique of money making and "capitalism," paraphrases: "The natural purpose of exchange, the more abundant satisfaction of wants, is lost sight of; the accumulation of money becomes an end in itself" (1973:33); rather than serve as an appeal for zero growth, this clearly displays a concern with the character and causes of economic growth. Thus, we have an opposition between the "more abundant satisfaction of wants," on one side, and the accumulation of money as an end in itself, on the other. From this point of view growth is as legitimate to an economy of *use-values* or want satisfactions as it is to an economy based on money profits and capital accumulation. It is not growth per se but the character and immense human significance of a society geared to accumulation for its own sake that is the cause for concern.

Instead of reducing the devil-beliefs to the desire for material gain, anxiety, "limited good," and so on, why not see them in their own right with all their vividness and detail as the response of people to what they see as an evil and destructive way of ordering economic life? Let us explore this notion that they are collective representations of a way of life losing its life, that they are intricate manifestations that are permeated with historical meaning and that register in the symbols of that history, what it means to lose control over the means of production and to be controlled by them. It would be a shocking oversight not to realize that these beliefs occur in a historical context in which one mode of production and life is being supplanted by another and that the devil dramatically represents this process of alienation. In so doing, the devil represents not merely the deep-seated changes in the material conditions of life but also the changing criteria in all their dialectical turmoil of truth and being with which those changes are associated—most especially the radically different concepts of creation, life, and growth through which the new material conditions and social relations are defined.

As such, the devil-beliefs suggest that the culture of the neophyte proletarians is in an important respect antagonistic to the process of commodity formation. In mediating the oppositions intrinsic to this process, such beliefs may even stimulate the political action necessary to thwart or transcend it.

The interpretation that I wish to elaborate is that the devil-beliefs form a dynamic mediation of oppositions, which appear at a particularly crucial and sensitive point of time in historical development. These beliefs can be thought of as mediating two radically distinct ways of apprehending or evaluating the world of persons and of things. Following Marx, I call these modes of evaluation *use-value* and *exchange-value*. Marx took this opposition from Aristotle and wedded it to Hegelian logic to create the anvil on which he forged his critical portrait of capitalism and its transcendence by the evolving patterning of world history. In exploring the distinct metaphysical and ontological connotations proper to each of these domains, use-value and exchange-value, we will inevitably be led to contrast precapitalist folk mysticism with that form of capitalist mystification Marx sardonically labelled *commodity fetishism*.

Attitudes to Wage Labor and Capitalist Development

In the sugarcane plantations of the Cauca Valley and in the tin mines of highland Bolivia it is clear that the devil is intrinsic to the process of the proletarianization of the peasant and to the commoditization of the peasant's world. He signifies a response to the change in the fundamental meaning of society as that meaning registers in precapitalist consciousness. The neophyte proletarians and their surrounding peasant kinsmen understand the world of market relations as intimately associated with the spirit of evil. Despite all the possibilities of increasing their cash incomes, they still seem to view this new mode of production as productive of barrenness and death as well. To them, therefore, this new socioeconomic system is neither natural nor good. Instead, it is both unnatural and evil, as the symbolism of the devil so strikingly illustrates. The meaning that is given to the devil in this situation is not unlike the definition that is given him by the Christian Fathers—"he who resists the cosmic process." As Joseph Needham notes, this comes close to the notion of forcing things in the interest of private gain without regard to what are seen as their intrinsic qualities (1956). This perception, with its passionate depth and sharpness, does not come out of the blue, so to speak, as the result of some mystical wisdom. Rather, it arises from a living context of coexisting ways of life: a peasant mode of production, in which the direct producers control means of production and organize work themselves, side by side with a capitalist mode of production, in which they control neither the material of labor nor its organization. Lived out daily, this actual and nonabstract comparison creates the raw material for critical evaluation. From this concrete condition of critical comparison the devil-beliefs emerge, as the situation of wage labor in the plantations and mines is contrasted with the drastically different situation that obtains in the communities from which these new proletarians have come, into which they were born, and with which they still retain personal contact.

The indifference or outright hostility of peasants and tribespeople the world over toward participation in the market economy as wage laborers has struck countless observers and entrepreneurs desirous of native labor. A theme of compelling concern to historians of the industrial revolution in Europe, as well as to sociologists of economic development in the Third World, is the seemingly irrational attitude of workers new to the modern wage-labor situation. The first reaction of such persons to their (usually forced) involvement in modern business enterprises as wage workers is frequently, if not universally, one of indifference to wage incentives and to the rationality that motivates *homo oeconomicus*. This response has time and again frustrated capitalist entrepreneurs.

Max Weber referred to this reaction as "primitive traditionalism," and much of his research was an attempt to explain its transcendence by the capitalist spirit of calculation. This primitive traditionalism survives into modern times, he noted in 1920 (1927:355). But one generation earlier the doubling of the wages of an agricultural laborer in Silesia who mowed land on contract to motivate him to increase his effort had proved futile. He simply reduced his work output by half because with this half he was able to earn as much as before. Malinowski noted that the white traders in the Trobriands faced insuperable difficulties in creating a native labor force of pearl divers. The only foreign article that exercised any purchasing power was tobacco, but the natives would not evaluate ten cases of trade tobacco as ten times one. For really good pearls the trader had to give native objects of wealth, and the traders' attempts to manufacture these arm shells, ceremonial blades, and so on, were met with scorn. The Trobriander, Malinowski thought, was contemptuous of the European's childish acquisitiveness for pearls, and "the greatest bribery and economic lures, the personal pressures of the White trader and competitive keenness of wealth, [could not] make the native give up his own pursuits for those foisted upon him. When the gardens are in full swing 'the god-damn niggers won't swim even if you stuff them with *kaloma* and tobacco,' as it was put to me by one of my trader friends" (1965, 1:19–20).

Among the "jealously egalitarian" Bakweri of the West Camer-
oon, the German and the British banana plantations found it difficult to obtain labor. The Bakweri were said to be apathetic, to waste
land, and to be disinterested in profit making. If they did accumulate
property, it was only to destroy it in potlatch-type ceremonies.
Those few who did associate themselves with the plantations and
become visibly better-off from their work were held to be members
of a new witchcraft association. They allegedly killed their relatives
and even their children by turning them into zombies who were
made to work on a distant mountain, driving lorries and so forth,
where their witch-masters were said to have a modern town. The
word *sómbî* means to pledge or to pawn; thus, under the new conditions of a plantation economy, it was believed that kinsmen became pawns or pledges so that a few might gain wealth. By stimulat-
ing the avarice of these new sort of witches, the incipient capitalist
economy was supposed to be destroying the youth and fertility of
the people. But in the mid-1950s, when the Bakweri villages un-
dertook to cultivate bananas cooperatively, and did so successfully,
this witchcraft was stopped. The Bakweri used their new source of
wealth to buy magic and develop curing cults that utilized expensive exorcists from the Banyang people. However, when banana
prices fell after 1960, indications were that the witches had returned. No money should be picked off the ground, the elders admonished, because it was being scattered to lure men to the water
side, where "Frenchmen" would employ them as zombies in the
construction of the new harbor (Ardener, 1970).

These and many similar reactions to incipient capitalist development provide dramatic testimony to the creative resistance of use-
value orientations. Summarizing his inquiry into the subject of labor commitment under modern imperialism, an anthropologist has
recently written:

> Recruited as plantation hands, they frequently showed them-
> selves unwilling to work steadily. Induced to raise a cash crop,
> they would not react "appropriately" to market changes: as
> they were interested mainly in acquiring specific items of con-
> sumption, they produced that much less when crop prices
> rose, and that much more when prices fell off. And the intro-
> duction of new tools or plants that increased the productivity
> of indigenous labor might only then shorten the period of nec-
> essary work, the gains absorbed rather by an expansion of rest
> than of output. All these and similar responses express an en-

during quality of traditional domestic production, that it is production of use values, definite in its aim, so discontinuous in its activity. [Sahlins, 1972:86]

This enduring quality of traditional domestic production based on the production of use-values leads to what we feel are bizarre and irrational responses to a system that is based on the production of exchange-values. It is important that these responses be specified in this manner and not buried in the obscure realm that is defined by categories such as tradition, the irrational, and primitive.

What we are given by these responses is the highly spirited clash between use-value and exchange-value orientations. The mystical interpretations and rhetorical figures associated with these two modes become enormously intensified when they are set into opposition by the spread of the cash economy and capitalism.

Manifested in popular culture, this opposition has inspired some of the greatest literature of our times. The spellbinding fantasy that irradiates the works of Miguel Asturias and Gabriel García Marquez, for example, concerning the United Fruit Company's banana plantations in Central America and Colombia, provides further testimony to the blending of poetic and political elements that concerns us here. It is precisely this aura of fantasy that so perplexes literary critics and Marxists who cannot understand the coexistence of fantasy and social realism. But as Asturias and García Marquez have repeatedly pointed out, it is this coexistence that constitutes reality in the "strong wind" and "leaf storm" of large-scale capitalist development in the Third World. The magic of production and the production of magic are inseparable in these circumstances. This is not testimony to the force of tradition or the glorious mythology and ritual of the unadulterated and precapitalist past. Rather, it is the creative response to an enormously deep-seated conflict between use-value and exchange-value orientations. The magic of use-value production draws out, magnifies, and counteracts the magic of exchange-value practices, and in this richly elaborated dramatic discord are embedded some rough-hewn proto-Marxist concepts.

As Christopher Hill has shown in his discussion of radical ideas during the English revolution of the mid-seventeenth century, this sort of proto-marxism exerted a strong force among the popular classes in Britain, too. Of course, the ideas to which I am referring were usually cast in religious terms. Yet, despite their lack of scientific metaphors they managed to confront fundamental issues of capitalist development in ways and with an intensity that are all too lacking today. "The Diggers have something to say to twentieth-century socialists," as do the many other radicals of the seventeenth century who refused to worship the Protestant Ethic, writes Hill (1975:15).

Today, the critical outlook engendered by incipient capitalist development has been largely superseded by the view that compliantly accepts capitalist institutions as natural and ethically commendable. Given this historically induced amnesia and cultural stupefaction, it is important for us to take note of the critique offered us by the neophyte proletarians of the Third World today, whose labor and products are relentlessly absorbed by the world market but whose culture resists such rationalization.

Hard-headed realists will scornfully dismiss this cultural resistance as of little importance, but the destruction of precapitalist metaphysics of production and exchange was considered by at least two influential social theorists as mandatory for the successful establishment of modern capitalism. Weber regarded the magical superstitions associated with production and exchange to be one of the greatest obstacles to the rationalization of economic life (1927:355), and in his essay *The Protestant Ethic and the Spirit of Capitalism* he reiterated the point. "Labor must . . . be performed as if it were an absolute end in itself, a calling. But such an attitude is by no means a product of nature. It cannot be evoked by low wages or high ones alone, but can only be the product of a long and arduous process of education. Today, capitalism once in the saddle, can recruit its laboring force in all industrial countries with comparative ease. In the past this was in every case an extremely difficult problem" (1958:62).

And as Marx observed, the transition to the capitalist mode of production is completed only when direct force and the coercive force of external economic conditions are used only in exceptional cases. An entirely new set of traditions and habits has to be developed among the working class until common sense regards the new conditions as natural. "It is not enough that the conditions of labor are concentrated in a mass, in the shape of capital, at the one pole of society, while at the other are grouped masses of men who have nothing to sell but their labor power. Neither is it enough that they are compelled to sell it voluntarily. The advance of capitalist production develops a working class, which by education, tradition, habit, looks upon the conditions of that mode of production *as self-evident laws of Nature*" (1967, 1:737; emphasis added).

Commodity Fetishism

If these "self-evident laws of nature" strike the neophyte proletarians with whom this book is concerned as unnatural and evil, then it is reasonable to ask why we regard our social form and economic process as natural. In suggesting an outline that an answer to this question might take, I will be charting the general problem with which this book is concerned.

At the outset some historical perspective is called for. It is too easily forgotten that at its inception industrial capitalism was described by an eloquent minority in Western Europe as profoundly inhuman and, in that sense, unnatural. With the maturation of the capitalist system, this sense of .moral outrage was dissipated, and eventually even criticisms of that system were phrased in the quasi-objectivist categories of order and nature that were laid down by the capitalist structure of comprehension. At their best, such critiques commonly concentrated on the anatomy and function of capitalism, the systems it elaborates for securing surplus value, the unequal distribution of its profit, and so on. The critical insights that were forced on sensitive personalities who were exposed to the beginnings of capitalism, critics who often invidiously compared capitalism with bygone eras, contained this class of criticisms, too, but did so within a metaphysic that could not for a moment entertain or acquiesce in the new definitions of person and work that capitalism engendered. In 1851, John Ruskin wrote that the perfection of industrial products was neither a cause for celebration nor a sign of England's greatness, "Alas! if read rightly, these perfectnesses are a sign of a slavery in England a thousand times more bitter and more degrading than that of the scourged African or helot Greek" (1925, 2:160). It was not that the new system necessarily made people poorer, but "this degradation of the operative into a machine" which led men into an incoherent urge for freedom. Above all, it was the sense of self-alienation that poisoned life under capitalism and spurred the class struggle, for, "It is not that men are pained by the scorn of the upper classes, but they cannot endure their own; for they feel that the kind of labour to which they are condemned is verily a degrading one, and makes them less than men." This was what so appalled Ruskin. In his vision the system became a living critique of itself. "And the great cry that rises from all our manufacturing cities, louder than the furnace blast, is all in very deed this—that we manufacture everything there except men; we blanch cotton, and strengthen steel, and refine sugar, and shape pottery; but to brighten, to strengthen, to refine, or to form a single living spirit, never enters into our estimate of advantages" (Ruskin, 1925, 2:163). The romanticism entailed in critiques such as Ruskin's. of industrial capitalism and of laissez-faire represented a focal point around which *both* conservative and utopian socialist critics converged, elaborating nostalgic myths concerning the primitive or precapitalist past as a way of combatting bourgeois ideology and of spurring people into political action. Scientific theories of history and scientific socialism developed in reaction to such romantic notions. Usually, however, their development was very one sided: they gave utopian ideologies such a wide berth that they in fact validated bourgeois ideals while appearing to negate them. The uncritical validation and even adulation of what was essentially a bourgeois concept of "progress" and of the natural science model of society are among the most salient manifestations of this.

The tension in early efforts to persuade contemporaries that the new economic system was baneful stemmed from one critical factor: increasingly, the system was seen as natural. The outrage and despair in Ruskin's writing stem not merely from what might be called the "objective" features of life under capitalism, but preeminently from the fact that these features came to be seen by its members as part of the natural order of things. To meet this tension, writers like Ruskin resorted to eulogizing medieval society, its idealism and religious principles, its basis in cooperation rather than in competition, and its absence of industrial exploitation and drudgery. Although they were well aware of the political coercion in medieval times, they still held the viewpoint that the critical lesson for the present lay in the greater control that the worker had possessed over materials, tools, and time. In his essay on the nature of the Gothic, Ruskin counseled his contemporaries not to mock at the fantastic ignorance of the old sculptors, for their works "are signs of the life and liberty of every workman who struck the stone; a freedom of thought, and rank in scale of being, such as no laws, no charters, no charities can secure; but which it must be the first aim of all Europe at this day to regain for her children." In many instances Marx himself, in developing a scientific and unsentimental critical analysis of capitalism, found that in the contrast between capitalist and precapitalist societies he could best drive home the cruel disfiguration of humanity that capitalism represented to him.

The use of the contrast between medieval and capitalist society was not just a romanticized rhetorical device. Quite apart from the critical lessons inherent in such a contrast, it is significant that peasants and craftsmen the world over have displayed similar reactions to the inner significance of capitalist organization. To understand this reaction it is helpful to analyze the salient differences between the use-value system that underlies peasant economics and the market basis of capitalism. Above all it is necessary to understand the way in which the market system of modern capitalism engenders a marketing mentality in which people tend to be seen as commodities and commodities tend to be seen as animated entities that can dominate persons. This socially instituted paradox arises because, unlike earlier forms of organization which joined persons into direct relationships for production and exchange (often predicated on their control over the means of production), the market interposes itself between persons, mediating direct awareness of social relations by the abstract laws of relationships between commodities.

The peasant mode of production differs from the capitalist mode in fundamental ways. Under capitalism the proletariat work force lacks the control over the means of production that peasants exercise. The peasant uses cash, not capital, and sells in order to buy, whereas the capitalist uses cash as capital to buy in order to sell at a profit, thus adding to capital and repeating the circuit on an ever-increasing scale lest the enterprise die. The peasant producer lives in a system that is aimed at the satisfaction of an array of qualitatively defined needs; contrarily, the capitalist and the capitalist system have the aim of limitless capital accumulation.

In the realization of this aim, capitalism stamps its products and its means of production with the seal of market approval—price. Only by "translating" all the varied qualities that constitute its products and means for creating them into one common "language," that of currency, can the generator of capitalism's vitality, the market, operate. Known as "commodities," goods and services under capitalism thus differ enormously from their counterparts in precapitalist systems of livelihood. Although they may in fact be the same articles, socially and conceptually they are very different. To take Aristotle's famous example, a shoe is a shoe, physically, whether it is produced for wear or for sale at a profit with the aim of accumulating capital. But as a commodity the shoe has properties that are in addition to its use-value of providing comfort, ease of walking, pleasure to the eye, or whatever. As a commodity the shoe has the exchange-value function: it can generate profit for its owner and seller over and above the use-value that it holds for the person who eventually buys and wears it. In its exchange-value the shoe is qualitatively identical with any other commodity, no matter how much they may differ in terms of their use-value properties—their physical features, symbolic attributes, and so on. By virtue of this abstraction, which is based on market exchange and the universal equivalence of money, a palace is equal to a certain number of shoes, just as a pair of shoes is equal to a certain fraction of an animal's hide. Absurd as it seems when thus stated, this socially necessary fiction is a commonplace that underlies the fictional naturalness of identities on which the society depends and that guarantees its concept of objects and objectivity.

According to the theory, phenomenology, and behavior of the market, the regulation of social activity is computed by men coldly calculating their egoistic advantage over one another within a context organized by the interaction of products depending on prices and profit margins. The organic conception of society is here dissolved by two synergistic processes: communality and mutuality give way to personal self-interest, and commodities, not persons, dominate social being. The exchange ratio of commodities mediates and determines the activities of people. Hence, social relations between persons become disguised as the social relations between things. What is more, the prices of commodities are constantly varying beyond the foresight and control of persons; thus, individuals are even more subject to the whim of the marketplace. People relate to one another not directly but through the mediation of the market guiding the circulation and relations of commodities. Their livelihoods depend on the relations established by commodities, and the market becomes the guarantee of their spiritual coherence. The market established basis of livelihood becomes in effect a constantly lived out daily ritual, which, like all rites, joins otherwise unconnected links of meaning into a coherent and apparently natural network of associations. The commodity paradigm for understanding humanity, social relations, and the world at large now predominates.

In the case of labor the transmutation in status and meaning that occurs with this shift in paradigm is highly critical. As a commodity, labor becomes the disguised source of profit to the employer in a transaction that appears to be the equal exchange of values so long as those values are judged as commodities. But labor is not only an exchange value, a numerical quantity of labor power. What the capitalist acquires in buying the commodity of labor power as an exchange-value is the right to deploy the use-value of labor as the intelligent and creative capacity of human beings to produce more use-values than those that are reconverted into commodities as the wage. This is Marx's formulation, and it is important that we clearly understand the two planes on which his argument works.

The capitalist system ensures the social institutions by which the free worker, bereft of the means of production, can be manipulated into working longer than is required for the production of goods necessary for his or her survival. In a twelve-hour working day, for example, the worker creates goods in six hours that are equivalent, as commodities, to the wages received. But the hidden mechanism that ensures the creation of surplus out of a situation that appears as nothing more than the fair exchange of equivalents is the movement back and forth of labor as an exchange-value and labor as a use-value. We tend to lose sight of this and the crucial importance of the noncommodity nature of labor if we adhere only to the simple arithmetic of the argument, which in this example displays a surplus of six hours labor-time. The commoditization process conceals the fact that within the matrix of capitalist institutions, labor as use-value is the source of profit. By the purchase of the commodity of labor power, the capitalist incorporates labor as a use-value into the lifeless constituents of the commodities produced. "Living labour must seize upon these things and rouse them from their death-sleep, change them from mere possible use-values into real and effective ones" (Marx, 1967, 1:183).

The ultimate consequence and meaning of these procedures is that the commodities themselves appear as the source of value and profit. The commodity definition of human labor and its products disguises both the humanly creative and social basis of value and the exploitation of that creativity by the market system.

The quantity of this disguised exploitation can be measured as surplus labor-time accruing to the employer, but the quality of that exploitation cannot be measured. The feeling of atomization and bondage which is the phenomenology of the market-based system is elusive because it is taken as natural. To the ideologues of the burgeoning capitalist system it appeared as efficient, natural, and good. But there was another view—a shocked disbelief that people could accept alienation as natural. "We have much studied and perfected, of late, the great civilized invention of the division of labour," wrote Ruskin in the mid-nineteenth century. "Only we give it a false name. It is not, truly speaking, the labour that is divided; but the men—Divided into mere segments of men—broken into small fragments and crumbs of life, so that all the little piece of intelligence that is left in a man is not enough to make a pin, or a nail, but exhausts itself in making the point of a pin or the head of a nail" (1925, 2:162–63). Divided psychologically by the market orchestration of the division of labor, producers are also separated from their products. Their labor creates and enters into the form of their products, which are then sundered from their grasp. In precapitalist economies, the embodiment of the producer in the product is consciously acknowledged, but in a capitalist system it is essential that this embodiment be "exorcised." Contrary views are outrageous, indeed, revolutionary. In his novel *Seven Red Sundays* concerning anarcho-syndicalists at the outbreak of the Spanish Civil War, Ramon Sender depicts a worker who was just released from jail hurrying to his old building construction site, a theatre, to glory in the finished building. "What-Oh! My good walls, noble lines, curving steel and glass! How the light sings in the round eye of a gable!" The manager refuses him entry. "But I worked on this job for more than six months." "If you did work, they paid you for it—clear out." The manager pointed to the door. The worker pointed to the inside staircase. "I'm going up. When I've seen everything, I'll look in to say goodbye. Or I'll stay here if I like. All this . . . is more mine than yours" (1961:20–21).

In his discussion of Maori exchange, Marcel Mauss concludes that the underlying basis of that form of society is the reciprocity that is associated with the belief that an article that is produced and exchanged contains the life-force (*hau*) of the person and objects in nature from whence the article derived. Indeed, if this were not acknowledged and reciprocity not insured, fertility itself would be jeopardized (1967).

However, in capitalist society this embodiment of person in product is exorcised in keeping with the norms of bourgeois private property. The embodiment is "paid for" by the wage or the selling price, just as "ownership" of any commodity is transferred at the time of sale. In the capitalist lexicon to buy or to sell means to claim or to lose all attachment to the article that is transferred. The relations of product to producer and to the productive social milieu, as well as to nature, are forever sundered. The commodity assumes an autonomy apart from human social activities, and in transcending that activity the relations between commodities subjugate persons, who become dominated by a world of things—things that they themselves created.

But this domination is mystifying. It is unclear what is happening. In fact it appears so natural that the issue of dominance rarely arises; in this sense the commodity form has truly subjugated the consciousness of persons who are endowed with a long capitalist heritage, but not, it would seem, the consciousness of those peasants with whom we are concerned—persons just beginning to experience capitalism. Instead, they are anthropomorphizing their subjugation in the figure of the devil, redolent of the power of evil.

By reacting in this manner to capitalist culture they are living testimony to the legacy of ideology through the ages that has assailed market exchange as something unnatural—a social form that undermines the basis of social unity by allowing creativity and the satisfaction of need to be subverted by a system that puts profit seeking ahead of people and that makes man an appendage of the economy and a slave to the work process instead of the master of it. As Marx noted, even in his later and less sentimental writings, the question in ancient society was always what form of society and economy could best serve the needs of man, and no matter how constrained and narrow that society may now appear to be, how much more satisfying and noble it was when man was the aim of production.

The distinction between use-value and exchange-value corresponds to these different forms of economic process: on the one hand, we have the aim of satisfying natural needs; on the other hand, we have the drive toward accumulation of profits. This distinction is usually traced back to the economic doctrine that was propounded by Aristotle, who saw a clear difference between what he called the correct use of an article, for example, a shoe meant for a foot, and the incorrect use of an article, production and exchange to make a profit. This was not an argument against exchange per se; neither was it an argument based simply on an appeal to ethical imperatives. Rather, it followed from the reasoned argument that found profit making detrimental to the foundations of a subsistence economy and destructive of the good society in general. This distinction between use-value and exchange-value, between the satisfaction of natural needs and the satisfaction of the profit motive, is a persistent theme in the history of economic theorizing in the West, especially in the writings of the medieval Schoolmen. Marx himself was heavily indebted to Aristotle's observations on the matter, as his many favorable comments in this regard bear witness. When Luther ascribed usury and the early manifestations of capitalism to the workings of the devil he was merely giving vent to the outrage and pain that many persons felt toward the flowering of the profit motive and the subjugation of social relations to the economic laws of commodities. For them this was certainly not a natural phenomenon.

Yet, in a mature capitalist system this fiction acquires the stamp of fact. The essential elements of its industrial enterprise—land, labor, and money—are organized in markets and are dealt with as commodities. From the use-value perspective, however, these elements are not commodities. "The postulate that anything bought and sold must have been produced for sale is emphatically untrue in regard to them," writes Polanyi. "Labor is only another name for a human activity which goes with life itself, which in turn is not produced for sale but for entirely different reasons." And he concludes, "The commodity definition of labor, land, and money is entirely fictitious" (1957:72).

Fictitious indeed! But then how does one explain the persistence and strength of this fiction? What makes it so real? How is it that labor, which "is only another name for a human activity which goes with life itself," is seen as a thing detached from the rest of life? In the Bolivian tin mines and in the plantation fields of the Cauca Valley this fiction is understood as a disturbingly dangerous and unnatural state of affairs and is credited to no less a figure than the devil, whereas to those of us who live in a well-developed capitalist culture this cultural convention has now become part of the state of nature.

The answer obviously lies in the way that the market organization of life's activities imprints reality and defines experience. Reality and the mode of apprehending it become defined in commodity terms that are based on the epistemological canons of atomistic materialism. Man is individualized, as are all things, and organic wholes are broken into their supposed material constituents. Irreducible atoms related to one another through their intrinsic force and causal laws expressed as mathematical relationships form the basis of this cosmology, and in so doing, embody and sustain the commodity fiction of social reality. This mechanical and atomistic view of reality, the basis of which was outlined in the works of Descartes and Galileo, found its most perfect expression in the physics and metaphysics of Isaac Newton, who may with all justice be regarded as the father of modern science and as the man who gave to capitalist apprehension the legitimizing and final smack of approval that only science can now endow.

If, in accordance with this outlook we regard our economy as natural, are we not construing a picture of our society in every way as fanciful as that of those newcomers to the commodity system who can understand it as the workings of the devil? If they can see the maintenance or the increase of production under capitalism as somehow bound up with the devil and thereby make a fetish of the productive process, do we not also have our own form of fetishism in which we attribute to commodities a reality so substantial that they acquire the appearance of natural beings, so natural in fact that they appear to take on a life-force of their own?

Take the capitalist folklore that fills the financial section of the *New York Times* (April, 1974), for example. We read of the "economic climate," of the "sagging dollar," of "earning booming ahead," of "cash flows," of treasury bills "backing up," of "runaway" and "galloping" inflation, of "climbing interest rates," of "bear markets" and "bull markets," of factories referred to as "plants," of "money growing" in accordance with investment, of how "your investments can go to work for you," and so on. The active mood predominates: "the London pound closed firmly at $2.402, up strongly from the opening of $2.337," and "weakness in the market was widespread and reflected the performance of the 15 most active issues." "Despite gasoline shortages and uncertain supplies, 10 of the 15 most active issues traded on Monday could be classed as travel-oriented." "Can the individual investor still find happiness in the market?" asks the muse, who on reflection answers, "Today there are dozens of ways to put your capital to work." A Chicago banker is reported as saying, "A general feeling seems to persist that something had definitely gone wrong with what had come to be regarded as the natural order of economic, financial and commercial life." The price of copper bears no proportion to the value of the coins into which it is minted; one spokesman for an important producer said, "While our selling price is killing us, we do have contractual and other obligations to deliver, whether we like to or not." Splitting his time between New York and his plant in Italy, Joe can't afford to waste time when he's dealing with his bank. That's where Bob comes in. "As far as I'm concerned," Joe says, "Bob *is* Chemical Bank." Hence, "Our Man is your bank—Chemical Bank. The businessman, when his needs are financial, his reaction is chemical."

These metaphors are common manifestations of what Marx referred to as commodity fetishism occurring in a developed capitalist culture, wherein capital and workers' products are spoken of in terms that are used for people and animate beings. It is money as interest-bearing capital that lends itself most readily to this type of fetishism. Capital appears to have an innate property of self-expansion, and this property diffuses into all economic life since in capitalism money is the universal equivalent and mediator between persons and all objects.

The concept of commodity fetishism is meant to point out for us that capitalist society presents itself to consciousness as something other than what it basically is, even though that consciousness does reflect the superficial and hypostatized configuration of society. Fetishism denotes the attribution of life, autonomy, power, and even dominance to otherwise inanimate objects and presupposes the draining of these qualities from the human actors who bestow the attribution. Thus, in the case of commodity fetishism, social relationships are dismembered and appear to dissolve into relationships between mere things—the products of labor exchanged on the market—so that the sociology of exploitation masquerades as a natural relationship between systemic artifacts. Definite social relationships are reduced to the magical matrix of things. An ether of naturalness—fate and physicality—conceals and enshrouds human social organization, the historical human significance of the market, and the development of a propertyless wage-earning class. Instead of man being the aim of production, production has become the aim of man and wealth the aim of production; instead of tools and the productive mechanism in general liberating man from the slavery of toil, man has become the slave of tools and the instituted processes of production. As Thorstein Veblen observed, industry has become synonymous with business and people have been duped into asking, "What is good for business?" rather than ask "What is business good for?"

In surveying the opinions of eighteenth- and nineteenth-century British economists and statesmen on the question of capital and interest, Marx sarcastically pointed out that in their eyes it becomes "a property of money to generate value and yield interest, much as it is an attribute of pear trees to bear pears. . . . Thus we get the fetish form of capital and the conception of fetish capital . . . a mystification of capital in its most flagrant form" (1967, 3 : 392). Elsewhere in the same chapter of *Capital* Marx quotes at length from economists and from economic journals of the mid-nineteenth century. He highlights the biological metaphors that their views of money so strongly suggest. "Money is now pregnant." "As the growing process is to trees, so generating money appears as innate in capital in its form as money-capital."

Benjamin Franklin's *Advice to a Young Tradesman* (1748) could just as well have been the target of Marx's irony. Franklin states: "Remember, that money is of the prolific, generating nature. Money can beget money, and its offspring can beget more, and so on. Five shillings turned is six, turned again it is seven and threepence, and so on, till it becomes a hundred pounds. The more there is of it, the more it produces every turning, so that the profits rise quicker and quicker. He that kills a breeding-sow, destroys all her offspring to the thousandth generation" (cited in Weber, 1958 : 49).

At the same time these fabulous fancies were systematically interwoven with the weltanshauung of *homo oeconomicus*, the supposed epitome of rationality. How could such a mutually reinforcing combination of rationality and fantasy so systematically coexist? What gave conviction to these biological metaphors? The answer lies in the peculiar and unique character of the social relations embodied both in capital and in the commodities produced in the capitalist mode of production.

Marx argued at great length and from a variety of viewpoints that these social relations of production impressed themselves on everyday consciousness in such a way that the entire process of production and the generation of the laborers' surplus value—the context in which capital works—is overlooked or slighted to the extent that the social process of capital reproduction and expansion may easily appear as a property inherent in the commodity itself, rather than of the process of which it is part. This socially conditioned appearance is a mystification in which the entire social context conspires, so to speak, to mask itself. In this process of decontextualization, profit no longer appears to be the result of a social relation, but of a *thing*: this is what is meant by *reification.*

Marx made his views on this very clear when he compared the formula for interest-bearing capital with what he called merchant's capital.

> The relations of capital assume their most externalized and most fetish-like form in interest bearing capital. We have here M-M', money creating more money, self-expanding value, without the process that effectuates these two extremes. In merchant's capital, M-C-M', there is at least the general form of the capitalist movement, although it confines itself solely to the sphere of circulation, so that profit appears merely as profit derived from alienation; but it is at least seen to be the product of a social *relation*, not the product of a mere *thing.* [1967, 3:391]

The same point permeates Marx's writings; for instance, in this passage from the *Grundrisse* he expresses his antipathy to the crude materialism that he sees as fetishism. "The crude materialism of the economists who regard as the *natural properties* of things what are social relations of production among people, and qualities which things obtain because they are subsumed under these relations, is at the same time just as crude an idealism, even fetishism, since it imputes social relations to things as inherent characteristics, and thus mystifies them" (1973:687).

Appealing to nature, to the paradoxical extreme wherein certain lifeless things are seen as animated, is merely one historically specific manifestation of that probably universal tendency whereby any culture externalizes its social categories onto nature, and then turns to nature in order to validate its social norms as natural. Durkheim saw this attempt to invoke the principle of biological determinism in the ideology of primitive society, and Marx spotted the same phenomenon in the genesis, acceptance, and use of Darwinism. "The whole Darwinist teaching of the struggle for existence is simply a transference from society to living nature of Hobbes' doctrine of 'bellum omnium contra omnes' and of the bourgeois-economic doctrine of competition together with Malthus' theory of population. When this conjuror's trick has been performed . . . the same theories are transferred back again from organic nature into history and it is now claimed that their validity as eternal laws of human society has been proved" (cited in Schmidt, 1971:47).

The same point might be made regarding Newtonian physics and the role of human beings who are subordinated to the impersonal controls of the self-regulating market, the central institution if not the "solar system" of capitalist economy. Newton's scheme earned the undying admiration of Adam Smith, the foremost theoretician and eulogist of the capitalist market. To Smith, Newton's system was "everywhere the most precise and particular that can be imagined, and ascertains the time, the place, the quantity, the duration of each individual phenomenon." It seemed to him to fit perfectly with the world of everyday experience. "Neither are the principles of union which it employs such as the imagination can find any difficulty in going along with." The Newtonian principles of union were not only applicable to gravity and the inertness of matter, but were "the same which takes place in all other qualities which are propagated in rays from a center." All of this amounted to "the discovery of an immense chain of the most important and sublime truths, all closely connected together, by one capital fact, of the reality of which we have daily experience" (1967:107–8). For William Blake, Newton was the symbol of market society and its oppressive use of technology and empire, and he assailed those very "principles of union" that Adam Smith found so congenial. Historians of science, as Margaret Jacob recently pointed out, have often presumed that the new mechanical philosophy triumphed in England because it offered the most plausible explanation of nature. Whether or not it does that, it was the correspondence of Newtonianism with the cosmology of the capitalist market that best accounts for its acceptance. "The ordered, providentially guided, mathematically regulated universe of Newton gave a model for a stable and prosperous polity, ruled by the self-interest of men" (1976:17–18). It was this reciprocating replication of market society in nature and of nature in market society that allowed Newtonianism to triumph and consummate the mechanical "principles of union" into a holy and scientifically impervious truth of all being. E. A. Burtt draws our attention to the following phenomenological features of Newtonian metaphysics, features which have direct implication for our discussion of commodity fetishism and its associated philosophy.

Here were those residual souls of men, irregularly scattered among the atoms of mass that swam mechanically among the etheral vapors in time and space, and still retaining vestiges of the Cartesian *res cogitans*. They too must be reduced to mechanical products and parts of the self-regulating cosmic clock. . . . Wherever it was taught as truth the universal formula of gravitation, there was also insinuated as a nimbus of surrounding belief that man is but the puny and local spectator, nay irrelevant product of an infinite self-moving engine . . . which consists of raw masses wandering to no purpose in an undiscoverable time and space, and is in general wholly devoid of any qualities that might spell satisfaction for the major interests of human nature. [1954:300–301]

The crucial point is that in the fetishism of commodities we encounter a general formula for the principles of union that apply to capitalist culture as a whole and guide social awareness, and this formula, according to Marx, is rooted in the relations of production and exchange as they impress themselves on consciousness in the work-a-day world. Briefly, this formula states that the social relation is consummated in the relationship of a thing to itself and that ontology lies not in a relational gestalt but squarely within the thing itself. Atomized, self-encapsulated things, what Burtt refers to as "raw masses," become the prime objects of analysis because their meaning and properties appear to lie within themselves alone. True explanation and understanding now rest on a conception of principles of union that reduce whole phenomena to their simplest parts, and ultimate causality is to be found in the unchanging movement of elementary physical atoms. This dominance of "thinghood" tends to obliterate people's awareness and to efface their capacity for moral evaluation of the bio-logic and socio-logic of relationships and processes, particularly socioeconomic activities and relationships. This is not to say that in this view things as such cannot be related to other things, and harmoniously related at that. Newton's scheme of the planets and Adam Smith's view of the self-regulating market are the outstanding examples of corpuscular interrelatedness forming a harmonious totality, much as modern systems theory does today. However, the binding relations are viewed as external to the individuated things, the identity and power of which is given in themselves alone.

From another point of view, however, this is a gross deception since these apparently self-bounded and potent things are merely the embodiments and concretizations of relationships that bind them to a larger whole. Their identity, existence, and natural properties spring from their *position* in an all-encompassing organic *pattern* of organization in which things are understood as but partial expressions of a self-organizing totality. The properties and activities of things may then be explained holistically and "structurally" as manifestations of their reticulate intelligibility as parts of an organic whole and not as products of mechanical causation and corpuscular collisions. If attention is focused on a single thing, as it must be at some point in any analysis, then that thing is seen as containing its relational network and surrounding context within itself; the thing is a system of relationships.

On the other hand, if the atomistic view prevails, as it does in our culture, then the isolated thing in itself must inevitably tend to appear as animated because in reality it is part of an active process. If we "thingify" parts of a living system, ignore the context of which they are part, and then observe that the things move, so to speak, it logically follows that the things may well be regarded or spoken of as though they were alive with their own autonomous powers. If regarded as mere things, they will therefore appear as though they were indeed *animate* things—fetishes. Capital, for instance, is often compared to a tree that bears fruit; the thing itself is the source of its own increase. Hence, reification leads to fetishism.

Fetishism: Precapitalist versus Capitalist

In contrast to this subordination of persons to things, persons in precapitalist societies and the products they create and exchange are seen as intermeshed. Yet, in these societies, too, such products may acquire lifelike qualities. Thus, products may become fetishes, but they do so for reasons completely different from those outlined above for a society based on commodity exchange. In the precapitalist mode of production there is no market and no commodity definition of the value and function of a good, and the connections between producers and between production and consumption are directly intelligible. Products appear to be animated or life endowed precisely because they seem to embody the social milieu from which they come.

For instance, in his analysis of Maori exchange Mauss said it was as though there existed a life-force (*hau*) within the goods and services exchanged, which compelled their reciprocation. According to Mauss, the Maoris believed that the very goods themselves were thought to be persons or pertain to a person, and that in exchanging something one was in effect exchanging part of oneself (1967). In his work *Primitive Man as a Philosopher*, Paul Radin discusses the Maori concept of personality together with examples taken from other primitive cultures and points out the insistence on multiple dimensions of the ego and its extension into past and future. The various elements can become dissociated temporarily from the body and enter into relation with the dissociated elements of other individuals and with nature. He concludes his analysis by stating that in such a philosophy the ego is intelligible only as it is related to the external world and to other egos. A connection is implied between the ego and the phenomenal world, and this connection assumes the form of an attraction and compulsion. "Nature cannot resist man, and man cannot resist nature. A purely mechanistic conception of life is unthinkable. The parts of the body, the physiological functions of the organs, like the material form taken by objects in nature, are mere symbols, *simulacra*, for the essential psychical-spiritual entity that lies behind them" (Radin, 1957 : 273–74).

In other words, the fetishism that is found in the economics of precapitalist societies arises from the sense of organic unity between persons and their products, and this stands in stark contrast to the fetishism of commodities in capitalist societies, which results from the split between persons and the things that they produce and exchange. The result of this split is the subordination of men to the things they produce, which appear to be independent and self-empowered.

Thus, the devil-beliefs that concern us in this book can be interpreted as the indigenous reaction to the supplanting of this traditional fetishism by the new. As understood within the old use-value system, the devil is the mediator of the clash between these two very different systems of production and exchange. This is so not only because the devil is an apt symbol of the pain and havoc that the plantations and mines are causing, but also because the victims of this expansion of the market economy view that economy in personal and not in commodity terms and see in it the most horrendous distortion of the principle of reciprocity, a principle that in all precapitalist societies is supported by mystical sanctions and enforced by supernatural penalties. The devil in the mines and cane fields reflects an adherence by the workers' culture to the principles that underlie the peasant mode of production, even as these principles are being progressively undermined by the everyday experience of wage labor under capitalist conditions. But until the capitalist institutions have permeated all aspects of economic life and the revolution in the mode of production is complete, the lower classes will persist in viewing the bonds between persons in their modern economic activities for what they really are—asymmetrical, nonreciprocal, exploitative, and destructive of relationships between persons—and not as natural relations between forces supposedly inherent in potent things.

PART II

The Plantations of the Cauca Valley, Colombia

Peasants! The sugar cane degenerates one; turns one into a beast, and kills! If we don't have land we cannot contemplate the future well-being of our children and families. Without land there can be no health, no culture, no education, nor security for us, the marginal peasants. In all these districts one finds the plots of the majority threatened by the terrible Green Monster, which is the Great Cane, the God of the landlords.

Peasant broadsheet,
southern Cauca Valley, 1972

CHAPTER 3

Slave Religion and the Rise of the Free Peasantry

T
wo generalizations are necessary to any discussion of black slave religion in Latin America. First, the whites were apprehensive of the supernatural powers of their subjects, and vice versa. Second, religion was inseparable from magic, and both permeated everyday life—agriculture, mining, economy, healing, marital affairs, and social relations in general. The Inquisition, for instance, regarded the occult arts that were drawn from the three continents not as idle fantasies but as the exercise of supernatural powers, including an explicit or implicit pact with the devil. The African slaves brought their mysteries and sorcery, the Indians their occult powers to cure or kill, and the colonists their own belief in magic (Lea, 1908:462).

The magical lore of the European was joined to that of the despised African and Indian to form a symbiosis, transformation, and adaptation of forms unknown to each group. This process was most obvious in beliefs concerning illness and healing. The Europeans had few efficacious medical resources, and their curing depended heavily on religious and magical faith: masses, prayers to the saints, rosary beads, holy water, and miracles wrought by priests and folk curers. The indoctrination of African slaves by Catholic priests focused on curing, which exploited the miracle-yielding power of the Christian pantheon to the utmost (Sandoval, 1956). Conversely, the Europeans availed themselves of their subjects' magic, which was not distinguished from religion. In fact, the Europeans defined African and Indian religion not merely as magic but as evil magic. "It is in this trance," writes Gustavo Otero, referring to the first days of the conquest, "that the conquerors became the conquered" (1951: 128). That restless dialectic of magical counterattributions persists in popular culture to the present day.

Colonization and enslavement inadvertently delivered a special mystical power to the underdog of colonial society—the power of mystic evil as embodied in the Christians' fear of the devil. The quasi-Manichaean dualistic cosmology of the conquerors coexisted with the polytheistic or animistic monism of the African slaves and Indians, so that the conquerors stood to the conquered as God did to the devil. Thus, the popular religion of Spanish America was stamped with ethnic and class dualisms of this momentous order —ever susceptible to mercurial inversions in accordance with the shifting currents of caste and class power.

The Inquisition was founded in Cartagena in the early seventeenth century for reasons that included the Church Fathers' judgment of the colony as the "most vicious and sinful in the Spanish Dominions, [with] the faith on the point of destruction" (Lea, 1908:456). Female slaves served as healers to such exalted personages as the bishop of Cartagena and the inquisitors themselves, while others were lashed when their occult powers were defined as evil, especially when epidemics of witchcraft were raging. Male sorcerers (*brujos*) became important leaders in the runaway slave camps (*palenques*) which caused the authorities endless concern (Borrego Pla, 1973:27, 83; Tejado Fernandez, 1954:117–32). As intermediaries for Satan, such leaders supposedly initiated their converts in a ritual that mocked Christian baptism and denied God, the saints, and the Virgin Mary in order to achieve salvation in the afterlife and wealth and power in the here and now. This system of belief expresses the specter of social inversion. Teleologically ordered by the Supreme God, the hierarchy of social forms defined by class, color, and sex engendered its mirror image in the fears or hopes of an underworld allied with Satan.

Blacks were notorious for their militantly anti-Christian outbursts, which were macabrely ritualized in the sine qua non of slavery, flogging; at such times it was not unusual for the victim to cry, "I denounce God!" (Medina, 1889:106; cf., Palmer, 1975). They also destroyed symbols of the church—hardly surprising in a society in which, for example, a woman slave owner might measure the duration of a flogging by the time it took her to recite her rosary (Meiklejohn, 1968:216).

Writing in 1662, the chief inquisitor attributed much of the sorcery and idolatry in the mining districts to the heedless materialism of the mineowners, who "live only for profit . . . and keep watch only that the slaves accomplish their daily labor and care for nothing else" (Medina, 1889:120). Ostensibly, this sorcery could not only kill and maim people but also destroy the fruits of the earth—a claim still heard in connection with alleged devil pacts made by plantation laborers in the southern Cauca Valley. The pact will increase their productivity and their wage, but renders the canefield barren. Yet, the same laborers, working as peasants on their own or their neighbors' plots around the plantations or as independent subsistence dwellers in the jungles of the Pacific coast, reputedly spurn such pacts. Zaragoza, the mining area referred to, was the scene of one of Colombia's greatest slave revolts, which, according to observers, attempted to exterminate the whites and destroy the mines, as well (Vázquez de Espinosa, 1948:341).

The spasmodic moment that bridged the lash and the cry of renunciation of the master's God epitomizes the slaves' devil. He can become a figure of solace and power in that war of attrition against the African's culture and humanity itself. In their devil worship, the slaves appropriated their enemy's enemy. Ironically, through its very attempts at suppression, the Church indirectly validated devil worship and invested it with power. By acknowledging fear of the slaves' spiritual powers, the credulous Spanish inadvertently delivered a powerful instrument to their bondsmen. The Spaniards believed that the devil had spawned the heathen African and that the slaves were part of his ministry. The sixteenth and seventeenth centuries were, after all, the most intense years of the witch cult in Western Europe, the Counter-Reformation, and the Inquisition—an epoch in which the whole of Christendom trembled before the threat of the diabolic and the magician's manipulation of nature.

Ambiguously but persistently, Europeans equated slave folklore and religion, African identity, with the devil (cf., Genovese, 1974: 159–284). But for the African slave the devil was not necessarily the vengeful spirit of evil. He was also a figure of mirth and a powerful trickster. As Melville J. Herskovits pointed out, West Africans understood the European devil as their divine trickster, and their moral philosophy resisted the sharp dichotomy of good and evil espoused by the missionaries (1958:253). Today, along the virtually isolated rivers of the Colombian Pacific coast, where blacks were largely left to fend for themselves after emancipation, they have, not one, but several devils, who tempt rather than threaten. The idea of hell among the blacks of the Raposo River only vaguely corresponds to the Christian idea; some people place it in the sky (Pavy, 1967:234). Finding their spirits defined as devils or one in particular defined as *the* devil, the blacks did not readily attribute evil to the "devil," at least not at first. And even if they did, the attribution could have signified hostility to the new order.

Describing the Apo ceremony among the Ashanti, William Bosman wrote during the late seventeenth century:

> Conjurors and Miracle-Mongers are no strange things amongst the Negroes: they firmly believe in them, but in a different manner from our European Ridiculous Opinionists; who are persuaded no Conjuror can do any feats without the help of the Devil. For on the contrary, the Negroes do not doubt but that 'tis a gift of God, and though in reality it is a downright cheat, yet they, ignorant of the Fraud, swallow it as a Miracle, and above Humane power; but that the Devil may not in the least participate of the Honour, they ascribe it all to God. [1967:157–58]

Whereas the Spanish ascribed it to the devil! Perturbed by the purely formal character of baptism and conversion, which impeded rather than sustained indoctrination, the outstanding Jesuit Father Alonso de Sandoval wrote during the early seventeenth century from his post in Cartagena: "They worship the devil . . . and when sick they invoke the names of Jesus and Maria" (1956:71, 82). As for "Guinea," he writes, there the devil held such sway and had so many aides that those few people inclined to the Christian faith died without remedy from sorcery or poison. Yet, by his own testimony, it was impossible to proselytize without reinforcing the pagan premises of the potential neophytes.

The enforcement of Christianity entailed those almost insuperable contradictions that made social control difficult for colonialists everywhere. The authorities constrained or suppressed some of the most public expressions of popular religion—for example, the feast days and funerals organized by the black *cofradías* (religious brotherhoods) and *cabildos* (councils)—which augmented the solidarity of slaves and free blacks, encouraged liberation, and maintained an African tradition in the New World (Acosta Saignes, 1967:202–5; Bastide, 1971:99). Yet, paradoxically, one of the reasons for allowing the formation of such *cofradías* and *cabildos* in the first place had been to further control over the black population (Bastide, 1971; Ortiz, 1921).

The scanty accounts of Christianization suggest that conversion and consolidation of belief remained little more than a formality throughout the entire epoch of slavery. Indeed, Sandoval (1956:198) echoed the common observation that the slave owners regarded

Christianized slaves as more rebellious and as poorer workers than those not indoctrinated and would pay less for them (Sandoval, 1956:198; cf., Bowser, 1974:79; King, 1939:16–17). Whites were not only disinclined to buy Christianized slaves but tried to prevent their conversion, at times telling them that baptism was bad. According to José Toribio Medina, slave owners, reluctant to pay the costs of lengthy inquiries and penalties, encouraged their slaves to disappear if they were on the Inquisition's wanted list (1889). As a result, an underground African or quasi-African religion seems to have flourished, at least during the early years, syncretized with ardent faith in the miracle powers of Christ and the saints—powerful spirits who could be appealed to for earthly succor.

In 1771 the Bishop of Popayán, capital of the Cauca region of southwest Colombia, complained bitterly that his attempts to catechize the slaves and prevent their being worked on Sundays and feast days encountered the firm opposition of the slave owners. He believed that clerical mine speculators were identifying too closely with the exploiters of their slave flocks (King, 1939:217). The right of the slaves to rest on feast days, of which there was at least one a week in addition to Sundays, was hotly disputed by the Cauca mine owners during the eighteenth century. Yet, in a study of the health of slaves in New Granada, David Lee Chandler concludes that for many slaves the Church's insistence on rest days "must have . . . prolonged their lives" (1972:238). On these days they could also earn the wherewithal to buy their freedom, but many Cauca slave owners responded by reducing the food and clothing ration of the slaves. In these circumstances the feast days may have inclined the slaves favorably toward the Church and added a religious rationale to their opposition to their masters.

Priests were in short supply, and few gave much attention to Christianizing slaves. "As a result," writes Norman Meiklejohn, "many of Colombia's Negroes were blithely ignorant of Christianity's true meaning and of its moral precepts" (1968:287; cf., Pons, 1806, 1:160). Yet surely this "ignorance" cannot be explained only by the shortage of priests. Black popular religion could hardly endorse slavery and all it implied, nor could the slaves remain content with equality in God's eyes but not in their own. But only with the breakdown of the colonial hegemony and the power of the Church could a radical interpretation of Christianity surface fully, as it did in the chiliastic doctrine espoused by the radical liberals from the 1840s onward.

In the opinion of Ramón Mercado, native of Cali and Liberal party governor of the Cauca region between 1850 and 1852, it was pre-

cisely Christianity in its true sense that was astir among the oppressed classes as a result of their condition and the authorities'
abuse of doctrine. The slave owners and their priests taught a perver-
sion of Christianity, which eventually facilitated their overthrow.
His accusation was leveled not against Christianity, which he saw
as innately liberating, but against the slave owners and the Church,
whose preaching "was reduced to the idea of a terrifying God so as to
exalt the large landowners, inculcate blind respect for the privileged
classes, . . . combat with the threat of eternal punishment in hell the
libertarianism threatening their hegemony, . . . and to erect as sins
the slightest action of the poor and devalued classes" (1853 : xi–xii,
lxxix). As Mercado astutely observed, it became a moot point who
was practicing idolatry, the rulers or the ruled. The tremendous
power of the slave owners, nowhere greater than in Cauca, engendered a religious fanaticism prone to violence.

With the impulse set afoot by the unsettling conditions of the
French Revolution and the Wars of Independence from Spain, the di-
abolical God of the slave owners spawned an antithetical vision of
the holy cause among the subject classes—a radical Catholic utopia,
anarchist and egalitarian, founded in the sacred ways of nature. Con-
fidently assuming the support of the masses, Mercado declared, "We
have to drag into the light of Christianity the iniquities that they
have committed against the people. The people know that their
rights should not be at the mercy of rulers, but that they are immanent in nature, inalienable and sacred" (1853 : lxxix).

Manumission, Laissez-Faire, and Regional Disarticulation

The significance of these prophetic claims emerges from
the nineteenth-century records of the largest slave estate in the
Cauca Valley, that of the Arboleda family. These records lie in the
Archivo Central del Cauca, Popayán, Colombia, and are yet to be
fully classified and indexed. Unless otherwise specified, all the following citations come from this source. In 1695 the originator of the
clan, Jacinto de Arboleda, had left only forty-seven slaves (Jaramillo
Uribe, 1968 : 22). In 1830, his descendants Sergio and Julio Arboleda
were among the wealthiest men in the republic, with some fourteen
hundred slaves rotated between their mines on the Pacific coast and
their gold placers and *haciendas* at the southern rim of the Cauca
Valley.

The country was vast, its inhabitants few, and effective control of runaways difficult. During the late eighteenth century, escapes and uprisings became a major social force along with the growing restlessness of free blacks and a general wave of discontent throughout the colony, which culminated in the war of the *comuneros* in 1781. In the Cauca Valley, plots were uncovered for large revolts, some of which included alliances with the Indians, and secret societies of slave *cabildos* were discovered also (Jaramillo Uribe, 1968: 68–71).

In the very southern part of the valley, near the Arboledas' domain, a mine owner and his son were killed by their slaves in 1761 (Arboleda, 1956, 2 : 306–7). Ensconced securely in a *palenque* deep in the woods along the Palo River bordering the Arboledas' vast estates, escaped slaves began cultivating high-grade tobacco during the last quarter of the eighteenth century and continued till abolition. Living as outlaws, they clandestinely produced about one-twelfth of the valley's entire crop. Police did not dare to enter the area. The runaways had amicable relations with the dissolute friars of the nearby monastery, who were said to be living with mulatto women, and worked with bands of tobacco smugglers in constant conflict with the government and its tobacco monopoly (Harrison, 1951 : 33–40, 132–40, 200–2).

Colonel J. P. Hamilton, who traveled through the Cauca Valley as an observer for the British government in the mid-1820s, stayed in the largest of the Arboledas' *haciendas*, Japio. He thought that their slaves were physically superior and healthier than those in other *haciendas* and mines in the valley, and noted with approval that the priest held confession. "If any conspiracy is plotting among the Blacks, the priest will, in all probability, find it out in the confessional chair" (1827, 2 : 130). His surmise proved incorrect. In the early 1840s, slaves from the Arboledas' *haciendas* joined the rebel army of Obando, who was sweeping southwestern Colombia with the promise of immediate abolition, and they sacked these estates. Obando's titles included "Protector of Christ Crucified," and he raised the standard of revolt to the cry of "Federalism and Religion." In 1841 he decreed that all slaves who joined his forces would be freed and their owners recompensed from the government's manumission fund or from his own resources if those proved insufficient. But the revolt failed.

In 1843 the provincial government estimated 400,000 pesos as the loss occasioned by the escape or death of slaves and the confiscation of cattle. The slave owners feared a recurrence of race war and attempted to pass a vicious penal code for blacks in 1843 (Helguera,

1971:192–93). A more businesslike reaction to rebellion and the plummeting price of slaves was to sell slaves abroad. Julio Arboleda marched 99 adults and 113 children over the Andes to the Pacific coast and sold them to Peruvian slavers for some thirty-one thousand pesos (Helguera and Lee Lopez, 1967)—a diaspora the blacks never forgot. Whatever peace the Arboledas enjoyed for most of the slave era, they bequeathed bitter memories that survive today. Blacks commonly say that the interior walls of the *haciendas* are permanently blotched by the blood of whipped and tortured slaves, which no amount of painting can conceal. At midnight on Good Friday people claim they hear the clatter of a mule carrying Julio Arboleda, vainly seeking repentance for his sins.

In 1851, with the avid support of the slave owners of the valley, the Arboledas led an unsuccessful civil war to oppose abolition. Against the rising tide of radical liberalism and class hatreds, they argued that labor would disappear. They were right. Gold mining in the southern Cauca Valley ceased soon after except for marginal peasant prospecting. Yet, despite their defeat and loss of slaves, the Arboledas maintained a semblance of their previous *hacienda* operations—a readjustment facilitated by their wealth and status and their location between two important and closely connected towns, Cali and Popayán. Most important, Sergio Arboleda, Julio's brother and owner of Japio, had prepared contingency plans for abolition—a policy encouraged by the national government's vacillation. By abolition in January 1852, the *hacienda* Japio and its subdivision of Quintero had prepared for the transition by institutionalizing a new category of workers, the *concertados*: blacks who, in return for a small plot of a few hectares, worked a certain number of days on the *hacienda*. Just before abolition, some 40 percent of the adult slaves had become *concertados*.

A neighboring slave owner, Joaquin Mosquera, who had been president of Colombia in 1830, wrote in 1852: "Up till now the general abolition has not produced any serious commotion; but I do see alarming difficulties because agitators have been advising the blacks neither to make work contracts with their former masters, nor to leave their lands, but to take them over" (Posada and Restrepo Canal, 1933:83–85).

Such incidents were common. Gilmore states that in the mining province of the Chocó, well to the northwest of the Cauca Valley, "property owners feared communistic expropriation of their property." Concerning the mines of Barbacoas, to the southwest, the famous geographer Augustin Codazzi reported that "perverted or ill-intentioned agitators had infused in that ignorant and uncouth people (Negroes and mulattoes) the idea that they should not work for whites, and the lands of the latter ought to be divided amongst them" (Gilmore, 1967:205).

Three months later Mosquera reported that his mines in the Caloto area resembled a town destroyed by an earthquake. He spent two weeks bargaining with the exslaves over the reorganization of the mines, most of which he rented out at "vile prices" to local white merchants and to blacks. The huts and plantain groves were divided up among the exslaves by family and distributed free of charge; the pastures were rented. The blacks, he wrote, "are now the owners of my properties, leaving me only a kind of dominion, allowing me but one-fifth of my previous income." And the same dilemma faced landowners throughout the valley (Posada and Restrepo Canal, 1933; Holton, 1857:381–82, 420, 511).

Returning to their estates in 1853, which had been temporarily confiscated by the victorious Liberal party, the Arboledas refined the *concertaje* system. They partitioned 330 hectares of virgin forest among the blacks of Quintero and provided them with "bread, clothing, and a roof." The blacks had to clear the forest, establish plantings for the *hacienda*, and pay off rents (*terrajes*) with five to ten days of labor each month. In a further effort to overcome the decline in the labor supply, Sergio Arboleda began a more capital-intensive production: brandy distilling, which became the main source of income of the *hacienda* and accounted for much of its economic success relative to other *haciendas* in the valley, then in steady decline.

The Arboledas tried to control their tenants tightly by restricting public meetings and work on rented plots. They had considerable success, but never consolidated the labor supply they so desperately needed. Years later, in 1878, Sergio Arboleda described his problems. While slavery had lasted, he had considered the woods along the border of the *hacienda* La Bolsa and the Palo River, which had so long been a refuge for runaway slaves, his own. But when the estates were confiscated by the Liberals in 1851, the slaves set free, and he and his brother forced to flee to Peru, "anarchy took over and when I returned in 1853 the political upheaval continued till 1854 and so great was the horror that infested those woods that nobody dared try to reach an agreement with the *terrajeros*. I myself was too afraid to enter in there." With the revolution of 1860, free blacks refused wage work even when offered generous terms. In their resistance the blacks took advantage of the national political turmoil, which rent the Cauca Valley more than any other part of the republic. Under either the Conservative or Liberal party banners, feuding elites fought savagely for state power in a region in which the sullen class hostility of the newly formed yeomanry tipped the balance of power.

Imprinted with the antagonisms of centuries of slavery, this new class of peasants found a precarious freedom in the disunity prevalent among their exmasters in a subsiding economy. The estate owners vainly strove to commercialize their holdings and to recoup their wealth during an economic contraction that isolated the Cauca Valley from the new markets, while the peasants subsisted on a generous soil.

As the republic became more involved in free trade on the world market, the national market became fragmented, each segment of the interior carrying on its principal commerce with Europe. It had become cheaper to bring goods to the western provinces from Liverpool than from Bogotá (Safford, 1965 : 507–8). While some areas like the tobacco-producing region of the Magdalena Valley were caught up in the current of free trade, the Cauca Valley became an economic backwater.

In 1857, Sergio Arboleda observed that the economy of Cauca was in far worse condition than it had been at the beginning of the century. Mines, public buildings, aqueducts, bridges, churches, and private houses lay in ruins. It was impossible to find artisans for reconstruction. The debris of neglected *haciendas* marked the countryside. Gold mining had collapsed. Prices of agricultural products had doubled since the definitive end to slavery in 1852, so that even though wages had also increased, the day laborer was worse off than before. Yet, "if we have lost our internal trade," he went on to note, "we have gained an external one. Today foreign imports are six times as great as before." Local industry could not compete with foreign, and local capital had been diverted to the purchase of foreign goods. He exhorted his fellow landowners to invest in agriculture and tropical exports—"tobacco, vanilla, rubber, sarsaparilla, sugar, and a thousand other products." But two problems remained: the shortage of labor and the insecurity of property. The lower classes disdained wage work, and there was no guarantee for "the sacred right of private property," which had received its first assault with abolition (1972 : 328–31).

Business confidence was also totally lacking. Sergio Arboleda perceived that slavery had engendered a moral climate antagonistic to the work ethic. That legacy and the distortions in capital investment induced by the new imperialism notwithstanding, he emphatically blamed the social malaise on the weakening of the Christian

religion, which alone could contain the lazy and ignorant population. "We have to return to Catholicism its empire, organize once
again the Christian family . . . re-establish the right of property . . .
and create a new permanent army" (Arboleda, 1972:207). Years before, slave owners had excused themselves from Christianizing their
slaves, whom they called too ignorant. Now, one of their leading
ideologues was making an analogous argument against bourgeois democracy by claiming that the ignorant masses could live in harmony only if they were Christians.

The unity of *hacienda* and chapel had been severed. The exslaves
retreated into the adjoining jungle to form a self-subsistent population of independent cultivators, free to create their own understanding of Christianity. Christianity, which landlords like Arboleda depended upon to contain the masses, was not weakening; rather, its
folk component was being liberated. The Church's latent function
had always been to coordinate distinct castes and classes around a
common ideological basis in which mysticism and official doctrine
congealed. The religion of the Mysteries, the miracles, the spirits of
the ancestors and the saints, together with the fear of the *malefici-
um*, had always held the souls of the blacks. And now, just as the
landlords' perception of the Church's function was changing, so was
that of the blacks, who no longer had to submit to their masters'
God in their masters' chapels as part of their holy family.

From its inception and not only when the Jesuits ran it, Japio was
as much a ceremonial as a production center. Indeed, its chapel was
the center of the vice-parish of Our Lady of Loreto. As large as the
owner's "big house," it was built of brick and tile, unlike all the
other *hacienda* buildings, which were built of adobe and thatch.
With stunningly jeweled and brocaded saints, silver crowns, and
gold and coral necklaces, the value of the chapel and religious ornaments amounted to 15 percent of the *hacienda*'s total capital, including slaves.

In 1753 the administrator had been instructed to take particular
care with religious observances—to compel instruction, prayer, and
singing each evening. In 1830 the visiting priest was contracted to
give mass once a month, to perform baptisms, funeral services, and
marriages for the slaves, and to undertake confession and first communion annually. He received a yearly stipend of 70 pesos, which
was two-thirds of the administrator's, and a per capita fee for deliver-
ing the sacraments. After the uprising of the early 1840s he ceased to
come.

After abolition, Sergio Arboleda contested the right of the Church to keep charging him the *primicias* or First Fruit's tax—usually one in seven bushels or animals—proclaimed the chapel to be his own, and bitterly denounced the changes in religious functions. While there had been slaves, he stated, the costs of religion had reaped him benefits, but now the Church no longer kept the blacks under control.

The parish priest replied in a tone unthinkable for the preabolition epoch. He revealingly alleged that after 1833 the slave owners had ceased to contribute to the costs of the sacraments and that up until abolition the priests had been forced to give monthly mass. He had continued as best he could, but it had become impossible because of lack of worshipers. The slaves had had so little free time to sustain their families that they had had to spend their Sundays cultivating their provision grounds. He berated the owner for ensconcing the chapel's ornaments in his house, so that the priest was forever at his mercy in organizing services. It was totally false, he said, that the chapel belonged to the Arboledas, that they had built it and paid for the ornaments. Rather, these had come from the Jesuits when they owned Japio. The very cemetery had been despoiled so that Sergio Arboleda could enlarge the *hacienda*'s patio. Finally, contrary to what Arboleda had said, the feast days could not be blamed for the fighting and general immorality of the blacks. The owner was to blame, with his distillation of brandy, the chief product of the *hacienda*, which he sold without scruple so long as he made money.

Church and religion acquired a new significance when the master-slave bond was ruptured. The landlords could no longer claim the Godhead, and given the supremacy of theology as the force sanctioning seignorial rule, all revolutionary doctrines and actions necessarily became religious heresies. By the same token, the underclass of society cast the landlords in the image of the antichrist and cast the worst aspersions on their faith. The culture preserved its intensely religious disposition; but now, inflamed by the social struggle over land, work, and freedom, a Manichaean consciousness was surfacing to buttress the fanatical division between the Liberal and Conservative parties, a division which wracked Colombian society from the mid-nineteenth century onward. The Liberals had dealt slavery its final blow. The blacks gave their fervent support to their most radical principles, just as the Arboledas remained devoted to the Conservative cause. Even though party leadership was notoriously fickle, here in the old heartland of slavery the social conditions ensured that the tempestuous ideological cleavage would sink deep roots.

Refractory Tenants: Idlers and Rebels

Although Sergio Arboleda repeatedly insisted that substantial rents and labor could be wrought from his tenants, he was forced to develop other means to secure labor and to maintain control. He rented large areas of pastureland to well-to-do cattlemen, many of whom were clergymen. The cattlemen could place their own tenants, provided the owner gave permission. This measure improved income and, perhaps more important, facilitated social control of the vast estate. He also established a laboring elite of whites. In his instructions to the estate manager in 1857 he said that the blacks worked too slowly in the mill and ruined the animals; only whites were to be employed there. Once proven, these whites were to be contracted for three years on a regular salary, he instructed, and to be given a plot to cultivate and on which to build a hut. They were not to be charged a rent, but had to work when called. If they did not, then they would be thrown off, and the *hacienda* would not pay for any of the improvements they had made to the land. They could not work for anyone else without Arboleda's permission.

Arboleda stressed that the working day of the blacks should be organized by piecework rates, never by time, and that it was better to leave work undone than to owe money. In the planting and harvesting of readily edible crops, like rice, only male peons from far outside the *hacienda* were to be hired, "but do this without people understanding that you do it intentionally." And, he added, beat down the wages of women.

There were two types of black tenants: those who paid rent by working one day a week for the *hacienda* and another more privileged group of 180 tenants who paid a pittance in cash annually—a sum that could be earned from a mere five to eight days labor. It would have been far more advantageous to the *hacienda* if these tenants had also paid in labor, but the Arboledas lacked the necessary power. This cash-paying group also provided the informants who kept a check on the constant thefts that plagued the *hacienda*.

By planting perennials like cocoa where there had been dense forest and by fencing in grasslands, Arboleda made further attempts to hem in the restless peasants. Thus, the monolithic, tightly centered slave *hacienda* gave way to a series of concentric spheres of authority, with a great variety of distinct but overlapping relationships to the central power. Large cattlemen who rented land, white peons, free contract workers, cash-paying tenants, and labor-paying tenants found themselves in a gridwork of oppositions to one another.

Slaves had constituted slightly more than one-half of the *hacienda*'s total inventory. Now the wage-labor bill was one-half of the *hacienda*'s running costs. The annual sales of brandy and cocoa turned out a handsome profit, which, however, proved unsteady. In the early 1860s and again in 1876 the *hacienda* was confiscated during civil wars in which Sergio Arboleda took a prominent and losing role.

The recurring struggle for land control is well illustrated in Arboleda's instructions to his administrator in 1867 and in 1871, when once again the balance of power tipped in his favor. His main concern in 1867 was the black tenants. They were to be divided into neighborhoods and successively called upon to pay their dues. A large renter was to be given the power to supervise rent collection in each neighborhood. Each September special vigilance would be required, according to the instructions, to stop tenants from clearing forest for planting corn without permission, and to ensure that those who did paid a rent. Immediate expulsion was to follow failure to pay, and no tenant was to be allowed to subrent or bring in outsiders. Artisans were to provide their own food. "I say this because experience has taught me: first, they charge the same whether you feed them or if you don't; and second, that almost all of them when they are assured food don't do in a month the half of what the food is worth, and at the end of a year's work, the task has been barely begun."

Some peasants responded angrily. In 1867, Arboleda received a letter about the rights to distil brandy:

Señor Arboleda:
Who do you think you are? By good fortune do you think that you are still in Quinamayo with your brother the Granadine Caligula and your army of bandits sacrificing the poor? Do you think that we will any longer tolerate your roguery? Alert, Doctor of Revenge; it is a scandal that a man like yourself that has so many ways to make money steals from the poor women their right to make brandy—their only means of livelihood left after you and your brother robbed us during the revolution. You are a public thief, an assassin, infamous and without shame! Take off your trousers and wear bushes. What have you come to do here? To rob us. Don't think that we have forgotten all the evil you have done. The hour of revenge will strike. We will never forget the firing squads of San Camilo and Palmira, nor the gallows in Piendomo or the orders of your brother to starve the prisoners to death. Do you think that you

are going to make us die of hunger too, quitting the income from the women? If that's what you think you are mistaken because here nobody has fear. Take care that the brandy isn't going to be the way you pay off your debts. Watch out that your wickedness and criminal life doesn't end up the same as your brother's [who was assassinated in 1862]; every Caeser has his Brutus. It's better to rob the government 300,000 pesos or more than make war on the women over brandy for this is very ridiculous. Look out or the people will fulfill their duty for we are free and sovereign; no longer are you Chief of State of the Goths [Conservatives] that can rob and kill as in 1861.

Some Masked Ones

By 1871, Arboleda's instructions concerning tenants had become lengthier and even more pugnacious. Squatters kept occupying land, and many tenants were refusing to conform. Arboleda instructed his administrator to make a census and expel those without documents if they would not pay rent. He advised caution. It would not be prudent, he said, to expel all refractory tenants simultaneously. The most rebellious should be dislodged first, to teach the others a lesson. All squatters were to be driven off by destroying their habitations, and all clearing of land in Japio by small tenants planting corn was to cease. The peasants retaliated by burning the cane fields and sabotaging the Arboledas' attempts to extend sugarcane cultivation so as to combat soil exhaustion.

By the late 1870s profits were well down. They remained so until the demise of the family and the beginning of large-scale commercial agriculture in the early twentieth century, when a railroad connected the Cauca Valley to the Pacific coast and thus to the international market. The intransigence of the black peasantry made it virtually impossible to survive the economic crisis. In 1882, Arboleda was trying to sell the estate. His son Alfonso, who took over the management in the mid-1870s, wrote despairingly to his father of theft, lack of labor, armed rebellion, refusal to pay *terrajes*, and the unremitting hatred of the peasants for the landlords. "These haciendas now produce nothing. . . . The only hope is with the *terrajeros*, but they refuse to pay. And the plantains! You have to place a guard beneath each tree so they aren't stolen." The production of cocoa was constantly threatened by theft. The blacks made paths throughout all the plantings, constantly tore down fences, and even blocked transport in and out of the *hacienda*. The political situation was desperate: the Liberal party faction of Hurtado "has assaulted our domain, stolen our arms, and is now taking on the oligarchy." The blacks in the Arboledas' lands along the Palo River were armed and fighting on the side of the Hurtadistas, but hardly as puppets. "The blacks around the Palo River," wrote Alfonso in 1879, "are constantly in arms. If they continue doing just whatever they please, and because here there are no forces to protect the landowners and no other way of making them see reason, then we will have to appeal to the Liberal government to see if they will apply force. For these blacks who are attacking the oligarchs are also a threat to the present government."

The blacks had a personal reason to arm and fight, for the Arboledas were trying to drive them out of their refuge along the Palo River. From the eighteenth century, runaway slave camps in this area had been an irritation to the Arboledas. With the *hacienda's* production slowing to a halt, the Arboledas now turned to these fertile lands in a forlorn attempt to break the independence of the smallholders and to sell their lands, as well.

The blacks constantly feared reenslavement. When Alfonso set by some stores of rice and plantain, a rumor spread that he and the government were about to take the blacks' children and sell them in another country, as Julio Arboleda had done in 1847. "From this," he wrote to his father, "you can calculate the hatred there is against us and you can infer that the stealing of the cocoa from the deposits comes from nowhere else than the cocoa buyers who propound these lies. The worst is that the blacks believe these tales and are alarmed."

Alfonso wanted to reequip the mill with modern machinery from the United States, but the constant threat of revolution paralyzed business. In 1882, with the collapse of the boom in quinine, the region's only export, money stopped circulating. The few workers that he could get for the mill enraged him because of their laziness and constant *fiestas.* "It's impossible to get workers even though one trips over idlers every day."

Contradictions of the Transition Period

The Cauca Valley now found itself at the margin of the commercial world as the market split the national domain into selectively discriminated satellites. Despite the *hacienda's* commercial success relative to others in the valley, it too eventually succumbed. Mercantilism and slavery had given way to attempts to create a free market. Yet, the exslaves could not be forced into wage labor. Refractory tenants, the convulsion of incessant civil war, and the restricted nature of the export market made large-scale commercialized agriculture untenable. Caught between two modes of production, the landlords tried to resort to a "neofeudalism" diluted by free contract labor. But land was abundant, the culture of servility had been transcended, and free contract labor proved too expensive with the national and export markets blocked.

Time and again, eyewitnesses described the tantalizing promise and general ruin of the valley; the problem lay in securing market outlets to the Pacific and in overcoming the allegedly lazy and surly disposition of the lower classes. In 1853, General T. C. Mosquera, thrice president of the republic and one of Cauca's most prominent sons, noted that the majority of the state of Cauca was black or mulatto. But whereas the whites were "intelligent, active, laborious, and moral," the blacks were "weak for labor, enduring, and suspicious" (1853:77, 97). Felipe Pérez, a Colombian geographer, pointed out that it was not merely laziness that was at issue but equality. The astonishing fertility of the soil meant that "to eat one does not have to work"; therefore, "people excuse themselves from serving others, and this spirit of social equality that predominates among the poor, drowns and tortures the aristocratic pretensions of the old mining feudocracy" (1862:212–13). Pérez insisted that "all that is necessary is that the idle hands which exist today stop being idle, and that social harmony, the best guarantee of work and business be allowed to prevail" (Ibid.:139).

But "all that is necessary" was far from possible. The characteristics noted by Mosquera, that the blacks were "weak for labor, enduring, and suspicious," and the spirit of social equality by which people excused themselves from serving others, as described by Pérez, had a material basis in the newly formed black peasant mode of livelihood. They sought refuge along the fertile river banks and in the dank forests, planting their staples of plantain, some corn, and a few commercial crops like cocoa and tobacco. Fishing and panning for gold were supplementary activities. Pérez, who pointedly refers to the decadence of all forms of agriculture and livestock raising in the valley, repeatedly singles out plantains and cocoa as the two crops of outstanding importance around 1862. These were primarily peasant crops, found along the wooded banks, swampy areas, and in the densely wooded regions inhabited by black peasants "refractory to the attacks of malaria" (García, 1898:28–29). This type of area abounded in wildlife, which the residents hunted and used as a source of meat (Pérez, 1862:140). E. Palau was of the opinion that the *"region privilegiada"* for cocoa was around the Palo River, the storm center of the black peasantry. Plantains were interplanted with young cocoa trees to serve as shade. According to García, in the late nineteenth century the best plantings of plantain in the entire valley were also located there (García, 1898:23). Palau described the plantain as "the most useful tree of the Indies" (1889:32). It is a semi-perennial producing fruit every eight to twelve months regardless of the time of year, and like all the peasant crops, it requires very little labor. Today, with a roughly similar ecology, a subsistence-sized peasant plot requires no more than one hundred days of relatively light labor. Evaristo García estimated that one hectare of plantains could supply twenty-four adults with their staple food requirements. He described how in his journeys through the valley he would enter the wooded regions to find inhabitants of the "Ethiopian race" sheltering in thatch huts surrounded by plantains and many other useful plants. Some families possessed small herds of cattle, horses, and pigs. Because they could thus subsist so easily, in his opinion, the peasants were loath to work on the cattle and sugar *haciendas*. For this reason, he wrote, there were few functioning large estates up till the end of the century (García, 1898:29).

In many senses these black peasants were outlaws—free peasants and foresters who lived by their wits and weapons rather than by legal guarantees to land and citizenship. The fearful specter of a black state was not lost on some observers. "In the woods that enclose the Cauca Valley," wrote the German traveler Freidrich von Schenk in 1880, "vegetate many blacks whom one could equate with the maroons of the West Indies." They sought solitude in the woods, "where they regress once again slowly to the customs of their African birthplace as one commonly sees in the interior of Haiti. . . . These people are tremendously dangerous, especially in times of revolution when they get together in gangs and enter the struggle as valiant fighters in the service of whatever hero of liberty promises them booty." With the revolution of 1860, the Liberal party's forces had destroyed the last restraints holding back the blacks. The majority of the valley's *haciendas* had gone bankrupt and suffered terribly from the persistent onslaughts of "fanatic" blacks. "The free black in the Cauca Valley," he wrote, "will only work under the threat of an excruciating poverty, and even so, is still likely to persist in his destructive ravages" (1953:53–54). And the worse blacks were those who lived in the southern part of the valley.

The peasants especially valued the *indiviso* (indivisable) and common lands, most used for cattle raising. Although the landlords claimed these as their own private property during the late nineteenth century, and more vigorously once the valley was opened to foreign markets in 1914, the peasants considered them communal and inalienable. In fact, they were more like no-man's-lands. Whereas the highland Indians held communal land under government sanction, the blacks of the Cauca Valley held commons informally and, if anything, provoked government disapproval. Pursued by a hostile gentry, denied political representation, deprived of the security of land tenure, denied the possibility of any representative village structure within the official framework of administration, the black peasants formed a new social class that stood outside society. Internally, their social organization appeared infinitely flexible and capable of endless permutations and combinations, as their kinship structure still attests. As a class, they had not evolved from years of patrimonial benevolence encrusted in manorial custom ensuring some minimal guarantees and protection. Thus, the new peasantry contained aspects of two different traditions: that of the slave and that of the slave-outlaw (*palenquero*). Violently excluded from society, the peasants were forced to challenge its institutions and views. In attacking the *haciendas*, they attacked what they saw as the cause of their suffering: they knew full well that so long as the *haciendas* existed, their owners would persecute them in search of their labor.

Shortly after abolition, police and "good and patriotic citizens" received wide powers to arrest so-called vagabonds and to force them to work on *haciendas*. As a result, the plains of Cauca became lands of brigandage and fear (Harrison, 1952:173). In 1858, Miguel Pombo, a leading government official, described the need for stricter laws to combat the increase in idleness and the high cost of food. The peasants were no longer bringing their foodstuffs to the town market and were neglecting their crops. Pombo suggested forcing them to work by placing them under the control of the police and the landlords. These measures, which would include starvation and flogging, were also to apply to the allegedly idle and drunken day laborers (*El Tiempo* [Bogota], Sept. 7, 1858:1; cf., Lombardi, 1971; Estado del Cauca, 1859).

The constantly harassed state could not achieve the ends so desired by the entrepreneurs. Much later, in 1874 for example, the heads of the tobacco industry complained to the town officials of Palmira, the most important rural town in the valley, that production was declining because of the lack and disposition of manual labor. "What is necessary," they urged, "are means that are coercive, prompt, efficacious, and secure" (*Estados Unidos de Colombia*, 1875:139).

Merchants, who formed a rising commercial class in the valley from 1860, began to act as intermediaries in the export of crops grown by smallholders and of products gathered by contractors. Many Colombian merchants took part, including Rafael Reyes, later president of the republic. The type of intermediary most likely to succeed as both merchant and landholder in the Cauca Valley was one with sources of foreign credit and accurate market information. Such was Reyes's close friend Santiago Eder, who as a United States citizen and consul with close kin in business houses in London, New York, Panama, and Guayaquil established himself in the southern part of the valley in 1860 (Eder, 1959). Weaving together a network of foreign and domestic commerce exporting tobacco, indigo, quinine, rubber, and coffee and importing finished goods, Eder built up the largest and most efficient sugar plantation in the valley. Its success owed much to mechanization. At the same time that the manager of Japio was forlornly recommending a modern mill from the United States as a way of alleviating the labor problem, Eder was installing a "Louisiana No. 1" mill, which was far superior to the one planned at Japio. Aloof from the internecine conflicts between Liberals and Conservatives, protected from confiscation by his status as foreigner and United States consul, he and men like him controlled the region's economy when the valley was opened to the Pacific in 1914. Immediately following abolition, Sergio Arboleda had advocated just this sort of development. But the ex–slave owners' incapacity to engage in foreign commerce, their ideological zeal, and their continual attempts to maintain an estate agriculture with unmanageable tenants ruined them.

Religion and Class War

Since the late 1840s, violent regional and national civil wars between the Conservative and Liberal parties have rent Colombian society, the latest being the *"violencia"* of 1948–58. Indeed, the parties seemed less political organizations than "hereditary hatreds," and the political culture was one that fostered an absolutist world view in which all controversy was conducted in quasi-religious and moralistic terms (Dix, 1967:211–12). Practically all explanations of the *violencia* focus on the competing elites and the patron-client relationship. The patron as a type of feudal warlord or *caudillo* acting through his broker or *gamonal* mobilizes his clients, the peasants, to war against another patron-client faction. The intense feeling of party attachment attributed to the peasantry is explained as the result of their dependency on their patron, transmitted down the generations, reinforced by the primary socialization of family life.

This Hobbesian view of society and human nature, the quintessence of the bourgeois experience of alienation and reification, interprets political ideology as the mechanical expression of the self-interest of opportunist *caudillos*. Yet it finds little support in the social history of Japio. In the southern Cauca Valley the peasants did not follow their erstwhile overlords. Rather than blindly follow a mystifying ideology imposed on them by an elite or be forced into struggle without moral conviction, they forced the elite to respond to a peasant anarchism fired by hatred of landlords and fanned by millenarian dreams. Heroically stimulated but forever crippled by vagueness of doctrine, this is the social basis that largely accounts for the bewildering tumult of *caudillo* realpolitik. Anarchism is most visible at the time of abolition and the millennialist fervor in the war of 1876–77. The absence of a vigorous bourgeoisie inclined the social struggle toward the populist form—the "people" versus the aristocracy. That the peasantry could not constitute itself as a class for itself, although it came close, does not justify theories that exclude class conflict and class alignments.

Frank Safford has argued, perceptively, that without detailed regional studies, the conventional occupational and economic class explanations of party affiliation and civil war in nineteenth-century Colombia must remain inadequate. But even he concedes that in the Cauca area "liberalism came to be an instrument of class conflict, representing the landless or dispossessed in their struggle against the large landowners, and often with leadership from a lower stratum of the upper class" (1972:361; cf., Bergquist, 1976).

These class struggles assumed a religious character. Orlando Fals Borda, summarizing a large body of scholarly opinion, writes, "The internal conflicts after 1853 that were fought ostensibly for the control of the budget, or for changing the Constitution, were really fought on religious grounds" (1969:108). The two parties became defined in Manichean terms. "One was either for or against the Church, on the side of God or the devil" (Ibid.:105). Contrary to the assumption that is often made, the Conservatives had no monopoly on religious passion. The Liberal extremists advocated a kind of romantic Christian socialism, as the Conservatives recognized. A prominent Conservative wrote of the uprisings at the time of abolition: "I have seen that demagogic socialism has appeared in some parts, as in the beautiful valley of Cauca, with the fatal furor with which the Anabaptists wanted to establish it in the sixteenth century. I am seeing the alarm which the gains of communism cause

in the very men who have fomented it in satisfaction of their ven-
geances, forgetting that it is not given to any agitator to contain the
revolutionary movement once he impressed it upon the misled multitude" (Gilmore, 1967:206).

In 1850 the official journal of the Archdiocese, *El Catolicismo*,
warned in a leading article "The Communism of the Gospel and the
Communism of Proudhon" that anarchists had misused the gospels
to persuade the people that "*communism* is the fundamental principle of Jesus Christ." It denounced a radical politician as an enemy
of property "who proclaims communism as a law of God" and asserted, "The Liberals profoundly reverence the sacred rights of communism, the sacred doctrines of Proudhon" (Gilmore, 1967:207–8).
The radical Liberals, who at mid-century propounded a confusing
form of libertarian socialism, acquired the name of "Gólgotas" from
the habit of their orators of referring to Jesus as the martyr of Golgotha. "Socialism is nothing else than the tear fallen from the Saviour on the hills of Golgotha," declared one of their spokesmen, José
Maria Samper (Gilmore, 1967:202). Liberal populism had firm roots
in a fervent anticlericalism, heir to the ideology of the French Revolution and the Wars of Independence (Giménez Fernandez, 1947).
United States diplomats in Colombia had no doubt that the civil
wars were basically religious. The Conservative party was the
Church party, and Church control of civil affairs provided "the only
vital internal political issue among the Colombian people" (Shaw,
1941:598).

The revolution of 1860 culminated in the complete separation
of the Church from the government and the disfranchisement of
the clergy. Many priests were banned from the country. More than
three-quarters of the Church property was confiscated. Education
fell under government control, although the bishops of Cauca, aware
of growing divisions among the Liberals, defiantly organized their
own schools. The church made attendance at public schools and
nonadherence to its political principles punishable by excommuni-
cation. The government then forcibly closed the Catholic Society of
Popayán, and similar societies in the Cauca Valley were closed by
groups independent of the government. Led by Sergio Arboleda, the
most popular figure in his party, the Cauca Conservatives, "in defense of our religious beliefs," began the war of 1876. To the battle
cries of "*Viva la religión. Viva el padre Holguín y el partido con-
servador*," and with *vivas* to the *Santísima Trinidad*, the bishop of
Popayán, and Pope Pius XI, who had condemned liberalism in 1864,
they attacked the town of Palmira. Priests armed only with cross
and rosary led insurgent battalions named "Bishop of Popayán," and

"Bishop of Pasto." In the most famous of all the battles at Los Chancos in the north of the valley, which left about 400 dead out of 7,500 combatants, the Conservatives were commanded by Sergio Arboleda (Briceno, 1878:241). His soldiers bore banners with pictures of Pope Pius XI and of Christ (Eder, 1959:267–86; Shaw, 1941:597; Briceño, 1878:228).

Accounts of the sacking of the principal town of the Cauca Valley, Cali, by Liberal troops in December 1876 provide a revealing glimpse of class, party, and religion (Eder, 1959:283–99). About two-thirds of the twenty thousand inhabitants were described as a vagabond population of blacks and mestizos imbued with intensely communistic doctrines. Unlike this rabble, the remaining one-third, whose property was devastated, was principally of Spanish origin and belonged to the Conservative party. The leader of the Liberal troops, David Peña, was said to be a communist visionary, a mystic lunatic, and an assassin blindly devoted to the maxims of the French Revolution and the Colombian Democratic Clubs founded in the 1840s. He allegedly initiated the movement to exile the bishops. Yet, he was a devout Catholic. He fought, he supposedly said, for glory and to exterminate all the Goths (Conservatives), who were to be swept out of his natal city in a flood of vengeance. His troops and the aroused mob destroyed Liberal as well as Conservative property—a lack of discrimination that turned the Liberal government against him. But there was little that it could do, for he commanded an enormous force and the loyalty of the lower classes. Armed bands of blacks were still roaming the streets eight months later. He led a lower-class populist upsurge with chiliastic overtones, which was directed against the property-holding class and the government machinery that supported it.

A Swiss professor, who taught for some years in Bogotá, visited the Cauca Valley in 1884, the same year in which Santiago Eder informed the United States ambassador that the "Valley was drowning in political and religious sectarianism" (Ibid.:304). To the professor, the typical Caucan was "a fanatic for his religion and will sacrifice everything, family, life and possessions, just for triumph. Because of this they are cruel in all conflicts and know no compassion. Here is the cradle of all revolutions, and here they generally end" (Rothlisberger, cited in Eder, 1959:265).

In 1875, Sergio Arboleda received a letter from his son, then managing Japio.

> In the last session of the local Democratic Club, mainly attended by blacks, they were saying that the aim of the Con-

servatives is to make a new revolution in order to re-enslave all the blacks. The Conservatives are believed to be saying "Slavery or the gallows for all Blacks." What is more, they state that the Conservatives are not true believers but feign Catholicism in order to deceive; the only true Catholics are the Liberals. In passing by one of the small shops . . . I heard a black saying "There in Mondomo we'll put the noose to their necks, apply the lash (making a gesture towards the sky) and then leave them to hang." . . . I fear greatly for you. You cannot return.

The Liberals stood to the true meaning of God, as the Conservatives stood to the devil. Religious ideas and mystical sentiment formed the essential nucleus of other political ideals. It could hardly be otherwise in this society saturated with religion and magic, and with the wounds of slavery still smarting in the souls of the now relatively independent but constantly persecuted yeomanry.

The letter from Japio was, after all, sent to the most popular Conservative leader in Cauca, commander of the Conservative troops and one of the most ardent, intelligent, and scrupulous devotees of the Church—the "*caudillo* of the Divine Cause," as pronounced at his funeral oration in 1888. The letter reflected the moral crisis in society, begat by anti-Catholicism and the ideals of the French Revolution and spurred by economic stagnation and political turmoil. Earlier, Sergio Arboleda had argued against the Liberal economic theory of the "invisible hand." He saw nothing in it except, as he put it, an egoistic bond incapable of constraining the violence of passion. The only hope lay in the Church's exercising dominion over a hierarchically organized society. Divine origin and infinite wisdom would prevent the Church from becoming tyrannical. True, Arboleda agreed, the Church's constitution was monarchical and despotic, but the Church's law was moral and thus protected and regulated democracy. "In short," he concluded in perhaps his most famous oration, delivered in Popayán in 1857 in response to the economic crisis, the Church "is the founder of liberty in the world. For her there are neither races nor classes, vassals nor kings, free nor enslaved. She recognizes them all and leaves them in their place. All are considered equal before God. Such is the Catholic clergy. The clergy can save us and nobody can save us but the clergy" (1972: 364).

The Cauca slave owners had used this sort of Christian doctrine as an argument against abolition. "Slavery is supported by the Holy Scriptures" began a particularly revealing passage in a broadsheet circulated in Cali in 1847, which cited Paul's famous epistle to the Ephesians (Jaramillo Uribe, 1968:264). The blacks feared reenslavement, and the Catholicism of the Church was the religion of reenslavement. Yet they had their own religious tradition, too: of folk belief, rural rites, and magic. As it had in the *palenques* of early colonial times, their leadership included sorcerers, such as José Cenecio Mina, their guerrilla commander during the War of One Thousand Days (1899–1902) who later so ably led the blacks' resistance to the Arboledas' usurpation of their lands. The peasants thought that he could transform himself into an animal or plant when pursued and that he was impervious to bullets. In doting on his memory they exult in the power of their folk heroes, as well as in their cultural autonomy from the larger society, the upper class, and the state.

The blacks of Colombia did not develop clearly defined syncretistic cults like voodoo, *santería*, or *candomblé*. Yet Thomas Price, who studied black folk religion in Colombia in the early 1950s, wrote: "There developed an integrated complex of Spanish Catholics and African usage, believed by the people themselves to be completely Catholic and therefore particularly immune to the efforts of priests who desire to banish the 'pagan' elements. This complex is a fundamental, functional aspect of their total way of life, and the adjustment they have made to their spiritual and practical needs is an adjustment unshakable by Catholic and Protestant missionaries alike" (1955:7).

This "little tradition" of the black peasantry related to the "great tradition" of the city and literati primarily through the doctrine of radical Catholicism assiduously expounded by radical Liberals like Ramón Mercado, one-time governor of the province.

For Mercado, the ideological currents of the European Enlightenment and the social changes effected by the Latin American Wars of Independence formed an explosive threat to the old institutions, which lingered on nowhere more tenaciously than in Cauca. Like Sergio Arboleda, he saw the root of social turmoil in a moral crisis. But for him this crisis resulted from the comprehension of the lower classes that the evolving essence of man was being negated. In the new social conditions, the toilers would no longer suffer their exploitation for the sake of the aristocracy, the army, or the clergy. In essence, he argued that Christianity had both a revolutionary and a reactionary potential. The revolutionary—and true—Christianity had originated before the Middle Ages as the religion of equality and fraternity. The reactionary form of the doctrine derived from the Middle Ages and feudalism, in which the Church had allied itself with the aristocracy against the common people, whom it allegedly defined as brutes or things, devoid of reason. But although the revolutionary implications of Christianity could be thus deflected, they remained ready to burst forth when times were ripe, to clarify the social struggle, and to stimulate action. "The instinct of which we speak derives from the ancient Christian revolution. This is the light brought from on high in order to enlighten and disentangle the gloomy chaos of inequalities and frightening abominations that they called the Roman world. The Christian revolution is the celestial explosion, the revelation of equality; this is the providential truth in the heart of a society that rests on privilege and slavery" (Mercado, 1853:iii).

As Mercado went on to say, a new age was dawning, relentlessly preordained in the march of reason and the essence of man, both embodied in Christ—who personified the Liberal creed. This messianic vision foresaw social equality in the divine inexorability of God's conquest of Evil. The God of the status quo, the false God of the ruling class and a corrupt clergy, systematically negates humanity. Now the time has come for the two forces that compose the social order to fight out the cosmological contradiction that engulf it. Equality versus privilege. Free inquiry versus authoritarianism. Nature versus cultural artifice. Reason versus Dogma. The lower classes, headed by the radical Liberals, were fighting the slave owners or ex–slave owners and the clergy—those conservatives who were holding back history and truth. To be a Conservative meant to conserve the old civilization. To be a Liberal meant to follow the true teachings of Christ—democracy and liberty—as summarized by Mercado:

> I saw during those solemn days, elderly people of eighty years spontaneously arm themselves and march to battle to defend the legitimacy and the regeneration of Democracy; elderly people barely clothed and trembling with their many years, but strong with their faith and throbbing with their enthusiasm for the Republic. I saw hundreds of young people and adolescents leave their homes, their wives, their children, and their belongings in order to offer their lives to the holocaust of the Holy Cause—to contribute to the triumph of Democracy and the redemption of the people. . . . We extinguish all the distinctions of rank because all men are brothers, and we all have the same right to enjoy the benefits of a society organized for welfare under the protection and guidance of Providence. [1853:lxxviii–lxxix]

The skirmishes, beatings, riots, and open wars that pulsed through-out the valley during the second half of the nineteenth century all seem to have been animated by such ideas and visions of the world. These conflicts between two multiclass parties, riddled with the factionalism of competing *caudillos* and their clients, were also genuine class conflicts, persistently channeled into unstable interclass alliances. Both the socioeconomic conditions and the ideology sustained the vigor of the underlying class antagonism. The black peasants were continually forced to defend what they saw as their rights to the land against a white elite that fought desperately to develop a commercialized estate agriculture based on wage labor and tenancy. The landed elite could force no more than a small minority of the peasants into peonage. The battle raged unremittingly.

Folk religion and class hatreds, if not class consciousness, had become symbiotically fused. The hatred of racial and class privileges was nourished by a radical reinterpretation of Catholicism in which the peasants' fight for land was sanctified by a complex cultural tradition evolved from the experience of slavery, the *palenque*, and the peasant-outlaw class sheltering in the jungles alongside the failing estates. The relation of God to the underworld remained forever fraught with the violence of the master-slave bond. When the blacks broke that bond, they recruited God to their side and let their masters go to the devil.

Ethnographic Postscript: 1970

Even today, peasants in the southern Cauca Valley, the descendants of the Arboledas' slaves, talk about the political parties and the Church in terms of the structure of sentiments beaten out on the anvil of contending social formations, when history provided a glimpse of alternate possibilities and transformations. "The priests? Some are less repellent than others." Christ gave liberally and founded the Liberal doctrine. The Conservatives wished to conserve evil and reenslave the blacks. An old peasant, Felipe Carbonero, on being asked in 1972 to explain the differences between the two parties responded in accents parallel to those of the radical Liberal intellectuals of the mid-nineteenth century.

The Conservatives wished to conserve the Law of the Spanish . . . to kill and enslave . . . to catch Negroes and sell them . . . to sell them from one *hacienda* to the other . . . to catch the Negro slaves and make them work night and day without paying them anything except their food—nothing more. This is what is called to *Conserve*; to conserve the evil law of the Spanish. From that comes the word "Conservative." The Conservatives wanted to make us into slaves again. That's why there were so many wars. The word "Liberal" is the word "free" [libre] that Jesus Christ spoke when he came into the world; freedom for everybody, Jesus Christ brought that when he came; freedom for all the world. This is what is called "Liberal"—a world of freedom and thought. . . . The Negro can never be a Conservative; neither can he humiliate himself. The Negro can only be a Patriot; never a Conservative. But it's not the rich who lead us. Here it's poverty. Here, in this region, it's the poverty that moves people, whether they be Liberal or Conservative, it's the poverty.

The fear of reenslavement, or worse, was still a factor in the *violencia* of 1948–58. On being read the letter from Alfonso Arboleda to his father, another elderly man commented: "Until today this exists. In a letter Dr. Laureano Gómez [the Conservative leader seen as instigator of the *violencia*] said he would finish off the blacks because most of them were Liberals. He would kill them or make them into Conservatives. That's why the *violencia* occurred and why it hit the black race hardest. Thus till today this letter of Arboleda's is significant."

The relationship between religion and politics, with the emphasis on free inquiry and the inalienability of land, emerged in a conversation in 1971 with another old peasant, now a cigar maker, Eusebio Cambindo:

Here the Bible was "artistocricized" or wicked and excommunicated as those people say. The Bible was good, but only for them; only for the priests. Anybody else who had a Bible was excommunicated; they went to hell. Listen! From where came the ignorance of the people, and the lack of understanding between *pueblos*, the hatred between blacks and whites, the big against the small? From where comes this egoism? It comes from the exploitation that one side doesn't want the other to know the truth about things—the truth in the Bible, the truth about life. . . . Well, God gave the land in common to all the world, to everybody . . . it says that God said, My land can be neither sold nor bargained for.

An eighty-four-year-old man, Tómas Zepata, a poet and now blind, who worked all his life on his small plot, commented on the differences between the two political parties whose struggles have tortured Colombian society for a century. First pointing out that the physical pressures of war would force you into the fray as a zealous partisan, he went on:

All is one,
And one is in all.
Into the one goes all,
For everything divides into two;
A single thing is always divided.

To which he added as an afterthought, "When Jesus Christ came, he said, 'Some of you are with me, and some of you are against me.' But it's the same thing really, because we all come from God."

A Manichean dimension is there. The world is split into two opposed and hostile parts—Good against Evil, Liberal against Conservative, Equality against Inequality. It is a natural law that things divide into two. Yet, "All is in one, and one is in all." The division will be transcended by a larger unity. Wholes are destined to become self-alienated subdivisions. Relationships become sundered into antagonistic parts. But that is only a moment in a larger and more inclusive process whereby unity is forged. The meaning of life and the force that animates the cosmos may be seen as a duel between God and the devil, the Liberals and the Conservatives, but they are all merely facets and oblique representations of the underlying truth of oneness and a common human destiny. "But it's not the rich who lead us. Here it's poverty. Here, in this region, it's the poverty that moves people, whether they be Liberal or Conservative, it's the poverty."

CHAPTER 4

Owners and Fences

"We are the owners and our fences are our titles"
Ricardo Holguin—owner of *hacienda* Perico Negro

The twentieth century ushered in a vast transformation that virtually broke the back of the peasant class. With the end to the devastating civil war, the war of One Thousand Days in 1902, the triumphant Conservative party was able to enforce a climate of "stability and progress," establishing the security for foreign investment, which entered Colombia on a scale unequaled for any other Latin American country (Rippy, 1931:152). Much of this capital was invested in the Cauca Valley. President Reyes, a close friend of Santiago Eder's, was in great need of funds to develop the valley where he himself had large holdings (Rippy, 1931: 104; Eder, 1959:221, 405). In 1914 the valley was opened to the world market by the rail line across the Andes to the Pacific and by the canal in Panama. United States advisors instituted a new banking and tax structure. In the southern part of the Cauca Valley there was an extremely sharp natural increase in the rural population and an even larger increase in the urban, increasing the demand for food.

As a result land values soared, and simultaneously, the large landowners secured the power to dislodge the peasantry and to initiate large-scale commercial agriculture. Peasants saw their plots expropriated, first for cattle raising and later for plantation crops, and they themselves were increasingly forced into wage-labor and the cultivation of cash crops on their shrunken holdings.

The large landowners now had the opportunity to make money from land; provided they could secure labor and submission from the unruly peasants. The ensuing enclosures of land were not only a bid to add acreage; they were also an attempt to deal with the problem of labor discipline afflicting the manager of Japio in 1882—"We cannot find workers even though one trips over idlers every day." In the words of the old *mayordomo* of the largest estate in the southern Cauca Valley, that of the Holguins', describing the return of the owners in 1913, "They came to dominate the negroes and expand their *hacienda.*" Rural proletarianization began in earnest. National censuses indicate that wage laborers constituted a mere fifth of the number of smallholders in 1912. But by 1938 the proportions had reversed. The wage laborers were a third larger than the number of smallholders and had increased fivefold.

Why wasn't a capitalist economy developed on the basis of commercial peasant farmers? Why did it develop by means of large estates and wage labor? The social organization of the peasants posed an obstacle to capitalist institutions. The working of land was shrouded in a maze of intensely personalistic relations based on different rights and obligations woven into a kinship system of multiple marital unions. To some extent the peasants produced for the national market, but consumed few market commodities. They were neither easily able nor zealous in expanding a surplus. Without the clearly drawn lines of private property in the modern bourgeois sense, they were refractory to the financial institutions and inducements that met and attracted the ruling classes. The peasants' bonds of kin and kind meant that capital accumulation was a virtual impossibility. Wealth, not capital, might be amassed, but only to be divided among the succeeding generations. Of course, merchant capital could coexist with this form of social organization, but since national capital accumulation demanded an ever-increasing domestic market, peasants who continued to practice self-subsistence were an obstacle to progress. Whatever the intricate calculus of the emerging system, its initial push was to destroy a form of social organization embedded in a nonmarket mode of using and sharing land.

Describing the beginning of enclosures, an old peasant tells how Jaime Gomez came. "He began to usurp, to rob, to damage, and to disquiet the residents of Barragán, Quintero, Obando, and so on. Then you had to flee or sell. In Barragán he broke the houses and erased the communism, the *comuneros*, because there were *comuneros* there." Systems of teamwork, festive labor parties and reciprocal labor exchange, were in force. "The *minga* [festive labor]. In that week you skin a pig, a chicken, a calf, or whatever, and invite your neighbors to work. They are working and others are preparing the meal from those animals. One or two days, whatever it is. One month or a week later I do the same. This we called the *minga.* It's like . . . a proletarian union. It was common. But today there is nothing because in this sector the owner peasants remain with no-where to work, with nothing to work . . . for a *minga.*"

An old man born in 1890 recounts:

> Around 1900 there were hundreds of *terrazgueros* [tenants]. There was hatred between the poor and the rich. The poor had no titles and the rich with the judges pushed the people off their *fincas* [farms]. This became very fierce in the War of One Thousand Days. Mostly it was done by the Holguins and the Arboledas. By the time Jaime Gomez came as a *hacendado* there were not many *terrazgueros* left. My father had 150 *plazas* on the other side of the Palo River [A *plaza* equals 0.64 hectares]. But the *terrazgueros* were kicked off into tiny lots of around half a *plaza* in the pastures of Los Llanos and became day laborers for the *hacienda.* They came with horses and lassoes and pulled the houses down without warning. I got a job feeding the horses and getting water. After, I cut cane for the animals. Then I went to work for Jaime Gomez as a milker and later on as a muleteer carrying the harvests of cocoa and coffee to Cali and Jamundi. I would take 12 mules at a time every two to three months and bring back barbed wire and salt. When they built the railway I only had to go as far as Jamundi. Another landlord was Benjamin Mera and he bought land from the Arboledas too. He was a black and a Liberal, while Jaime Gomez was white and a Conservative. But it was the same thing. Lots of Liberals did the same as the Conservatives. There wasn't much resistance here in Quintero. The rich brought in the law, the authorities, to get rid of the blacks and they didn't even pay five cents for the land.

"Man is one thing, law is another; two things very different. One thing is law and another thing is man," says Tomás Zapata, an old blind peasant, illiterate, and a poet. "In the War of Independence everyone fought together, rich and poor, blacks and whites, Conservatives and Liberals. But after we had triumphed the poor were left waiting at the door and the land was divided amongst the heavies, the rich. The poor were left in the street. Nothing. And then the poor began to revolt. But when the rich understood that the poor were going to take back the land they imposed the *política* [politics] so that there wouldn't be any union amongst the poor."

The invigorated entrepreneurial class seized the so-called common lands as well—those large pastures that people used in a type of communal tenure, the legal status of which was most complex.

Often these common lands were called *indivisos* because they could not be divided, use-rights being inherited from generation to generation without partition so that by 1900 hundreds of households could claim usage. From the early 1900s onward local newspapers contain reports and official notices of the partition of such lands. Typical was the *indiviso* "Bolo de Escobares," in which around 440 "owners" were involved. It was located just to the north of the Puerto Tejada area and was valued at 40,000 pesos. The newspaper *El Comercio* announced to the "sharecroppers" of this *indiviso* on 16 June 1904 that lots from twenty-five to one hundred hectares were now on sale. Inalienable land became alienable. Land became a commodity as never before, and what peasant could pay? Peasants had customarily exchanged land by buying and selling improvements—the *mejoras*—not the land itself. But now, secure ownership required purchase of land, and few could afford that. At the same time the large landowners were rarely in a position to pay for the improvements. Thus, both parties became locked in conflict. Increasingly, one finds advertisements for barbed wire. It had been introduced into the valley in the late 1870s together with new types of grass. Small wonder that one of the more common advertisements in newspapers around the turn of the century reads: "The most useful book ever published in Colombia is *The Household Lawyer*." And, as Phanor Eder noted in 1913, "Cattle prices are going up continually. Profits are large."

Tomás Zapata talks of the *indivisos*.

Indiviso land consists in this. When the discoverers found America the land was then guarded by the Indians that were here in those times. Then the discoverers began to take their lands, because all the poor people were held by them as slaves. All the poor class were enslaved by the people who took the land. This owner would have that land over there, and another owner would have another portion of land over there, and another owner would have another portion of land over there, and there was still a lot of land without any owners at all. Thus they uprooted those who were here first, the Indians, but never got round to selling all the land that remained. They just sat content with their arms folded and a lot of land that they possessed was never sold and it became impossible to sell it. This is what they called an *indiviso*, and such land could never be alienated. They also called these lands *comuneros*; that was the land where you and I, and he, and someone else and someone else, and so on, had the right to have our animals.

The animals were divided by their brands; no bit of land was divided by fences. There were some *comuneros* with eighty families. They were lands where you could place yourself as an equal with everybody else. Here almost all the land used to be like that. But after the War of One Thousand Days, the rich came along and closed off the land with barbed wire. From then on they began to take ownership of the lands, even though it was not theirs. If you had your portion of land or share of land and it was not fenced in, they would come from afar, and as they had wire, they would close it off and you just had to get out of there because the law would not shield you. That's how it started; the rich kept coming and coming, throwing people off the land, stripping every poor person of their possessions. Then they planted grass for pastures. That is why the people who were here had to either leave or go to work for the rich, because there was no law for the poor. They felled the poor. Even the *mejoras* had no value; when they closed you in, you had to get out. And thus the *mejoras* that you had—they ravished them without paying.

The memory of the assault is vivid and lives on in popular legend as a holocaust. The memory of a Golden Age is equally tenacious, recalling a time of plenty, self-sufficiency, and neighborliness. An old woman describing the 1920s recounts this sense of irretrievable loss. "Before the rich invaded here there were only us peasants. Each family had its cattle, two or five. There was much milk and meat and plantings of rice, corn, plantains, and some cocoa and coffee. There were no machines for pulping coffee. We did it with a stone. We made very little chocolate because it gives you colic. We grew tomatoes next to the house, onions and manioc too. But today! No! Where could we plant?"

Eusebio Cambindo talks about the past as we sit in his one-room shack in the township of Puerto Tejada fronted by the green slime of the open sewer. His grandchildren help him roll cigars, his only way of earning a living now that they have no land. As the candlelight flickers on the crumbling mud walls, he insists that Don Tomás Zapata's account needs to be complemented with his own, for Zapata is a philosopher, whereas he lives for literature.

Before the rich entered with force, the peasants had large *fincas*. There were big plantings of cocoa. Now it's all gone, all of it. Milk was very abundant. Meat was abundant without preparation. You didn't have to stew it, just a slab on its own. The plantains; big and more than enough. Fruit; whenever you wanted it. If you didn't want it then someone else could have it. Life was more than easy. You would arrive at whatever place and they would serve you food and give you hospitality and ask you to stay. The only thing we bought here was salt, and sometimes clothes, something to cover yourself in. From here to there was nothing else because the peasant produced all. You never bought food. Soap was made from ashes and tallow. Candles were made in the home. Animals, like horses? If you needed one it was lent. Little exploitation there was at that time; people loaned everything. I needed your bull to reproduce cow's milk; you would lend it. You needed my horse. I would lend it, and so on, successively.

He adds, "God gave the land in common to all the people. Why was it necessary that one or two or three thieves became owners of enormous quantities while there were other people that also needed land?"

The Holguin family, whose sons thrice assumed the presidency of the republic, returned to reassume their domain in 1913—"to dominate the Negroes and expand their *hacienda*" inherited from the Arboledas. Maria Cruz Zappe, daughter of Juan Zappe, a general famous for his exploits as a guerrilla chief in the War of One Thousand Days, saw it all.

They began to get rid of the peasant farms. Right up to the banks of the Cauca was in cocoa. They cut it all down, quit, quit, thus, no more owners. They came with their peons and planted grass all around the house and cut down the farm and as the Conservative government of Caloto came to protect them there was no law for us. They wanted to widen themselves, to make pastures. There were blacks with pasture and they were all thrown off. They had their pastures for their cattle and they had their farms and they were all thrown off. That place they call Palito. That was a little village by the side of the river. They tore it all down without recognition of anything, without paying even one cent. They put pasture right into our beds because Popayán would not help the race. Caloto neither. They were against us.

Where they could not or did not want to dislodge peasants, the Holguins levied rents, first on the land and then on each cocoa tree. The bandit Cenecio Mina assumed the leadership of the groups that formed the resistance. "For example," continues Zappe, "there was a struggle against the Cambindos in Barragán. They were opposed to paying rents while at the same time other groups arrived here in Puerto Tejada; from the sides of Serafina—a señor Balanta; from the side of Guachene—a señor Santiago; from Sabanetas—some other señor; and so successively. So the groups formed to deliberate amongst the wisest blacks. They were self-defense groups aimed at liberating the tenants so that they wouldn't be thrown off and so that cattle wouldn't be put into their farms and so that people could keep what they had had before." Through this organization the peasants were largely able to revoke the rents imposed on cocoa trees. To have their customary use-rights and *mejoras* made rentable was to them the final straw.

Mina was a powerful sorcerer. He could change himself into an animal or plant to elude the police and the *hacienda* guards, and he was impervious to bullets. He did this through his knowledge of the *ciencia cabalística*—the Jewish mystical doctrine of the Cabbalah, which entered into Renaissance thought and magic via the Hermetic tradition. Hidden deep in the woods, he lived on his large farms with many concubines. An old peasant dotes on his legend.

> When they began to tear down the peasants' trees around the *vereda* of Palito the people called on Cenecio Mina to defend them because all the lawyers for miles around were with the Holguins and none would help us. Thus, as he was a Negro, they called on him. The Holguins tried to raise rents by charging rent on each tree of cocoa; four pesos per tree. The people wouldn't stand for that because it was they who had planted those very same trees. They would pay for the right to use the land, but for the trees, no! And so the people got together and said they would do nothing.
>
> Cenecio Mina wasn't educated in the university, but he was a man of natural talent, gifted with science; natural science. He hadn't had even a week in the school. He was a colonel in the War of One Thousand Days. The people around here loved him a lot and he had a band of over 100 men. Thus he came to defend us against the *hacienda* of Periconegro, the Holguins' *hacienda*, and those who were defended went with him to defend other blacks in trouble way over in Ortigal.
>
> They captured him and took him prisoner to the capital, Popayán, but as he was a man of means, I guess he bribed the police, because he got away soon after that. That man could break open mountains and go wherever he wanted to and nobody knew how he did it or where he was. The day he broke

out of prison was celebrated around here like the birth of a newborn child.

He knew the law. He knew how to defend himself, and he defended all the rest of us. They chased him and chased him. Another time they got him but he wouldn't let them keep him. He wouldn't let them. He just slipped away all the time. It was the rich who got him in the end. They paid a friend to poison him at a *fiesta*.

A granddaughter of the Holguins who were supervising the estate at that time relates that in retaliation for the fencing in of land and the sowing of pasture, Mina and his followers killed cattle and left the carcasses with a sign stating, "Mina did it." Such men had risen to fame and proven their mettle as guerrilla commanders during the War of One Thousand Days, nearly always on the side of the Liberal party.

In 1915, some two years after the Holguins returned to the region to reclaim their patrimony, the alarm at Mina's activities was so great that the government dispatched a permanent body of National Police to remain in the Puerto Tejada area in an attempt to track him down (Gobernador del Cauca, 1915:2).

In his 1919 annual report the governor of the department of Cauca complained bitterly about the degree of social instability in the Puerto Tejada area, which he ascribed to the "economic abnormality" of the times, the difficulties people faced in feeding themselves, and the lack of a penal colony. He urged the formation of a special corps of police that "would give guarantees to the *hacendados* and the business of cattle dealing" (Gobernador del Cauca, 1919:4).

During the provincial elections of 1922 (according to government reports) the police narrowly averted a slaughter of white Conservatives by black peasants in the district of Guachene, some five miles to the southeast of the township of Puerto Tejada. In the same year the police were directed to contain the attacks against landlords in the Tierradura district, six miles to the east. The peasants were intent on invading and occupying lands that had been fenced off (Gobernador del Cauca, 1922:4, 6). The land in question had been taken by the Eders' company, La Compañía Agricola del Cauca, and today this land is one of the largest sugar plantations in the entire republic, El Ingenio Cauca—owned by the Eder family. The peasants claimed (and still do) that the land belonged to the local smallholders because it was an *indiviso*, and since 1922 the area has known repeated land invasions by these peasants and their descendants, in the mid-forties, for example, and also in 1961 (cf., Instituto de Parcelaciónes, 1950).

The Commercialization of Peasant Agriculture

The bandit-led struggle was transformed into a more modern political movement in the 1920s as peasants created militant syndicates. These spread over Colombia in the 1920s and early 1930s, but subsided thereafter with the election of a reformist national government (Gilhodes, 1970:411–22). At the same time peasant cultivation became increasingly oriented toward cash crops. In 1833, according to a census of the province of Popayán, the annual production of cocoa in the Puerto Tejada region was a mere 11.4 metric tons and there was no coffee (compare this with figures for the 1850s in Codazzi, 1959, 2:69). In 1950 all peasant plots were planted in cocoa and coffee with, of course, some plantain as well. Around 6,000 tons of cocoa were produced annually, all of it from peasant holdings. Monsalve's (much criticized) census of 1925 reported 59,000 coffee trees in the municipality of Puerto Tejada. The National Federation of Coffee Growers reported 576,000 in 1932; an increase of almost 1000 percent in seven years. As peasants turned to more intensive cash cropping, they also became more dependent on money, to the detriment of their earlier autarky; they boarded a treadmill on which they sold most of what they produced and bought much of what they consumed. Increased production of cash crops was caused by the declining size of plots, by the new monetary demands of landlords determined to squeeze out in rent what they could not get through dispossession, and by the legal and de facto security to land that perennials bestowed. Cash cropping was also a response to the inducements and pressures of incoming merchant traders representing large business houses, the tentacles of which sprouted from the national capital and the northern hemisphere.

A part-time resident of the valley and descendant of the Eder family, Phanor Eder, has left us the following description of rural commerce around 1910. He said that the bulk of the country's business was done by general stores, which functioned as exporters and importers, wholesalers and retailers. Foreign trade worked through commission houses of the United States and Europe. Even a large part of the gold and silver went through the same firms. In the coffee trade, the larger planters shipped directly to the commission merchants, to whom they were often indebted for advances. The smaller planters sold to the general stores, which financed the purchases by

sixty- and ninety-day drafts on the commission houses. Local dealers had agents, who scoured the countryside. In some cases these local dealers were independent, but more often they were in close relationship to the purchasing agents of the foreign houses, many of
which owned a number of plantations that they had taken over for
debts (Eder, 1913:124–25).

By the second decade of this century, the commercial and population center of the southern part of the valley had shifted to black
territory in the depths of the "dark jungle" (*monte oscuro*), as it had
been called by outsiders (Sendoya, n.d.:83). Here, at the junction of
two tributaries of the Cauca, the blacks evolved a flourishing market, linked to the city of Cali by the river system. Municipal status
was granted by the government in 1918. By the late 1920s this center, called Puerto Tejada, became part of the road network, which allowed for a freer and different movement of goods, took a good deal
of the transporting away from blacks since they had controlled
riverine transport, and indicated, above all, the region's commercial
coming of age. The annual reports by the governor of Cauca during
the 1920s mainly concerned the construction of bridges and roads
connecting the Puerto Tejada region to the main centers of commerce. Built mainly on the money paid over by the U.S. government
as indemnification for the "secession" of Panama, the railway line
between Cali and Popayán had reached within walking distance of
Puerto Tejada by the mid-twenties (Ortega, 1932:198–206). Road
and rail construction became an obsession for enterpreneurs, who
constantly chafed at the high freight costs (Eder, 1913:151).

Plantains were the basis of peasant self-subsistence. Surpluses
were taken by bamboo rafts down to Cali, and during the last decades of the nineteenth century the region was famous for the abundance of its plantains. Today, most plantains are imported from fara-
way areas. Cocoa became the peasants' mainstay. It flourished under
local soil and climatic conditions as few other crops could, and the
peasants had been used to its cultivation since slavery. It had a good
selling price and formed a natural and legal impediment to landlord
predators greedy for pasture and sugarcane land. Cocoa slowly
emerged as a cash crop in steady proportion to the decrease in the
subsistence crops on which the peasant lived while waiting the five
years for the cocoa to mature. But from the 1930s and 1940s the
planting of cocoa without capital became increasingly difficult, for
the plots were generally too small to achieve such a balance.

It should also be observed that when the land was abundant and
cheap, cocoa was a better-paying proposition than coffee. But when
land became scarce and expensive, coffee became the more lucrative

alternative. The initiation of coffee planting by peasants in the 1920s was a response to this.

The merchants who flocked to Puerto Tejada in the 1920s and 1930s to buy peasant cash crops also acquired great political control. They were whites, generally from Antioquia, and members of the Conservative party. The black-owned shops around the central *plaza* were replaced by theirs. These middlemen held agencies or commissions from the large cocoa- and coffee-buying firms. Conveniently entangled with these large firms, they were just as conveniently disentangled from the peasant producers, whom they could exploit with little fear. Although outsiders could act as businessmen, there were reasons why this was not so easy for locals. As an old peasant points out:

> The black is more afraid of big business deals. He fears to put even 20 cents into a business because he thinks he will lose it. The black is less of a financier than the white. He's just not the same as a "Paisa" [Antioqueño]. The "Paisa," if he has 20 cents, he invests them, and gets out 40 or nothing. The blacks here are agricultural people. They aren't acquainted with business, with the bringing in of a pack of clothing or establishing a cocoa-buying agency. And what is more, if I set up a shop here, then it's not long before the gossip and the maliciousness starts; the envy of man against man. And then I slowly enter ruin because I have to live by trust. "Here, take it, pay me to-morrow! Go on, take it, tomorrow will be alright!"
>
> And then you, for reasons of race, or because you are a *compadre*, or for friendship, just never pay me. In that way I would become ruined. I would lose all my capital. But the white man, no!; because he gives me credit within the bounds of business—he gives me credit of 40 cents because he has already robbed me of 80 on the same deal. He already has 80 cents profit. Thus he gives me 40. If they are lost, he really hasn't lost anything!

By the late 1930s, land pressure seems to have become acute. The sugar industry and large-scale commercialized agriculture were becoming firmly institutionalized in the social fabric through more stable financing and powerful landlords' associations, welded together by a common fear of the peasantry and the need to control marketing and infrastructural development (cf., Gilhodes, 1970: 417; Fals Borda, 1969:141; Dix, 1967:323–26). Technological uplift with improved varieties of sugarcane and other crops, together with new livestock species and methods of breeding, was introduced or restimulated by the Chardon mission and the opening of the Palmira agricultural school in the Cauca Valley in the early 1930s (Chardon, 1930). The Rockefeller Foundation gave further stimulus to capital and energy intensive agriculture by establishing the national government's institute of agronomy in 1941.

A local black schoolteacher wrote an impassioned appeal to the government in 1945:

> Since a long time now many people are being forced off the land here. Most people have only two to ten acres and nearly all grow cocoa exclusively. Most of the peasants are illiterate and only know how to work their plots. During the first decades things went well because the soil was so rich and there were no plagues. But now there are too many people. Minifundia and mono-production have emerged with all their dreadful consequences. The occupants of each plot doubled and tripled in a short time and the plots became smaller. In the past 15 years the situation has changed threateningly. Today each crop gets smaller and smaller and the harvest is preceded by a long wait; thousands of physically active people are forced into idleness. . . . Usury increases, stealing increases; life is now a pendulum oscillating between misery and forlorn hopes. The peasants of Puerto Tejada are suffering a situation without parallel. It is obvious that it is not possible to limit this situation as more and more people are deprived of their patrimony.

The Violencia

The horrendous Colombian civil war from 1948 to 1958, aptly known as the *violencia*, further accelerated the enclosure of peasant lands by the burgeoning plantations as their owners took advantage of the frightful insecurity of those times. Peasants claim that the large landowners used the aerial spraying of herbicides to destroy their cocoa, a tactic used in other parts of Colombia in the 1960s, as well (cf., Patiño, 1975 : 181–83). Peasant plots were flooded as large landowners manipulated irrigation and drainage canals, and access to plots was blocked by sugarcane. As a result, the production of cocoa, the mainstay of the peasant income, dropped by 80 percent from 1950 to 1958 (Wood, 1962).

The spark that set the *violencia* flaming throughout Colombia was the assassination of the Liberal party *caudillo*, Gaitán, in Bogotá on the famous Ninth of April, 1948. Cities like Bogotá and Cali erupted, but Puerto Tejada was the only rural settlement to react in the same way. An uncontrollable mob sacked the stores in the afternoon and evening, but there was little personal injury. Nevertheless, the report that reached the outside was grotesque. Supposedly nuns were raped, and Conservatives (generally whites) were decapitated and the blacks played football with their heads in the *plaza*. Such fantasies of Puerto Tejada complement its portrayal as an inferno of violent thieves and vagabonds—an increasingly compacted reservoir of black malcontents in a political geography dominated by white rulers. The fantasies perpetrated about the *violencia* of Puerto Tejada stem from the fear generated by exploitation and racism.

An eyewitness relates:

> I was preparing adobe when I heard on the radio that the leader of the people, Doctor Jorge Eliécer Gaitán, had been assassinated. At that time Nataniel Díaz (a black leader from Puerto Tejada) was in Bogotá, and with a group of students they took the national radio station. That was when Nataniel Díaz said on the radio, "Alert *macheteros* [people of the machete] of Cauca! Take vengence on the blood of the *caudillo* Jorge Eliécer Gaitán." Almost all the stores were owned by white Conservatives, who fled or barricaded themselves. Within moments rockets were lit calling the peasants from around the town. They left wherever they were. From all the rural neighborhoods they came. They took the official liquor store at four in the afternoon. They drank *aguardiente*, rum, and all that. Everyone got drunk. Everyone took a bottle and had a couple more in their pockets and then began sacking the stores. It was incredible. Mainly they went for the stores of the political chiefs who ran the town. They took sugar, rice, candles, soap. . . . But here the people didn't want blood like in other places where they killed Conservatives. No! Here they wanted to rob; nothing more. They also robbed the rich Liberals.

This was not an organized uprising. It was a spontaneous outburst of the people, led by years of humiliation and outrage. This was anarchy, but it was founded on generations of oppression and clearly focused morally. The *pueblo* was always ruled from the outside and from the top down. There were no formal organizations that the people could call their own. Small wonder that when the levees of state control gave, the flood that had been mounting for years poured wildly, taking with it the goods that not so many years before the people had prepared on their own plots: "They took sugar; they took rice; they took candles; they took soap."

Within days the army quelled the riot and military law provided the cover with which the plantations appropriated peasant farms. With the aid of World Bank and U.S. financing the plantations have continued their remorseless expansion across the flatlands (Fedesarrollo, 1976 : 344). Whereas only 2,000 tons of sugar were produced in the region in 1938, some 91,000 tons were produced by 1969.

Local land sales and tax records (supported by peasant oral history) show that the modal peasant holding decreased from 4.8 hectares in 1933 to 0.32 in 1967. This fifteenfold decrease was accompanied by no more than a doubling of the local population. Land shortage cannot be blamed on the "population explosion" as the Rockefeller Foundation experts try to claim (e.g., Wray and Aguirre, 1969).

Government censuses show that by 1970, whereas some 80 percent of the cultivable land is owned by four sugar plantations and a few large farms, 85 percent of the holdings are less than six hectares and ownership is becoming increasingly concentrated. The majority of the holdings are so small that their peasant owners are forced to work on the large estates. According to my own census in 1971, 8 percent of the rural inhabitants are virtually landless, and another 63 percent have less than the two hectares necessary for subsistence.

A local agronomist pointed to the economic function of this pattern of land distribution in which the peasant mode of production coexists with that of the large-scale capitalist. "The poor peasants supply the labor closest to the plantations. As they possess their own houses they save the plantation the cost of constructing housing and the transport of a very large number of people. Moreover, their economic necessities tie them indefinitely to the plantation outside of which it would be difficult to obtain work (Mancini, 1954 : 30).

The Dual Nature of the Proletariat

Unlike conditions in most sugar-producing areas of the world, the climatic and soil conditions of the Cauca Valley permit year-round aseasonal production. The notorious instability of the labor situation cannot be ascribed to ecology but to the political action of the plantation owners taking advantage of the fact that many of the workers also have small plots of their own.

In the early 1960s the militant trade union structure was broken by the growers, who established a dual system of labor recruitment and employment. This was accompanied by a switch from growing all their cane themselves to buying more than half of it from independent large farmers by 1974. Faced with serious labor unrest and the need to expand production as never before—to fill the gap in the U.S. sugar import quota subsequent to the embargo on Cuban sugar—the Cauca Valley cane growers stimulated the development of a labor contractor system, by which formally independent intermediaries are paid to recruit small gangs of casual workers for set tasks.

Around a third of the workers on the sugar plantations and nearly all those on the large farms are recruited and supervised by labor contractors. These contractors can largely avoid the costly social security benefits and can pay even lower rates than the agribusinesses pay permanent workers. Casual labor like this cannot form or join trade unions; thus, they are often employed to break strikes. The contracting system atomizes the work force, facilitates the control of workers, lowers the overall labor bill, undermines the political strength of *all* workers, causal or permanent, and helps ensure an elastic reservoir of labor to cope with fluctuations in demand—a fluctuation that is very marked even in the sugar industry.

Ease of recruitment and organization of contracted labor relies heavily on the co-optation of existing social networks among the poor. The hidden source of strength of the contracting system is the capacity of poor people to organize themselves into wage-working gangs. The efficient harnessing of labor to the labor market is indebted to nonmarket modes of social relationships. Furthermore, the contracting system facilitates the predominance of the piecework system in capitalist agriculture, which in turn bolsters the contractor system. Compared with a time-work system of payment, the piecework system allows the employer far more opportunity to wear down the daily wage, to intensify labor, and to heighten the individualism and competition among the workers. This creates a vicious circle in which the lowering of the daily rate makes the piecework mode of payment and the contracting system more appealing to the workers. Since they are unable to act collectively on the wage structure, the workers at least have in the contractor piecework system the chance of exceeding daily rates by intensifying their labor. And, because many of the contracted workers prefer to move back and forth between the peasant sphere and the plantations, the contractor system becomes more appealing. A plantation ditchdigger who was paid by the cubic meter dug relates:

> With food prices so high and wages so low, workers are forced to work their very hardest to make ends meet. Some don't even stop for lunch. When a man fell down with stomach pains the other day, a Saturday, the others barely paid him any

attention. The foreman demanded that he keep working. The man asked for water, but the boss said he should get up and work. He was still lying in the cane field when the truck came to take the workers back to town, and they forgot him. He laid there all weekend. When they came back on Monday he was almost dead. They took him to hospital and gave him serum. But he died a little later. The workers are so preoccupied with getting enough money to live on that they just concentrate on what they are doing. They don't have time to think about anybody or anything but what they are doing.

Shortly afterwards, the man who recounted this left the plantation and devoted himself full-time to his mother's plot. He reasoned that although he made less money it was worthwhile because the intensity of the work was so much less.

In the valley over the past fifteen years a fivefold to tenfold increase has occurred in the large-scale cultivation of crops other than sugarcane, and these crops are exclusively worked by the contractor system—the difference with the cane being that a high proportion of workers in these crops are local women and their children. The labor contractors prefer to employ women and children. They say they are "more tame," will work for less, and do as they are told. They have to, because the burden of child care and feeding increasingly falls on the women, who are painfully conscious of the hungry infants awaiting their rice at nightfall. Life histories and genealogies indicate that the two-generational single woman-headed household and short-lived liaisons between women and men have become increasingly common over the past thirty years. The marriage rate has halved since 1938. These women and children laborers are often known as *iguazas* in reference to the migratory ducks that pick the seed lying in the fields. Some people derive most of their income from such gleaning, eating or selling the grain they find loose in the soil. But despite what the contractors say, these women do strike on occasions and do so directly and spontaneously without organized leadership, walking off the fields when the rate offered is insultingly low.

The majority of the casual laborers are locals of peasant descent and born in the area. To varying degrees they rely on their plots for some of their livelihood. Many oscillate between peasant farming and working for contractors, whereas others have their immediate families supplying part of their subsistence from their plots. Around three-quarters of the so-called permanent fraction of the wage-laboring force are black immigrants from the relatively isolated jungles of the Pacific coast. Most of them alternate between the coast and the plantations; they remain at the latter for one to three years and then return to their households, coming back to the plantations again after a year or so, usually leaving their spouses and children behind.

The wage laborers on the plantations and large farms are not "pure" proletarians with nothing to subsist on apart from the sale of their labor-time. Whether casual or permanent, whether locals or immigrants, they are generally part-time proletarians whose subsistence and that of their dependents rests on their complementing proletarian labor with the fruits of peasant cultivation or of similar types of income opportunities.

The Art of Peasant Farming

The cool groves of the peasant farms provide a sharp contrast to the enormous, hot, and treeless fields of the agribusinesses. Tiny islands of straggling forest life, the plots lie squeezed by the sugarcane of the plantation. They are composed of cocoa, coffee, citrus, and plantains interplanted amid a profusion of shrubs, plants, and red-flowering shade trees. The difference in aesthetic forms, peasant and plantation, comes down to this: peasants have some control over materials, tools, time, and land; wage laborers have control over none of these. Tomás Zapata put it well: "My sons and daughters are uninterested. They are only concerned with getting by daily and grabbing the money in the afternoon; to go to work in the dawn and return at nightfall. They live day by day. But agriculture is an art, and they don't understand that. For this art the first thing is constancy and land." What is more, judged strictly on economic criteria, the peasant form of farming is in many ways more efficient than the large capitalist farms. The poverty that so cruelly afflicts the peasants lies neither in their mode of production nor in their rate of reproduction. Instead, it lies in the inefficiencies of large-scale capitalist agribusiness. By virtue of its greater political power and monopoly over land, agribusiness can compensate its inefficiencies by taking advantage of the efficiency of peasant farming.

The main tasks in peasant agriculture are the harvesting, which occurs every two weeks, and the weeding, which is done once or twice a year. Both tasks are light and require little time. Around two hectares cultivated in this way provide a subsistence living for the peasant household and demand no more than one hundred labor-days a year. Only a machete and a light spade are used. Firewood, house-building materials, cordage, wrapping leaves, packing, gourds, a little corn and manioc, and many medicinal plants are also obtained from the plot, on which poultry and pigs are maintained as well. Commercial as it is, this type of agriculture preserves most of the preexisting ecosystem in its vast diversity of cultigens, and the soil is constantly nourished by a compost of the fallen leaves, which equals that found in tropical rain forests. The flowering shade trees are said to be essential for the health of the perennial crops, and in blocking the sun they inhibit the weed growth that proliferates in open-field tropical farming and causes much extra work. The abundance of tree life breaks the winds and absorbs the heavy rains; moreover, the trees hold moisture and slowly release it in the dry seasons.

The plantains yield their fruit eight to ten months after planting, regardless of the time of the year, and through their suckers they continue producing for five or more years. Cocoa and coffee are harvested every two weeks. Both have a six-month cycle, and the cycles are complementary: when coffee wanes, cocoa waxes, and vice versa. Hence, a steady trickle of income and labor input is maintained during the whole year. There is very little capital maintenance, if any.

Women own and manage one-third of the peasant farms, and no sharply defined division of field labor by age or sex exists, as it does in the agribusinesses. Areas tend to be divided into kindreds centered on a rich male peasant with ten or more hectares of land. He calls on his neighboring siblings, cousins, concubines, and their children to assist in the work that his own household cannot handle, pays them on a daily rate, and is always susceptible to their claims for loans and gifts. On his death the large farm is usually divided among these persons, and the quasi class pyramid collapses, to be slowly reformed by the emergence of another hierarchical kindred. Reciprocal ties based on family mold labor relationships. Redistribution of wealth along kinship molds class structure. The national market affects labor and the distribution of wealth within the peasant sphere, but it is not constitutive of that sphere's inner structure and function. Commercial as it is, this peasant mode of livelihood is not a microcosm of the market economy. It is not rationalized in the capitalist sense whereby the rule and weight of commodity formation permeates the metabolism of social life in the productive process and colonizes life outside the workplace, as well.

Since 1971 when many peasants and landless laborers were organizing invasions of plantations to take over lands by force, this traditional style of peasant farming became subject to a "green revolution" wrought by the Colombian government and the United States

Agency for International Development (USAID). This new and convenient wisdom of development agencies was an attempt to increase peasant productivity, rather than institute land reform, as a solution to rural poverty. Effectively, this meant uprooting the perennials and replacing them with an expensive, risk-prone, mechanized, open-field system of mono-cultivation of soya, beans, or corn. Around a third of the peasant farmers accepted the loans to develop this new system. Invariably, they were males because the financial and rural extension services naturally gravitated to them and because women were generally hostile to the idea. The result of the innovation has been to increase astronomically peasant indebtedness, to virtually eliminate the local subsistence base of plantains, and to increase the rate of land acquisition by the plantations. Under the new system, income is jeopardized because mono-cropping is susceptible to plagues, winds, and flooding. Moreover, income is derived, if at all, only once every four to six months. Capital inputs rise dramatically because of the need for new varieties of seed, tractors, fertilizers, pesticides, and increased labor inputs, which are necessary despite the use of machinery. Cultivating in the new manner, peasants have become employers of labor as never before, and the character of the peasant class structure has evolved away from the kindred formation into a stereotypical capital/labor structure. Rich peasants absorb their neighbors' land, and the economic leveling that used to occur on a rich peasant's death now happens only rarely, for they sell or rent out their land to the plantations. Women have lost the supply of traditional foods that they used to gather in the old-style plots to sell in the towns and have become more dependent on men than ever. They provide a ready labor pool for the labor contractors or for the urban wealthy who use them as domestic servants.

The Articulation of Modes of Production

It certainly cannot be claimed that agribusiness development in this food-rich area has improved the standard of living. Such development has meant a growing rupture between agriculture and nutrition. Whereas subsistence crops and peasant farming has withered, the profits of the expanding sugar plantations are very high (averaging around 40 percent between 1970 and 1974, expressed as net income over costs [Fedesarrollo, 1976:340–346]). Yet, some 50 percent of children are said to be malnourished (Community Systems Foundation, 1975). Moreover, it appears that the nutritional balance that must be achieved by working adults is maintained at the expense of pregnant women and children and that people are now eating far less than they did before agribusiness development. The environmental health hazards attributable to this development compound the nutritional problem. The mills discharge their effluents into the rivers, the main supply of drinking water, and all sources of water are fearfully contaminated with fecal matter, according to repeated surveys by bacteriologists. Infestations by hookworm (in 50 percent of the population), *Entamoeba histolytica* (25 percent), *Strongyloides* (20 percent), and *Ascaris* (70 percent) abound. The sewage system is abysmal, and people commonly go barefoot. None of the wealth of the agribusinesses is invested in the public services that are needed to overcome the damage wrought by agribusiness.

Political tension and crime are a constant preoccupation. Official "states of emergency" are in force more often than not. In such situations, which are common in much of Colombia although the country is formally a democracy, military law prevails most of the time, preventing, for example, popular assembly and group meetings. The owners of large estates like the two sugar plantations closest to town have to travel with armed escorts of police and soldiers for fear of kidnapping. For the same reason, their high-level administrators have their jeeps fitted with two-way radios connecting them to the army in Cali. The plantation workers' trade unions are nowhere weaker than in this area, and salesmen for John Deere claim that the amount of sabotage of mill machinery and field equipment is staggering—higher here than in the rest of the valley where there are far fewer peasants.

Contrary to all the propaganda of the large landowners, it is by no means true that this large-scale farming provides a more efficient use of land, labor, energy, or capital than does peasant farming, even though yields are generally higher due to the capital and energy intensive character of their inputs. Efficiency can be computed in many different ways, but it is surely significant that the sugar plantations supply fewer jobs per hectare and less cash return to the worker (and the owner) per hectare, and demand a far greater human energy output per day than do peasant farms, traditional or modern (see Table 1). Traditional peasant farming in this area is some six times more efficient than that of the sugar plantations in energy yielded in food compared with the energy input required to produce that food. Furthermore, even though the yield per hectare of peasants growing modern crops (such as soya) is only around half of that of the large-scale farmers growing the same crops, production costs of the peasants are so much lower that their return on capital in-

TABLE I:
Comparisons between peasant farmers and plantation workers in the Cauca Valley, Colombia, 1970–76

| | Peasant Farmer on Two-Hectare Plot | | Plantation Worker |
	Traditional	Modern	
Annual net income, 1971 (Colombian pesos)	$10,000	$ 8,000	$10,000
Number of hectares per worker	1.0–2.0	1.0–2.0	3.2
Labor days required per year	105	243	275
Individual's labor energy output per working day (kcal)	1,700	1,700	3,500
Individual's labor energy output per year (kcal)	173,000	415,000	804,000

Note: Data on traditional peasant farming come from my monitoring of four plots every two weeks for nine months in 1971. Data on modern peasant farming come from similar on-site fieldwork in six plots in 1972 and 1976. Data on plantations come from Fedesarrollo (1976) and from personal interviews with plantation personnel. Labor energy expenditures (7.4 kcal per minute) for plantation workers were calculated by Spurr et al. (1975:992) using respirometry techniques on local cane cutters and loaders; those for peasant labor were indirectly calculated from tables in Durnin and Passmore (1967). An alternative lower assessment for plantation workers by Spurr et al. was ignored, as this was derived by methods conflicting with and not comparable with those used by Durnin and Passmore. Sugar plantation energy efficiency is calculated only on the basis of its three main energy inputs (and therefore has been overestimated): (a) human labor, 197,000 kcal per ton of sugar; (b) electricity, 112,000 kcal per ton of sugar; (c) fuel oil, 452,000 kcal per ton of sugar. Traditional peasant farming energy efficiency is calculated only on the energy input-output ratio involved directly with cocoa production, assuming a low average yield of 290 kg per interplanted hectare, as determined by fieldwork. Household tasks, such as drawing water, were not included as energy inputs. The ratios came to 5 : 1 for sugar plantations, and 30 : 1 for peasant cocoa farming.

vested—their "capital efficiency"—is the same as or higher than that of the large farmers (depending on whether or not one budgets the peasant landowner's own labor as a cost). This is just as true when we compare the profit rates of the peasants on the new crops with those of the sugar plantations. If we were to make the comparison with the traditional peasant mode of production based on perennials, the capital efficiency of the peasantry would be infinitely better than that of agribusiness since capital inputs are negligible. Large-scale farming here is not inherently more efficient than peasant farming—whether efficiency is defined as output over input, in currency, or in calories.

So long as a substantial proportion of the agribusiness labor force is composed of workers who own or share in small plots, the costs to the agribusiness sector of maintaining and reproducing wage labor are lower than they would be if that sector had to meet such costs on its own. For not only does the self-provisioning by the workers cover part of these costs, but as stated earlier, the workers put their capital to work on their own farms in a more efficient manner than does agribusiness.

We must take leave, then, of those popular prejudices that naively exalt the efficiencies of scale and postulate a purely economic motor of material relationships of "efficiency" displacing one mode of production by a supposedly more efficient one. Instead, we must call attention to the role of social relationships and political force in forging a functional fit between two coexisting modes of production, agribusiness and peasant, and in so doing be alert to the manifold social contradictions that such an articulation engenders.

In the evolution of the relationship between agribusiness and peasant farming in the southern Cauca Valley, agribusiness is less efficient than peasant production on several crucial criteria. But because of its monopoly over land, agribusiness can compensate for its own inefficiencies by taking advantage of those peasant efficiencies. By reducing peasant farm size below a certain minimum, the capitalist class is able to accumulate surpluses. Bigness and modern technology are not in themselves inherently more efficient. Rather, they provide the muscle necessary to coerce a labor force into being, as well as the discipline and authority necessary to exact surplus value from that labor.

Until the capitalist class was able to obtain the political power necessary to reduce peasant holdings to a certain small size, less than that required for subsistence, wages in the capitalist sector of agriculture were high because peasants could subsist from the use-value production of their own plots. The high cost of labor here was due to the low value of labor—value of labor defined as the value of commodities necessary to maintain and reproduce labor. As capitalist farmers used the political power channeled their way by the entry of U.S. capital and by openings on foreign markets beginning around 1900, they were able to expand over and forcibly appropriate peasant land. They were motivated by the desire for more acreage for their crops and by the need to reduce peasant holdings so that peasants would be obliged to become wage laborers—semiproletarians—who provided part of their subsistence from their peasant farming and, in some cases, used their wages as remittances to sustain the peasant farm.

This type of articulation between the two modes of production is part of a larger determining context, that of neocolonial underdevelopment: specifically, the smallness of the domestic market and the underdeveloped division of labor. This structural feature of peripheral economies, whose market lies at the centers of the world capitalist system, means that concern with increasing workers' purchasing power is secondary to the drive for unlimited expansion of production. Hence, reducing the value of labor and purchasing power or maintaining it at a low level makes for fewer problems than it would in developed capitalist economies. Semiproletarianization of the peasantry, as opposed to complete proletarianization, is in keeping with such a structure. Moreover, this same structural feature precludes the conditions necessary to sustain a "pure" proletariat (especially in the countryside)—that is, a class of people who have nothing to fall back on but their labor power, which they are forced to exchange on the market for wages. The peasant adjunct to wage labor is therefore necessary both to capitalists and to wage workers, for whom a capitalist wage is rarely sufficient for survival.

This moment of social history and this fact of social structure have to be firmly grasped if we are to appreciate the moral nature and social significance of the sentiments that underlie peasant-worker existence: the history is one of enclosures, barbed wire, sugarcane, and hunger; the important component of the social structure is the laborer who stands between two epochs and in two worlds, proletarian and peasant. It is all too easy to idealize the margin of precarious independence that blunts the full play of market forces on the peasant. Yet, as Raymond Williams reminds us, we must be alert to the implications of just such a breathing space in providing a critical distance from the ever-dominating wage economy (1973: 107). The experience handed down from generations of struggle against land appropriation is tied to the daily experience in fields and woods of two utterly distinct forms of life. This pattern of history and the contrast that is lived out within two antithetical modes of production prevent the development of a capitalist working class, "which by education, tradition, habit, looks upon the conditions of that mode of production as self-evident laws of Nature" (Marx, 1967, 1:737).

CHAPTER 5

The Devil and the Cosmogenesis
of Capitalism

O f all work in the region, wage labor in the agribusinesses is held to be the most arduous and
least desirable—even when the daily cash return is high. Above all, it is the *humillación*,
the humbling authoritarianism, which agi-
tates the workers, while the large landowners and their foremen complain of the workers' intransigence and fear their sporadic violence.

Lower-class people feel that work has somehow become opposed
to life. "On the coast we have food but no money," mourn the immi-
grant workers from the Pacific coast. "Here we have money but no
food." Locals contrast work in the poverty-stricken peasant sphere
with that on the plantations, saying, "I would rather be fat without
money, than old and skinny with money." They say that they can
see how plantation work makes people thin and prematurely old in
comparison with even the least remunerative peasant occupation.
They fetishize the sugarcane, describing it as a plant that dries or
eats one up.

In 1972, on their own initiative, people organized invasions of
plantations and large farms. A broadsheet prepared for public distribution by a group of people who combined working on plantations with working peasant plots reads as follows:

   We peasants reject the sugarcane because it is the raw material of slavery of the peasant people. We peasants are disposed
   toward changing the sugarcane for crops that we can consume
   here—like plantains, cocoa, coffee, rice, potatoes, and corn.
   The sugarcane only helps the rich and the government to buy
   more and more tractors to give luxury to themselves and their
   families.

Peasants! The sugarcane degenerates one; turns one into a beast, and kills! If we don't have land we cannot contemplate the future well-being of our children and our families. Without land there can be no health, no culture, no education, nor security for us, the marginal peasants. In all these districts one finds the plots of the majority of the peasants threatened by the terrible Green Monster, which is the Great Cane, the God of the landlords.

We emphatically reject the cultivation of sugarcane for the following reasons:

—the bad faith that these captains show by flooding our parcels of land with the water they use for their cane.

—even more! The fumigation that does damage to the peasant crops leaving us in the most tremendous misery, paving the way for them to send in their agents to buy up our land.

—the landlords took our lands from us for this purpose. Still there exist ancient people born at the beginning of the century who can physically narrate the imperialist history of these *señores* landlords. The holdings of our forebears are now concentrated into great *latifundia* reducing the recent born to the worst misery.

The Devil and Proletarian Labor

According to a belief that is widespread among the peasants of this region, male plantation workers sometimes make secret contracts with the devil in order to increase productivity, and hence their wage. Furthermore, it is believed that the individual who makes the contract is likely to die prematurely and in great pain. While alive, he is but a puppet in the hands of the devil, and the money obtained from such a contract is barren. It cannot serve as productive capital but has to be spent immediately on what are considered to be luxury consumer items, such as fine clothes, liquor, butter, and so on. To invest this money to produce more money— that is, to use it as capital—is to invite ruin. If one buys or rents some land, the land will not produce. If one buys a piglet to fatten for market, the animal will sicken and die. In addition, it is said that the sugarcane thus cut will not regrow. The root will die and the plantation land will not produce until exorcized, plowed over, and replanted. Some people say that although the money obtained through the devil contract cannot buy the aforementioned goods, it should be shared with one's friends who are able to use it as ordinary money. The contract is supposed to be made in the deepest secrecy, individually, and with the aid of a sorcerer. A small anthropomorphic figurine, referred to as a *muñeco* (doll), is prepared, usually from flour, and spells are cast. The male worker then hides the figurine at a strategic point at his place of work. If he is a cane cutter, for example, he places it at the far end of the rows of cane that he has to cut and works his way toward it, often chanting as he cuts his swath. Sometimes, a special prayer is said just before beginning the work. Another aspect of the belief is that the man working with the *muñeco* does not need to work any harder than the other workers.

Many foremen and even administrators believe in the use of the *muñecos*; they are afraid and would fire a suspect immediately. When this has happened, it is said, the worker has submitted without resistance. All foremen keep a sharp lookout, and they are very suspicious of anyone producing well above average. Some people note that the agribusinesses do not like workers to make more than a small fixed amount. The sensitivity of all concerned can be acute, and the belief permeates daily activity in a variety of forms. Plantation workers may chide a gang member who outpaces the rest, saying, "What a way you have come with the *muñecos* today!" In passing, it should be noted that the belief is held not merely by the most illiterate and credulous. Peasant-worker militants, leaders of modern political groups, also believe that these devil contracts occur.

Because the stories and accounts of the devil contract are told with a great deal of circumspection and in a narrative style that refers such contracts to other persons' doing, a cultural outsider like an ethnographer cannot be sure whether such contracts really do occur or are merely thought to occur. For my purposes it does not matter, because I am concerned with a collective belief. However, it can be stated that devil contracts are really made, although I suspect that they actually occur with less frequency than people assume. I know two folk healers rather well who will arrange such contracts, and one of my closest friends related the following account concerning his twenty-two-year-old cousin who recently made a devil pact. I have no doubts about the authenticity of this story. This cousin was born on the Pacific coast and came to the plantation town of Puerto Tejada as a young boy. In his teens he worked intermittently on the plantations and also made a few visits to his father on the Pacific coast, where he acquired knowledge of magic. He became increasingly resentful of plantation work and decided to make a pact with the devil. To add to his already considerable magical lore he bought several books on magic from the plantation town marketplace and studied them. One day he went into a sugarcane field and eviscerated the palpitating heart of a black cat over which he cast his spell (*oración*, or prayer). No sooner had he done so than a tremendous wind came roaring through the sugarcane. Terrified, he ran away. "He did it in order to sell his soul to the devil, so that he could get money without working," said my informant.

Modes of Interpretation

What, then, is the meaning of this? This highly secretive, individualized, and rare occurrence is purely a supposition on the part of people. Nobody claims to have ever seen it, but nearly everyone has some hearsay evidence and firmly believes that it occurs, albeit, rarely. Like art at the beginning of history, magic and ritual, it is an experience set apart from the rest of life—in order to exercise power over it. Like the occasions of birth or death, the work situation as portrayed by the alleged proletarian devil contract is one of those situations that a society can seize upon to express its character.

We must see the devil-belief then not as an obsession or as a norm that ineluctably and directly guides everyday activities but rather as an image illuminating a culture's self-consciousness of the threat posed to its integrity. An image of this sort cannot be fitted like a cog wheel into a structural-functional "place" in society. Instead, the belief in the proletarian devil contract is a type of "text" in which is inscribed a culture's attempt to redeem its history by reconstituting the significance of the past in terms of the tensions of the present. "To articulate the past historically," writes Walter Benjamin, "means to seize hold of a memory as it flashes up at a moment of danger. This danger affects both the content of a tradition and its receivers: that of becoming a tool of the ruling classes. In every era an attempt must be made anew to wrest tradition away from a conformism that is about to overpower it. The Messiah comes not only as the redeemer, he comes as the Antichrist" (Benjamin, 1969:255). In the case of the devil contract in the plantation cane fields, this imperiled tradition exploits the antichrist to redeem the mode of production of use-values and to wrest it from the alienation of means from ends under capitalism.

Our reading of the text offered us by the culture in the form of the supposed devil contract made by male proletarians will focus on the culture's concept of cosmogony and on the meaning this concept creates when confronted with the radical transformation of the society's mode of production.

Let us first consider situations in which such a contract is supposed *not* to occur: peasants working their own plots or those of other peasants for wages; women, even when engaged in proletarian labor; market vendors; and the Pacific coast immigrants back home in the relatively self-subsistent nonmarket economy of the coast.

The Coast

Muñecos are a customary item of magic on the Pacific coast of Colombia, from where many migrants working in the valley come. But they are not used as they are alleged to be used in the valley's plantations. Instead, people use them in curing rites, as protection against theft, and as protection against sorcery. They are used not for gain but for alleviation of misfortune and for protection. In fact gain is what leads to illness and misfortune. As one anthropologist describing coastal black culture has written, "The resulting ethic is the antithesis of success" (Pavy, 1967:279)—"success" being viewed here as market achievement.

On the coast blacks sometimes make recourse to Indian shamans, and it appears that Indians have absorbed some African magic too. S. Henry Wassén claims to have discerned African features in some of the equipment used by Chocó Indian shamans, especially their curing figurines (1940:75–76). The figurines offer strong testimony of the plasticity of tradition and of the magical power of foreign influence, for in addition to dolls with African features there are dolls that are carved in the form of Europeans of the colonial period and others influenced by icons of Catholic saints. It is likely that the dolls referred to in the proletarian devil contract in the Cauca Valley are descendants or transformations of these same figurines, which embody the tutelary spirits of the shaman. It bears noting that the general cultural area surrounding the Cauca Valley at the time when African slavery was introduced was one in which the use of such figurines was common. Moreover, Nils M. Holmer and Wassén have noted the widespread distribution of these figurines among Indian cultures ranging across the north of South America from the Pacific coast to the Atlantic (1953:84–90), and Gerardo Reichel-Dolmatoff states that the Chocó Indians, inhabiting the northern half of the Colombian Pacific coast, formerly inhabited many regions inland and that even today some small groups have survived *east* of the Cauca River (1961:230).

Drawing on the pioneering work of Holmer and Wassén, Reichel-Dolmatoff describes the use of dolls by Cuna and Chocó Indian shamans. Made from wood or clay in the form of humans or, less commonly, of animals (often distorted), the dolls form a central role in curing by exorcizing animal spirits or the influence of a vengeful shaman that has abducted the soul of the patient. Among the more accultured Chocó Indians, most disease-afflicting spirits are thought of as spirits of the dead, and Indians under mission influence refer to such spirits as devils (Ibid.:229–41, 494).

Reichel-Dolmatoff argues against those anthropologists who attribute a fertility function to the use of these dolls. In his opinion their use in pregnancy is not to increase fertility or to magically induce reproduction. Instead, they are critical to the ritual regulation of the process, concerned with preventing malfunction during reproduction. The Cuna Indian curing song and rite employed to relieve obstructed birth, published by Holmer and Wassén (1953) and made famous by Claude Lévi-Strauss in his essay "The Effectiveness of Symbols" (1967a), support this claim in full. Thus, insofar as there is a resemblance, we must be alert to the implication that the use of the dolls in the Cauca Valley plantations is not to be explained primarily as a desire to increase yield; it is the regulation of a dangerous process that is at issue.

This raises the importance of the analogy between production and reproduction. In use-value economies production is often metaphorized as reproduction, and both spheres are understood or expressed in the same ontogenetic concepts. Aristotle and the Schoolmen constantly extended the concepts of biological reproduction to the spheres of material production, exchange, and monetary exchange. Like these philosophers, the lower classes of the southern Cauca Valley find that metaphors and symbols in one sphere readily pertain to the other: for example, increasing production under incipient capitalist relations of production yields barrenness in nature and lack of reproductive power in wages gained. Interestingly, the everyday parlance of mature capitalist economics also utilizes biological metaphors (the "growth" of capital, factories referred to as "plants," and so forth), but these metaphors exalt capital by endowing it with fertility.

The Local Peasants

It is crucial to realize that the local peasantry are not thought to make contracts with the devil to augment productivity on their own plots. The logic of the belief preordains this. As the peasants point out, such a practice would be self-defeating because the money gained in this way cannot be reinvested in equipment or land and because the contract renders the land barren. Despite the poverty that cruelly afflicts them and despite their desire for greater income, peasant proprietors therefore are said not to enter into devil contracts. Only when they are engaged in modern proletarian labor on the large capitalist farms are they thought to do so. Even those who work for wages for other peasants are not considered to make these contracts.

Allegedly, the only magic used in connection with peasant plots is good magic linked to the souls of the virtuous dead and the Catholic saints, and such magic is aimed at protecting the plot against theft and malign mystical influences. It is not used to increase production. For example, one rite ensures that, upon entering the plot, a thief will fall asleep until discovered by the owner. In another rite the owner leaves a sharpening stone, a machete, and a gourd of water, and the thief is forced to sharpen the tool and commence working until apprehended. In yet another rite the owner might have a snake—a fantastic terrifying snake which only a thief can see—that prevents entry and theft.

Women

Women working for wages on the plantations are generally thought *not* to make devil contracts. Again, this follows the logic of the belief because women are held to be the main, if not sole, providers for the household in general and the children in particular. Like those involved in Aristotle's category of a "householding economy" (*oeconomia*), they are understood to be embedded in a productive enterprise the end of which is not sheer increase. "In household management the people are of greater importance than the material property, and their quality of more account than that of the goods that make up their wealth" (Aristotle, 1962 : 50–51). Since the money derived from the plantations through a devil contract induces sterility and destroys growth, one obviously cannot use it to raise one's children.

Women are heavily implicated in magic, it is said, in the use of sorcery against the lovers of their male consorts or, less commonly, against the unfaithful consorts themselves. In the majority of such cases the sorcery occurs when one of the women concerned is pregnant or giving birth. This redemptive sorcery is directed at the process of reproduction, not at material production as in the male proletarians' devil contract. When a man is directly afflicted by this love magic, he is transformed into a lovesick fool, forever tied to the woman who casts the spell. An example of such a secret rite aimed at "tying" an unfaithful lover, who, as happens so often, was declining to provide for the upkeep of the children he had fathered, went as follows.

The woman obtained a cigar, a complete candle, four matches, and a candle stub. The ritual is most efficacious if the cigar and the complete candle are bought with money from the faithless spouse and if the remaining items are loaned by someone notoriously mean. Three of the matches were rolled into one and used to light the cigar. As she began to smoke it, the complete candle was cut into halves. When the cigar was half smoked, the candle stub was lit and then the half-candle was lit. Then the cigar was smoked at a furious rate, emitting large clouds of smoke over the candles, and she concentrated deeply on the man in question, whose name was Catalino. When the ash dropped she stamped on it, chanting, "*Catalino, hijeputa, Catalino hijeputa, Catalino, hijeputa*" (Catalino, son of a whore . . .). Variations on this procedure include reversing the cigar so that the lit end is in one's mouth while puffing, using four cigars but only smoking two, throwing them in the air so that they somersault, and chanting, "*Venite hijeputa, Venite hijeputa; parete hijeputa, parete hijeputa*" (Come, son of a whore . . . stay, son of a whore . . .).

Although some of the symbolism is obscure, much is obvious. Contagious magic is present in the buying of the items with the money of the man at whom the spell is aimed and also with the money from someone notoriously mean. Behind the principle of contagious magic one discerns that, in certain situations, an exchange of goods and money involves the notion that they embody and transmit a person's spiritual essence. The reversals and cutting in half of the ritual objects also follow laws of sympathetic magic, which are aimed at reversing the social situation implicating the woman and the man. The candle and the cigar, both alight, presumably symbolize the man's sexual potency. The candle is cut in half and the ash or seed that falls from the lit cigar is stamped on and destroyed, thus symbolically destroying his potency and seed in other women. At the same time the spell curses him in no uncertain terms and demands his return. The magic is not aimed at increasing yield. The rite is directed toward the destruction of the man's potency as it is extended beyond the bounds of his reproducing partner, at which point it becomes akin to the investment of capital aimed at sheer increase. This man can and must be kept within the bounds of *oeconomia,* providing for his spouse and children, and prevented from irresponsible multiplication. An exchange system between a man, a woman, and their offspring is threatened by his embarking on a vastly different system of exchange based on endless gain or yield. Faith in the magical rite is a manifestation of the virtue of the former system and the illegitimacy of the latter.

Cosmogony

If economic success is regarded as dangerous on the coast and envy channeled through sorcery is rampant not only there but also in the plantation zones as a means of thwarting such success, then Tawney's reminder of the moral revolution underlying the birth of capitalism becomes extremely apposite. "The life of business, once regarded as perilous to the soul," he writes, "acquires a new sanctity." What is significant, he noted, "is the change of moral standards which converted a natural frailty into an ornament of the spirit, and canonized as the economic virtues habits which in earlier ages had been denounced as vices" (1958:2–3).

The issue is clearly stated. There is a moral holocaust at work in the soul of a society undergoing the transition from a precapitalist to a capitalist order. And in this transition both the moral code and the way of seeing the world have to be recast. As the new form of society struggles to emerge from the old, as the ruling classes attempt to work the ruling principles into a new tradition, the preexisting cosmogony of the workers becomes a critical front of resistance, or mediation, or both.

Cosmogony deals with the fundamental bases of creation: change and the beginning and end of existence. It is to be found, as Mircea Eliade reminds us, as a living memory in myths of origin and salvation. These may take a myriad of forms, large and small, such as the New Year's Day celebration when the world is symbolically created anew, the coronation of a new king or queen, the marriage ceremony, or the formalities of war and peace. The myths are worked out in more everyday concerns as well—in saving a threatened harvest or in healing the sick. The profound significance of these rites, Eliade points out, is that "to *do* something well, or to *remake* a living integrity menaced by sickness, it is first necessary to go back *ad origenem,* then to repeat the cosmogony" (1971:157).

In referring this to the culture of the southern Cauca Valley, it is well to remember Evans-Pritchard's warning against assimilating so-called primitive *thought* to the realm of modern Western mysticism. In the greater part of primitive and peasant everyday life, supernatural powers are not attributed to either persons or things, and the mystical assumptions and connections assumed are not the product of *mind* but of rite and collective representations inherited from generation to generation as *culture*. Above all, "We must not be led astray by Lévy-Bruhl into supposing that, in bringing in mystical causes, primitive man is thereby explaining physical effects; rather he is explaining their human significance, their significance for him" (Evans-Pritchard, 1965 : 115; 1933; 1934).

Only with these important qualifications can we concur with Eliade's view that the primitive ontological conception is one in which an object or an act becomes real only insofar as it imitates or repeats an archetype of the original creation and that what lacks this exemplary model is meaningless and therefore lacks reality.

Even so, what tends to be overstated in Eliade's formulation is that the imitation involved is merely passive repetition of an archetype. To rectify this we need to stress that cosmogonic rites actively create reality and that their persuasive power lies precisely in the special type of knowledge that comes from creating.

Giambattista Vico's New Science might be appropriate here. It was a science of history formed in the wake of Renaissance magic and against the growing power of positivist-like doctrines. Against the atomism and utilitarianism of positivism, in which society is apprehended by instrumental rationality utilizing the epistemology of the physical sciences deploying the logic of scarcity and maximizing inputs, Vico saw man as a collective being, as the ensemble of social relations. People act as they do because of their membership in society, and their sense of this relation is as basic as are their material needs. Their experience of everyday life, their modes of expression, their sense of purpose, their fears and hopes—all these important aspects of human experience fall well outside the net cast by natural science. Like the Renaissance *magi*, Vico saw man as creator of himself and the social world. Like the Schoolmen, Vico took the view that one can only truly know what one creates and that to know something is in some important sense to become it, to become united with it. This parallels the magician's acquisition of power over the object by entering into it, achieving the unity of experience that is identical with creation (Berlin, 1977 : 14). It was God who created nature, and our knowledge of nature would always be "external," a play on the surface of things. But what we could know from the "inside" was history and society, for we had created them. In Vico's own words:

In the night of thick darkness enveloping the earliest antiquities, so remote from ourselves, there shines the eternal and never failing light of a truth beyond all question: that the world of civil society has certainly been made by men, and that its principles are, therefore, to be found within the modification of our own human mind. Whoever reflects on this cannot but marvel that the philosophers should have bent all their energies to the study of the world of nature, which, since God made it, He alone knows: and that they should have neglected the study of the world of nations or civil world, which since men had made it, men could come to know. [1970:52–53]

Now, more than two centuries later, it is not the neglect of the civil world by the natural philosophers at which we should marvel; rather, we should marvel at the engulfing of the understanding of the civil world by the canons of knowledge used in the physical sciences, so that, for instance, the exploitative relation between capitalists and workers becomes reified in the categories of capital and labor-time or, merely, capital. As Weber emphasized, this way of seeing society through the eyes of "formal rationality" was coincident with the rise of capitalism and with its very form, in which cause met effect in a self-enclosed interplay of meaning—the capitalist market, the separation of business from the householding economy, rational bookkeeping, and, above all, the capitalist organization and exploitation of "free labor." Proletarianization ushers in a new order of nature, "An immense cosmos in which the individual is born, and which presents itself to him, at least as an individual, as an unalterable order of things in which he must live" (1958:54).

Creation, life and death, growth, production, and reproduction—these are the issues that preoccupy cosmogony. They are also the preeminent processes in the curing rites, in the sorcery, and in the alleged proletarian devil contract in the southern Cauca Valley, where peasants are being proletarianized. Yet, this new cosmos is still in the process of becoming. In this process the lower classes are liminal beings, neither peasant nor truly proletarian. Like the liminal personae in the rites of passage made famous by Victor Turner (1967:93–112), their condition is one of contradiction and ambiguity, in which bizarre symbolization of death and birth is preeminent, symbols that are isomorphic with the historical status of the proletarianized peasants. As liminal beings—neither what they were, nor yet what they will become—the position of these half-peasants, half-proletarians is both negation and affirmation of all structural positions. We should therefore expect that they will thrust into prominence the salient contrasts of the structures that enclose them, peasant modes of life and proletarian modes, and that theirs is the realm, as Turner puts it, of "pure possibility from whence novel configurations arise" (Ibid.: 97). The creation of the proletarian devil contract is one such novel configuration. To better understand it, we need first to sketch in the outlines of the local cosmology and its cosmogonic rites.

Cosmology Enacted

The popular cosmology of the Cauca Valley derives from that of the Catholic Church. No matter how odiously the Church is regarded, its religious impress has been and continues to be firm. Preeminent is the Christian myth of creation and salvation. This is constantly reenacted in the Church rites of Easter and of baptism, as well as in the folk rites of death, folk healing, and sorcery. Indeed, this fundamental aspect of Catholic cosmogony is repeated for more people more intensely in folk rites than in the Church itself. The Fall and the transcendence of evil as figured in the Resurrection can be said to be the basis of folk rites and magic.

The official Church vision of the cosmos as trisected into hell, earth, and heaven is greatly modified by the belief in the spirits of ancestors and by the very literal belief in spirit forces. These ancestor spirits are known as *ánimas* or "souls" (*almas*) or simply as "spirits" (*espiritus*). If unquestionably bad, they exist in hell or roam in the air, although the majority inhabit a special room or part of the sky. Every person has a spirit, which can desert the body and wander, especially at night. A young friend of mine drinks water before sleeping at night so that his spirit will not get thirsty and wander. At death, one's spirit tends to remain close by or to return to the earthly realm. The elaborate funeral rites and anniversaries for the dead are held to purify the spirit and to ensure that it achieves and retains its destiny in heaven. If, like Julio Arboleda the infamous slave and *hacienda* owner of the early nineteenth century, the dead person was unremittingly evil, then his spirit must constantly wander. He returns especially during Easter week when he can be heard urging on his mule train near Villa Rica. The *ánimas* of one's family tree, particularly one's mother and her mother, serve as intermediaries with God, the fount of nature, as people say. When one is in danger, one asks the *ánimas* for help. The appeal is made to thwart danger rather than to gain good fortune. The latter request is more properly directed to the saints, as when one buys a lottery ticket. The saints, it is said, have more "respect." But if, for example, one is robbed, one appeals to the *ánimas*. Their role is redemptive. They are of the people. It is said, "The saints live in the Church; the *ánimas* live with us." The way in which the *ánimas* function in magic and in sorcery is not clear, but specialists venture the opinion that some sort of link is established between the spirit of the magician or sorcerer, spirits such as *ánimas* or evil spirits possibly including the devil, and the spirit of the victim.

The rites of death articulate these ideas concerning the *ánimas* with the archetype of Christ's death. They are the rites of greatest public communion and draw vast numbers of people to the house of the deceased, especially for the first and the last night—the ninth. The body is displayed the first night in an open coffin, upon which even the very poorest families will spend an enormous sum, perhaps even selling the family farm. Singing led by female kin lasts through the first night and eight more. The songs are Church derived, focusing on Christ's death and ascension, endlessly reiterating the drama of salvation and the analogy between the deceased's passing away and Christ's triumphant passage over death and life, suffering, and evil.

Easter rites attract a larger attendance than any other Church ritual. Easter Friday is the occasion of many taboos. Those who defy the prohibition of work risk harm, and blood may run from the plants they cut. The river must be avoided. The eerie and utterly strange silence that descends on the town is shattered at midnight on Easter Saturday when the dance halls and bars open once more to an exultant shriek of sound and gaiety.

In the folk rites for curing households one clearly sees the cosmogony reenacted. These rites are the most common form of magic. Even when only one person in a house has received the sorcerer's sting, the entire house as a living entity or as a small community is afflicted. The household is not only the social cell of the economic form, *oeconomia*, but also the appropriate moral entity for the sorcerer's envy. People in an ensorcelled house commonly complain of one or more of three things: they work hard, but gain nothing; they suffer constant theft; or they are always sick.

There are many specialists in house curing, and most people can perform minor curing themselves. Prophylactic cures are also common. Even middle- and upper-class people in the cities have their homes cured, and at New Year, the women from the southern Cauca Valley sell large amounts of the aromatic plants used in the rite. Factories and large shops in the city also resort to such curing, according to these country women.

Only when I had the chance to witness the archbishop of Colombia with several of his bishops and many priests consecrate a new cathedral in the highlands of western Colombia did I realize how the folk rite of house curing is merely a scaled-down version of church consecration. (Or could it be that the Church rite came from the folk?) The phased form of the events, the ritual elements of salt, holy water, and incense, the chants, and, above all, the exorcism of the spirit of evil are all more or less identical. Small wonder that the Indians there regard Christ as one of the original shamans. The theme of exorcism aggressively directed against the devil, demons, and "the enemy" in order to achieve health of body and soul, protection, and salvation is particularly strong. For example, at the entrance to the cathedral the archbishop blesses the salt: "I exorcise you, salt, in the name of our Father Jesus Christ, who said to His apostles: 'You are the salt of the earth', and repeated by the apostle; 'Our conversation is always spiced with the salt of grace.' It is sanctified for the consecration of this temple and altar with the aim of repelling all the temptations of the demons so as to defend body and soul, health, protection, and the surety of salvation. . . . Bless this salt to make the enemy flee, impart healthy medicine for the benefit of body and soul for whoever drinks it. For Christ our Father, Amen." The holy water is prepared with ashes and wine, then sprinkled around the interior walls by the archbishop while the assembly incants, "Let us go to the house of the Lord. . . . Let this temple be sanctified and consecrated in the name of the Father." As he blesses the burning incense, the archbishop chants, "Lord bless this incense so that with its fragrance will banish all pain, all sickness, and all the insidious attacks of the enemy will be distanced from your child whom you redeemed with His precious blood. Let Him be free of all the bites of the infernal serpent."

Considering but two of the critical elements involved in the southern Cauca valley, salt and holy water, one can begin to see what happens in the conversion of official religion to folk rites. The essential ingredient in ensorcelling a house is *"sal"* (salt). It consists of a mixture of earth and ground-up bones and skulls from the cemetery, which is than "planted" in the vicinity of the house being ensorcelled. Holy water is essential in curing sorcery. It is obtained from the priest at Easter, after baptism, upon request or illicitly. The priests may bless water brought by any person at any time, but are hesitant to do so. In their own words, such usage may be fetishistic.

Yet they are forced to accede as a way of buttressing their power, and in so doing stimulate the pagan roots of their religion. A teenage boy, the son of a cane cutter, lists the following uses of holy water: "You sprinkle it in a house when a bad spirit such as the devil is present. You use it with incense when making 'a sprinkling' (*riego*) in a house for good luck. It is used in baptism. You use it to bless a person who has been ensorcelled. You use it to cure a house salted with witchcraft. It is used to prepare medicines, especially when a person is suffering from sorcery. You use it in any situation against sorcery."

Houses can be protected from sorcery by "planting" three crosses in front and three behind: "One never knows from where envy is going to come, from in front or from behind." The crosses come from a tree called "the tree of the cross" because of its cross-shaped grain. They are planted with "essences," costly perfumes bought in the marketplace. The full-scale curing rite is synchronized by the critical times associated with Christ's death. There have to be nine cleansings, just as there have to be nine nights for funeral rites, and this figure is supposed to be associated with his death. "Jesus suffered a punishment of nine days: Thursday to Sunday plus five more of great suffering." Moreover, the cleansings have to occur only on Fridays and Tuesdays, the days that people associate with the crucifixion and resurrection. These are the days most propitious for magic and sorcery throughout Latin America (Stein, 1961:324; Madsen, 1960:146; LaBarre, 1948:178; Métraux, 1934:90), and it is on these days that sorcerers and witches not only perform their evil deeds but also can most clearly discern actions taken against them. Old people say that these are the preferred days for planting crops, too. They are also considered to be "privileged days" because on them "the saints and the planets bestow great beneficence to the households that believe in this." Furthermore, the very hours most propitious for curing, midday and three o'clock, are supposedly those hours corresponding to the critical hours of Christ's drama on the cross.

Having divined that the house or person is afflicted with sorcery, the curer prepares medicines and incense. The medicines, known as the "irrigation" (*riego*), contain many ingredients and vary with the practitioner. Aromatic plants are commonly used, such as the seven varieties of *albaca*, verbena, and sometimes the hallucinogen, *datura*. Verbena is crushed on Easter Friday and is called the "ash of Easter Friday"; it has the property of exorcizing evil. Eliade draws attention to the idea that the potency of some medicines can be traced to prototypes that were discovered at a decisive cosmic moment on Mount Calvary; they receive their consecration from having healed the Redeemer's wounds. Eliade cites a spell addressed to verbena in early-seventeenth-century England: "Hallowed be thou Verbena, as thou growest on the ground,/For in the Mount of Calvary, there wast thou first found./Thou healest our Saviour Jesus Christ, and staunchest his bleeding wound;/In the name of [Father, Son, Holy Ghost], I take thee from the ground" (1959:30). Holy water and nine drops of a strong disinfectant are added, together with nine drops of *quereme*, a rare and somewhat mythical perfume, which is said to attract members of the opposite sex. Sugar, lemon juice, and aspirin (known as *mejoral* [bettering]) may also be mixed in. A spell ("conjuration"), usually derived from old books on magic, is cast over the mixture together with a strophe such as this one referring to the plants: "You whom God left and the Virgin blessed, for all the centuries and the centuries, Amen." A practitioner comments: "The plants have great virtue. They have spirit. They reproduce seeds and themselves. That is why they have virtue. They produce aroma. This is an important part of their power." Typical of the conjurations are those in the book *The Most Rare Secrets of Magic and the Celebrated Exorcisms of Solomon*. A curer friend tells me, "Solomon is a great magician who was born at the beginning of the world."

Followed by a retinue of household members the curer exorcises the house, sprinkling the medicines on the walls and the floors, often in the form of the cross, and paying special care to doorways, windows, and beds. First, the house is cleansed from inside outward, then from outside inward. The house is then not to be swept for three days thereafter—"until the medicines penetrate." Incense bought from a pharmacy is burnt and wafted in the same way. Simultaneously, the curer chants songs referring to the creation, death, and resurrection of Christ. An oft repeated refrain goes: "Go away evil, enter goodness, thus Jesus Christ entered the house of Jerusalem." Another chant is this: "House of Jerusalem in which Jesus entered, I ask our Lord, Go away evil and enter goodness, because thus entered Jesus, triumphant in the sanctified house of Jerusalem, with these plants that the same God gave us, and that the Virgin blessed. God helps my intercession, because God is for all His children, and for all the centuries."

The curer usually has a bottle of other medicines, which is drunk with the household members. The household head provides brandy, which is added to a mixture that contains many of the ingredients used in the irrigation plus other plants sometimes including *chon-dur*, an aromatic root obtained from wandering Putumayo Indian herbalists and magicians, in whose curing rites it has a central importance. The largest herb stall in the local market of this predominantly black region is managed by a Putumayo Indian, and insofar as there is a hierarchy of curers, Putumayo Indians stand at the apex. Not only do local black curers obtain plants and charms from these Indians, but many of them have been cured and thus educated and sanctified by the Indians, whose rites they then partly imitate. Both blacks and whites attribute vast magical powers to these outsider Indians because they see the Indians as primitive, bound to the natural world and creation of first things. Local tradition may also associate these Indians with Renaissance magic and the mysticism of Mediterranean antiquity in the Cabbalah.

By means of these and other manifold connections, local cosmology as enacted in rites of cosmogony recreates the history of European conquest in which whites, blacks, and Indians forged a popular religion from Christianity and paganism. From its inception this religion sustained beliefs attributing magical powers to the different ethnic groups and social classes, according to the role they played in the conquest and in society thereafter. Taken as a whole, this popular religion is a dynamic complex of collective representations—dynamic because it reflects the dialectical interplay of attribution and counterattribution that the distinct groups and classes impose on each other. Thus, in a restless dialectic of the conquered transcending their conquest, the social significance of inequality and evil is mediated through the immersion in the pagan of the conquerers' myth of salvation.

Incredulity and the Sociology of Evil

The sugar plantation agribusiness towns are notorious for the amount of sorcery said to exist in their midst. For this reason curers far and wide refer to these centers as "pig sties"—sorcery being commonly called *porquería*, piggish filth. Sorcery (and its curing) cancels inequalities in this society of insecure wage earners in which competition pits individualism and communalism against one another.

The commonly cited motive for sorcery is envy. People fear the venom of sorcery when they feel that they have more of the good things in life than others do. Sorcery is evil, but it can be the lesser evil when it is directed against the greater evil of exploitation, failure to reciprocate, and the amassing of ill-gotten gains. Those who are better off constantly fear sorcery and take magical steps to prevent its penetration. And with good reason. A close friend of mine told me how his desperately poor mother and her three children were evicted by a landlord for not paying rent. In fury she retaliated by ensorcelling the house. Nobody dared live in the house thereafter. In another case a friend of mine and his fellow worker in the plantations tried to bribe a tallyman into recording more work than they had done. The tallyman refused, and they solicited an Indian magician so as to dispose of him through sorcery.

Although murky premonitions of class struggle can be seen in this envy-laden sorcery, not all sorcery is directed by the poor against the better off; neither is sorcery directed against the true ruling class— the plantation owners or the heads of government, for example. People give two reasons for the absence of sorcery against the feared and hated ruling class. First, the rulers don't believe in sorcery. Second, even if they did, they could employ superior magicians because they are far wealthier. These are interesting reasons because in areas of southwest Colombia that have less capitalist development, such as the *hacienda* areas in the mountains, the *hacienda* owners do in fact believe that many of their misfortunes are due to the sorcery of their peons. These *hacienda* owners combat such sorcery by making expensive pilgrimages to Indian shamans whose fees or remoteness puts them beyond the reach of the peons (who, nevertheless, persist with their mystical form of class warfare). This does not occur in the agribusiness areas; hence, I conclude that the more critical of the two reasons given above is the one that the people emphasize: agribusiness owners do not believe in this sort of sorcery.

This indicates that the people who believe in sorcery recognize that the sorcerer's power depends upon the existence of a shared culture, through which medium sorcery achieves its end. In acknowledging the incredulity and hence immunity of their rulers, the working class of the plantations thus acknowledges and discriminates changes in the culture of classes as such cultures change in accordance with the transformation in the modes of production—from *hacienda* production to agribusiness.

In the proletarian devil contracts the plantation owners are not aimed at or afflicted, at least not directly. It is alleged that by means of the contract the worker in the capitalist mode of production, and only in this mode, becomes more productive—more productive of income and of barrenness. As we shall see in chapter 7, such a belief is the logical outcome of the confrontation of a philosophy based on use-value and the capitalist mode of production. The magic in the devil contract is directed not at the plantation owners but at the sociohistorical system of which they are part. The proletarian neophytes have lost a class enemy susceptible to magical influence, but they stand to win a new world in their realization of that enemy's disbelief.

CHAPTER 6

Pollution, Contradiction, and Salvation

Two secular images in the language of sorcery materialize its magical aura: sorcery is person-made, and it is "filth." Although invisible powers forming an indistinct hierarchy led by the devil are prominent, the emphasis in sorcery is on the creative will of persons. Sorcery is the *maleficio*, the evil made, or it is, dramatically and simply, the "thing made," the *cosa hecha*. It is not seen as fate or as an "accident of God." The soul of sorcery lies in the poisoned breast of envy, and its dominating motif is filth.

Following Douglas's interpretation (1966), ideas of filth and pollution are a reaction that protects cherished principles and categories from contradiction. What is being cleansed in Cauca Valley curing rites that evoke the creation, death, and salvation is that which is unclear, or contradictory, or both. Seeing "dirt" as contradiction allows us to deepen our understanding and to move beyond the spellbinding surface of the sensational keywords, dirt, envy, and evil.

Before doing so, however, it is essential to grasp the significance of the concept of "contradiction" in this context; for without its clear understanding the iconography of the devil and other symbols in popular culture remains elusive. Here it is helpful to refer to Marx's method of analysis. As Karl Korsch points out, the reader of Marx's *Capital* "is not given a single moment for the restful contemplation of immediately given realities and connections; everywhere the Marxian mode of presentation points to the immanent unrest in all existing things." The concept of contradiction is here embedded in a method that includes in its affirmative recognition of the existing state of things the simultaneous recognition of the negation of that state, of its inevitable breaking up (Korsch, 1971 : 55–56). Sensitivity to contradiction makes us aware of the unstable and tensioned interplay between opposites, which otherwise assume the aura of fixed and meaningful things in themselves. This is the case with the dichotomies of the Western Church, which reify good apart from evil as essences symbolized by God and by Satan in a quasi-Manichean world view. The concept of contradiction urges us to consider, as a cardinal principle, that God and Satan are not opposed essences. Rather, they represent two operations of the Divine, "the shadow and light of the world drama" (Watts, 1968 : 80–81). In Blake's idea of the marriage of heaven and hell, "good" and "evil" are reunited as angel and devil in the lower depths. The divorce of heaven from hell is tantamount to the suppression of life's energies by lifeless regulations and precisely mirrors the difference between Church and folk religion. In Blake's words: "Without contraries is no progression. Attraction and Repulsion, Reason and Energy, Love and Hate, are necessary to human existence" (Blake, 1968 : 34).

Based on the mythology of the Fall and salvation, the folk religion and magical curing of the southern Cauca Valley are just this affirmation of the dialectical oneness of good and evil. The devil symbolizes the antithetical processes of dissolution and decomposition, on the one hand, and growth, transformation, and reformulation of old elements into new patterns, on the other. Thus, in the devil we find the most paradoxical and contradictory process, and it is this dialectic of destruction and production that forms the basis of the association of the devil with agribusiness production—living death and florescent barrenness. With the proletarian devil contract, wages grow, yet they are barren and redolent of death. Under these conditions production and destruction become interchangeable and interchanging terms.

The alleged proletarian devil contract is more than an ascription of evil to agribusiness. Over and beyond that, it is a reaction to the way in which the system of market organization restructures everyday life and the metaphysical basis for comprehending the world. This reaction registers not only alienation but also its mediation of the contradiction between antithetical modes of production and exchange. This mediation can be expressed in many ways. I choose to analyze it both as the antithesis between use-value and exchange-value and as a response to the contrasting modes of precapitalist and commodity fetishism.

The Antinomies of Production

The plantation and peasant farming society of the southern Cauca Valley is composed of two antithetical exchange systems operating simultaneously: on the one hand, the system of reciprocity and self-renewal; on the other, that of unequal exchange and self-extinction.

Although it has been commercialized in many ways, the perennial-based peasant agriculture still replicates the natural ecology of the tropical forest, provides food for the cultivating household, and yields produce throughout the year. The agricultural labor is done without any strict division of labor by either sex or age, and is, in the truest sense of the phrase, a "householding economy." Compared to labor on the agribusiness plantations, work on the peasant plots is felt to be far less intense and far more pleasant, for physical as well as for social reasons. What is more, this perception applies even for the wage laborers—referred to as peons—who work for peasants. For instance, when employed in weeding, a peon covers around one-tenth of an acre per day, and in 1970 received around 20 pesos a day. Working for an agribusiness, on the other hand, the same person covers about one-third of an acre and receives around 30 pesos. In other words, as more elaborately calculated in chapter 4, the agribusiness laborer can earn a higher daily wage, but has to work a great deal harder for each peso of income. The decision confronting an economically pressed worker who must choose between work for a peasant or work for an agribusiness is an excruciating one. Sooner or later, the worker finds out that there is little choice: either agribusiness labor has to be abandoned because the piecework system extends one's capacities beyond their limit, or such labor has to be suffered as a type of slow death brought on by chronic fatigue and illness. The agribusiness laborer ages fast. The high spirits of youth fade quickly into the dejection of a present with no promise for the future. Adolescents may at first desire to work for the plantations because of the chance of making more money. But within a few months to a year they are back working peasant plots for less money because, as they say, "I would rather be fat without money, than old and skinny with money." Workers with families to support come to the same conclusion as they are ground down by tiredness and sickness and the constant struggle with foremen over piecework rates in the plantation fields. The state of their bodies, as indicated by their concern with fatness and thinness and by the sicknesses subsequent to such exploitation, tells them what the two modes of production are about. For them self-renewal and self-extinction are more than mere metaphors for contrasting the two systems. These principles are engraved in the flesh and contours of their bodies, and the people themselves perceive this. The contrast is evident, and self-critical, precisely because they directly experience the inescapable contradiction between peasant and agribusiness labor. Each is necessary, yet each is insufficient for life.

Social differences, as well as physical differences, distinguish the two systems. Within the peasant sphere of production persons are united directly through their own personal bonds, which encompass a common kinship, neighborhood, and culture. Work relationships are the dimension of these personal bonds that channels labor, payment, and job control. As Marx writes in his chapter on the fetishism of commodities: "Personal dependence here characterizes the social relations of production . . . for the very reason that personal dependence forms the ground-work of society, there is no necessity for labour and its products to assume a fantastic form different from their reality." In contrast to the reified form that labor acquires as a commodity in matured market conditions, "the social relations between individuals in the performance of their labour, appear at all events as their own mutual personal relations, and are not disguised under the shape of social relations between the products of labour" (1967, 1:77). The labor contracts between peons and peasant employers express personal relations, not market relations, and are subject to agreed changes according to codetermining life histories, household ties, personal problems, and fluctuations in physical conditions of the work situation. Peasant employers dare not press their hired labor too hard. Peons are usually paid on a daily or a contract basis, rarely by piecework rates, and punctuality and discipline are not the concerns that they are on the plantations. There, in sharp contrast, the relationship is felt as impersonal and oppressive. The workers are victimized by the foremen, fined or laid off if late, and subjected to sudden drops in pay scales, over which they have no control. Often, the workers are nameless or exist merely as numbers on pay packets, and it is not unusual for them to give a false name as an insurance against retribution. Even though they may make more money, the workers constantly say that they are being cheated; yet, they never say this about peasant work. Above all, agribusiness work is considered humiliating and *muy obligatorio* (very obligatory), a perception that derives from the contrasting experiences of the two situations, peasant and proletarian.

Of course, conflict and inequality exist among peasants and are not restricted to the agribusiness-peasant relationship. Yet, in the peasant sphere they have a totally different character. Distinctions of wealth between peasants are mitigated by redistributive and reciprocal mechanisms, which conflict serves to regulate, and the ideological distinction between a rich and a poor peasant is further diluted because all peasants define themselves as poor (*pobres*) in contrast with the rich (*ricos*) who manage the agribusiness sphere. This sense of a common oppressor exists because nobody expects the rich to be concerned with reciprocity or redistribution, and that there is little that can be done to get even with them.

The pervasive sense of historical injustice enforces these contrasts. Plantation development robbed the peasants of their lands and continues to do so. "The landlords took our lands from us for this purpose. Still there exist ancient people born at the beginning of the century who can physically narrate the imperialist history of these *señores* landlords. The holdings of our forebears are now concentrated into great *latifundia* reducing the recent born to the worst misery." This sense of injustice extends beyond the immediate issue of land per se. Land is a way of referring to a way of life. Its appropriation by agribusiness signifies moral as well as material plunder. Countless examples can be given, but the following text from a letter written by a group of peasants to a government agency in 1972 should suffice. "For a long time we have been suffering from the enormous damages inflicted upon us by the industrial lords dedicated to the benefit of sugarcane . . . for which they remove water from the Palo River without any type of control . . . without practicing nor respecting the sacred norms as written in the law books. So long as justice based on equality, justice as the voice of God, is still in motion, we ask for your attention."

Of course this is rhetorical. The appeals to the "sacred norms," "justice based on equality," and "justice as the voice of God" are a means of making the argument more persuasive. But to dismiss these tropes as cynical manipulation is to forget that this mode of expression was chosen because it was believed to be effective. The issue concerns the use of land and water in a way that violates the sacred norms, justice, equality, and God. In other words, the issue concerns the moral revolution that, according to Tawney, is required for the birth of the modern capitalist system: "It is the change of moral standards which . . . canonized as the economic virtues habits which in earlier ages had been denounced as vices" (1958:2). Similar to this letter of peasant protest is Mercado's principle expressed in the heady days of the anarcho-religious uprisings of 1849: "The people know that their rights should not be at the mercy of rulers, but that they are immanent in Nature, inalienable and sacred." The plantations, owned by the "industrial lords," show no respect for these rights. What is more, the industrial lords are seen as dedicated to sugarcane—to a thing—and not to people. Repeatedly, this refrain is heard from peasants recounting their history: "God gave the land in common to all the world, to everybody. God said that 'My land can neither be sold nor bargained.'"

These ideals and those concerning the sharing of wealth and labor increasingly diverge from the practices of everyday life. The Golden Age of plentiful land and food, mutual aid, labor exchanges, and *fiesta* work parties is invoked all the more heartrenderingly as the ideals of equality and reciprocity are subverted. But it is these ideals that give force to the moral outrage and censure of the community. Sorcery is but one manifestation of this moral code in action. Wealth should be shared, as should the means of production. Fear of sorcery is tantamount to fear of having more than others, and having more indicates failure to share. Sorcery is evil. But its roots are embedded in legitimate concerns in areas in which competition pits individualism and communalism against each other. The shopkeepers who constantly employ magic to exorcise their businesses out of fear of rivals and of the poor are a clear example of this. The alleged proletarian devil contract is a different manifestation of the same repertoire of concerns. Since inequalities are inevitable, particularly with the new economic conditions, the contradiction between making a living and being equal is inescapable. Such is the basic nature of the filth that is exorcised by curing rites; filth is the contradiction that assails the *idealized* principles of equality.

But what is meant by equality? In his essay "Ideology and Conflict in Lower Class Communities," Jayawardena distinguishes between two radically different conceptions of equality. On the one hand, he presents the equality of persons deriving from their intrinsic personal or human worth, rooted in the human condition and in the capacity of all human beings to feel, to suffer, and to enjoy. He argues that this notion of human equality is usually dominant in a subgroup to the extent that that group is denied social equality by the wider society or by its dominant class. On the other hand, he gives us the equality derived from the concept of equality of rights and opportunities, as analyzed by Alexis de Tocqueville in his discussion of egalitarianism in the United States. This idea of equality ignores the total human being and concentrates instead on one facet of a person's existence; thus, equality can be measured quantitatively. As Jayawardena notes, the same point was made by Marx in his "Critique of the Gotha Programme," in which he attacked the principle of "equal wages for equal work" adopted by the German socialists because this evaluated the worker by only one aspect of his existence. Because of differing individual capacities and conditions, Marx considered this principle a bourgeois formula for perpetuating inequality. Inequality could be overcome only if equality were based solely on human needs (Jayawardena, 1968). The difference between these two ways of evaluating equality stems from the difference between use-value and exchange-value. Only with the exchange-value paradigm can the criteria of equality be reduced to prices and money, at the cost of reification.

In a situation in which a use-value economy like peasant householding coexists with and is felt to be imperiled by an exchange-value system, these modes of evaluating equality are at loggerheads. Hence the contradiction signified by "filth" is not only an issue concerning inequality: filth also puts at issue the market paradigm of equivalence.

The foremost principle of *oeconomia*—the householding mode of production—is to provide for the needs of the household. The sale of surpluses need not destroy self-sufficiency nor imperil the integrity of the principle of production for use. In denouncing production for gain as unnatural, Aristotle made this crucial point: capitalist-oriented (chrematistic) production threatens the very basis of society. The fundaments of human association should not be subjected to the raw economic motive of gain in and for itself.

An identical economic philosophy can be found in the pattern of motifs presented by the southern Cauca Valley today. The peasant crops give little, yet they give constantly and regularly within a social and ecological nexus that continually refurbishes its own roots. However, for plantation workers the archetypal exchange structure as symbolized by the proletarian devil contract is radically different. The worker makes a lot of money by selling his soul to the devil, but this is reciprocated by nonrepetitive and final events: a premature and agonizing death and the barrenness of soil and wages. Rather than an exchange that reinforces and perpetuates a set of perennial reciprocal exchanges like the peasant's relation to the tree crops, the devil contract is the exchange that ends all exchange—the contract with money which absolves the social contract and the soul of man.

This is but one expression of the fundamental contradiction that structures local society from the viewpoint of the lower classes. Two opposed systems of production and exchange operate simultaneously: a system of reciprocity and self-renewal together with a system of unequal exchange and self-extinction.

This structure of opposition can also be seen *within* the peasant sphere of production. It stands out clearly in the opposition between women and men in the procreation of children and in the rejection or acceptance of the technology of the "green revolution," which is replacing traditional practices. The obligation to raise the children falls to the women, but the children reciprocate that care later in life; while the fathers are referred to as flies, "those who sting, and fly away, leaving their eggs in old meat." The few advocates of the techniques of the green revolution and the further commercialization of peasant agriculture are men. The women bitterly oppose the uprooting of the perennials that such an innovation requires. "They give us little, but they give!" say the women, who are alienated from the new technology. Only men drive and own tractors, and men are favored for loans and dealings with the government. Women fear the new financial ties, fear indebtedness, and fear a mode of cash cropping that provides income only once or twice a year, if at all. They fear that their offspring will die of hunger while waiting for the harvest, and they fear the eventual loss of their land. The developmental cycle of the peasant household focuses on the reproduction of the maternal line. As a young household grows older, the proportion of females living in it increases, concentrating women and land into one productive unit. Males move into extrahousehold occupations and residences, while the women cling to the cultivation of the perennials. Women lend and receive between households and manage the distribution of foodstuffs. Through the women households are sewn together by the ties of children from many fathers. Both the pattern of material production to which women wish to adhere and the social pattern of reproduction of offspring in which they are implicated are cyclical, self-perpetuating exchange structures. However, the male peasants' pattern of exchange, in both procreation and in the new mode of material production that they espouse, is far less cyclical and reciprocal and tends to the extreme portrayed by the male proletarian devil contract—the exchange that ends all exchange.

But only when the region is considered as a whole is this antithesis clearly established, starkly experienced, and projected into the contrast between peasant householding and agribusiness production. A preexisting pattern of ideas immanent in culture, if only barely and confusedly borne in consciousness, is all the more securely fixed by the new experience which threatens the roots of that pattern. The experience, as Lévi-Strauss suggests, would remain intellectually diffuse and emotionally intolerable unless it incorporated one or another of the patterns present in the group's culture. "The assimilation of such patterns," he proposes, "is the only means of objectivizing subjective states, of formulating inexpressible feelings, and of integrating inarticulate experiences into a system" (1967a:166).

In this case the system is an organized contradiction, the opposite poles of which are mutually animated by their contrasted reflection in each other. On the peasant side is the ideal of reciprocity and cyclical exchange, guaranteeing production, reproduction, and fertility. On the plantation side, by contrast, exploitation, barrenness of human relations, and death coexist with the production of wealth. The former mode is felt to be self-perpetuating, whereas the latter is self-extinguishing. It is the transaction that ends social interaction by bargaining away sociability for thralldom to the kingdom of things. As layer after layer of its various manifestations are peeled off, the underlying nature of the contradiction is revealed: the meaning of personhood and thinghood is at issue as capitalist development reworks the basis of social interaction and subjugates that interaction to the fantastic form of relations between things.

What Polanyi meant by the "commodity fiction" is precisely this socially organized confusion of persons and things that is established by the assault on the lower classes in the southern Cauca Valley by the rule of commodities. Yet, for all its fictional nature the commodity fiction is real and effective in a specific form of social organization: it supplies the vital organizing principle of a market society. It is the social principle that simultaneously organizes and erodes the society of man, and, as Marx reminds us, drains the creative power of socially active man into a world perceived as redolent of magically active things, the fetishism of commodities. This critique of the market and commodities parallels an earlier critique of God. Man creates God in a self-alienating act the consequence of which is such that God is seen as having created man. The product of man's creative imagination enthralls the creator. Man becomes the passive offspring of a power that he himself creates, a power that is anthropomorphized and animated to the degree that man denies authorship of his own creation. As with God, so for the market and commodities—social entities created by men, yet working in the collective imagination as animated beings endowed with the life that men deny themselves. Man's collectively created products enshroud his life with phantom objectivity.

But in the popular culture of the southern Cauca Valley the phantom objectivity of commodity structures concealing the world of social relationships does not distort the collective consciousness in this way. When the industrial landlords are described as dedicated to sugarcane instead of to people, when "we peasants reject the sugarcane because it is the raw material of slavery of the peasant people," and when the cane is fetishized as "the terrible Green Monster, which is the Great Cane, the God of the landlords," the system in which production has become the aim of man is decried and contrasted with the ideals of the use-value economy in which man is the aim of production.

In place of a person-centered cosmos we find a system centered on the Great Cane, the God of the landlords, who renders man a slave. People are reduced to things. As in Burtt's description of the metaphysics of the scientific revolution that accompanied the birth of capitalism, "Man is but the puny and local spectator, nay irrelevant product of an infinite self-moving engine, which existed eternally before him and will be eternally after him, enshrining the rigour of mathematical relationships while banishing into impotence all ideal imaginations" (1954:301). The issue is more than Tawney's formulation concerning the canonization of economic habits that an earlier age had denounced as virtues. What is also at stake is the moral transformation of cognition itself.

The advance of market organization not only tears asunder feudal ties and strips the peasantry of its means of production but also tears asunder a way of seeing. A change in the mode of production is also a change in the mode of perception. The organization of human sense perception is determined by historical as well as natural circumstances. The change to capitalist society enshrines the rigor of mathematical relationships and banishes into impotence all ideal imaginations such that personhood is the reflex of thinghood. In this transformation of society and metaphysics, the perception of the socially constituted self gives way to the atomized perception of the isolated maximizing individual as a unit of mass-space—a mechanical product that maximizes utility through the infinite self-moving engine, the market, of a mechanomorphic society.

As this transformation unfolds, human intention, imagination, and understanding—capacities that are dependent on social interaction and beyond the reach of laws pertaining to nonhuman things—are irrelevant and inferior; yet profoundly suspect. Like the economic vices of concern to Tawney, the new mode of sense perception also has to be canonized and enshrined; the earlier fetishism of religion is replaced with the fetishism of commodities. The new mode of perception is no more natural than the mode it displaces. It, too, is but one of many ways of seeing the world, in which conventionally agreed upon connections masquerade as facts of nature. Ultimately, even this construction is revealed to be a magico-religious world, in which the arbitrary but conventional character of the sign is daily consecrated in rituals affirming its naturalness. So it is that people's daily participation in the market becomes the guardian of their spiritual coherence.

But this coherence can never be achieved. The quest for the significance of things is a tenacious one and reaches out beyond the excruciatingly narrow straits of the new axiomatic structure that defines thinghood. Market rationality succumbs to its self-induced irrationality, and commodities become animated with human significance.

The new social form may turn men into numbers, but it also turns plantation crops like sugarcane into monsters or gods. Life, distorted to be sure but life nevertheless, surges into things, transforming social products into animated beings. All ideal imaginations, Burtt writes, are banished into impotence. But are they? In their subjugation these ideal imaginations struggle against the fetishism of commodities: the sugarcane of the plantations becomes "the terrible Green Monster," the "Great Cane," the "God of the landlords," an animated being that is said to slowly devour the men who bring it to life.

Fetishism and Hermeneutics

Against the rationalizing mystique of our times, Benjamin insisted on applying his hermeneutic urge to read and understand "texts" that are not texts in any conventional sense. "The ancients," as Peter Demetz elaborates, "may have been 'reading' the torn guts of animals, starry skies, dances, runes, and hieroglyphs, and Benjamin, in an age without magic, continues to 'read' things, cities, and social institutions as if they were sacred texts" (1978: xxii). He did so, it needs emphasizing, motivated by the viewpoint of historical materialism. If his enterprise appeared to oscillate constantly between magic and positivism, as his friend Adorno chided, then the comparison of this type of hermeneutics with that of the neophyte proletarians of the southern Cauca Valley is all the more appropriate.

This reading of things as though they were sacred texts, this penetration into and articulation of what Benjamin called the "silent language of things," was, in his own eyes, conditioned by melancholy and that this was something more than neurotic self-indulgence. It was an intellecting mood that was forced on one who confronted the dialectic of freedom and necessity written into historical materialism. One thinks here of the slogan that was advanced against the paralyzing mysticism that is intrinsic to the Marxist evolutionary-determinist position—Antonio Gramsci's combative adage, "Pessimism of the intellect, optimism of the will"—as a somewhat similar attempt to locate a stance that privileges both the inexorable movement of history and the necessity for active human intervention in that movement. Historical materialism is a mode of historiography in which the painstaking scientific mind is driven by a passion rooted in sadness to structure a conception of the world as a self-activating totality of coherent parts. Melancholy establishes and confirms the distance separating subject from object, a distance that is necessary for objective analysis, while it simultaneously registers the need to transcend that alienation, which is also the alienation of man as created by history. Melancholy is the gaze that penetrates the images of the past, transforming them from dead objects into images vibrant with meaning for the revolutionary encounter with the present, the history of which would otherwise become a tool of the ruling class to mystify the victims of history. In every age, Benjamin asserted, the attempt has to be made to wrest tradition away from the conformism that is about to overpower it. Nothing could be further from the conservative nostalgia for the past. The issue is that a class cut off from its own history is far less able to act as a class than one that is able to situate itself in history. Yet history is essentially catastrophic; it triumphs at the expense of its human agents. The claim that the past exerts on the present, Benjamin wrote, is messianic, and cannot be settled cheaply. Historical materialists, he appended, are aware of that.

Fredric Jameson describes the mood of Benjamin's searching the past for an adequate object that will redeem the present without falling either into fascist mythopoesis consecrating the irrational or into the consummation of history through statistical data processing. It is the mind of private depressions, dejection of the outsider, and distress in the face of a political and historical nightmare (1971: 60).

To read things as though they were sacred texts, to fill them with the penetrating sadness of the loser and dejected outsider, projecting the distress that arises in the face of a political and historical nightmare—this is also the dying wail of a peasant class over whom the wave of "progress" is about to roll. As Barrington Moore suggests, it is in this wail, rather than in the aspirations of classes about to take power, that the wellsprings of human freedom lie (1967:505). Not all historical materialists are aware of that.

To read things in this way, as though they were sacred texts, is also to indulge in a sort of magic, which we can call "precapitalist fetishism." It is to strive for a unification of experience otherwise unobtainable. It is the stubborn compulsion to see things and persons as reciprocally interwoven to the point at which things are meaningful because they embody interpersonal relationships even when (in an age without magic) those relationships lie concealed behind a reified exterior.

Concerning exchange in precapitalist societies, Mauss asks in his essay "The Gift," What force is there in the item exchanged that makes reciprocity so compelling? "This bond created by things," he replied, "is in fact a bond between persons, since the thing itself is a person or pertains to a person." And he elaborates on this apparent confusion of persons with things: "In this system of ideas one gives away what in reality is part of one's nature and essence, while to receive something is to receive part of someone's spiritual essence" (1967:10).

The practice of the modern market system strives to deny this metaphysics of persons and things reflected in social exchange and to replace the type of fetishism indicated by Mauss with the commodity fetishism of capitalism as interpreted by Marx. The former type of fetishism derives from the antiquated notion of reciprocity, the metaphysical depths of which are suggested by Mauss and the keynote of which lies in the unity felt to exist between persons and the things that they produce and exchange. The latter type of fetishism, commodity fetishism, derives from the alienation between persons and the things that they produce and exchange. Codified in law as much as in everyday practice, this alienation results in the phenomenology of the commodity as a self-enclosed entity, dominant over its creators, autonomous, and alive with its own power.

The fate of the peasant who is caught in the commercialization of agriculture, particularly where this involves large agribusiness production, is to bear witness to the clash between these two forms of fetishism. The belief in the proletarian devil contract, as well as other instances of fetishism is the outcome of this clash. The devil is more than a symbol of the new economy: he mediates the opposed meanings and sentiments that the development of this economy engenders. For if the peasant or use-value outlook were superseded by market culture, there would be no basis for fabulations like the devil contract. The emergence of this trope is occasioned by the meaning that a use-value culture ascribes to the tropes generated by the market organization of society, production, and exchange. The devil contract registers the human meaning of this type of organization and stamps it as evil and destructive, and not the result of morally neutral forces that are naturally inherent in socially disembodied things.

The manifestations of the culture in magic, in beliefs about plantation crops, and in the contrast of peasant with agribusiness production, are subject to a dialectical reading of things as sacred texts. On the one hand, there is the reading made by the lower classes themselves, a reading beholden to the metaphysical principles of use-value, as those principles are confronted by commodity culture. On the other hand, there is the reading imposed by the analyst, and this is an inescapable activity. The two readings converge, emblazoned in the texts that the neophyte proletarians have themselves provided.

CHAPTER 7

The Baptism of Money and the Secret of Capital

The Baptism of Money and the Birth of Capital

According to the belief in *el bautizo del billete* (baptism of the bill) in the southern Cauca Valley, the godparent-to-be conceals a peso note in his or her hand during the baptism of the child by the Catholic priest. The peso bill is thus believed to be baptized instead of the child. When this now baptized bill enters into general monetary circulation, it is believed that the bill will continually return to its owner, with interest, enriching the owner and impoverishing the other parties to the deals transacted by the owner of the bill. The owner is now the godparent of the peso bill. The child remains unbaptized, which if known to the parents or anybody else would be a cause of great concern since the child's soul is denied supernatural legitimacy and has no chance of escaping from limbo or purgatory, depending on when it dies. This practice is heavily penalized by the Church and the government.

The baptized bill receives the name—the "Christian name" as we say in English—that the baptismal ritual was meant to bestow on the child. The bill is now referred to as Marlene, Jorge, Tomás, and so forth—whatever name the parents had decided to call the child. To set the baptized bill to work, the godparent pays the bill over as part of a routine monetary transaction, such as when one pays for some goods in a store, and mutters a refrain like the following:

José   (José
¿te vas o te quedas?   Are you going or staying?

¿te vas o te quedas?   Are you going or staying?
¿te vas o te quedas?   Are you going or staying?)

Referred to by its name, the bill is asked three times whether it is going to return to its godparent or not. If everything works as it should, the bill will soon return to its godparent, bringing a large amount of money with it. This transferral is accomplished invisibly.

A black middle-class family owned a corner store in the village. Halfway through the morning, when the wife was alone, she went out the back and then quickly returned because she thought she heard some noise in the till. Opening it, she found all the cash gone. She then remembered some peculiar behavior on the part of one of the customers earlier on in the morning and then realized that someone had passed her a baptized bill. As soon as she had turned her back, this bill had made off with all the money in the cash register.

In a busy supermarket in the nearby large city, a shop detective was startled to hear a woman standing near a cash register chanting under her breath: "Guillermo! ¿Te vas o te quedas? ¿Te vas o te quedas? ¿Te vas o te quedas?" He promptly surmised that she had passed a baptized bill and was waiting for it to return to her with the contents of the register, and he immediately arrested her. She was taken away and nobody knows what happened thereafter.

One of the few successful black store owners in the village was saved from a great loss only by a most unusual coincidence. Serving in his shop, he was startled to hear a strange noise in his cash register. Peering in, he saw two bills fighting with one another for possession of the contents, and he realized that two customers, each with their own baptized bills, must have just paid them over and were awaiting their return. This strange coincidence allowed him to prevent the spiriting away of his cash.

In precapitalist societies, commodity exchange and the market are absent. Animism, magic, and various forms of fetishism flourish. But is that fetishism the same as the fetishism of commodities that is found in a capitalist system of socioeconomic organization? Marx, for one, was clearly of the opinion that the two were very different and that in posing this question one was well on the way toward demystifying the illusions that the commodity form of exchange induced. "The whole mystery of commodities, all the magic and necromancy that surrounds the products of labor as long as they take the form of commodities," he wrote, "vanishes therefore as soon as we come to other forms of production" (1967:76). Yet we should add that when the commodity system encroaches on a precapitalist social formation, the two forms of fetishism, the magic of reciprocity exchange and the magic of commodity exchange, impinge on one another and coalesce into a new form.

The belief in the baptism of money in the southern Cauca Valley is that through this illicit religious mechanism—illicit in that it deceives the parents, the child, and the priest and spiritually mutilates the child by annihilating its acceptance into the citizenry of God—money will breed money, that money will grow. This is merely an exotic expression of the standard Marxist formula for capitalist circulation, M–C–M' (money–commodity–more money) or simply M–M', as opposed to the circulation that is associated with use-value and the peasant mode of production, C–M–C (commodity A–money–commodity B, or selling in order to buy). The problem that Marx set himself, the mystery of capitalist economic growth and accumulation of capital in which capital appeared to breed more of itself, is in this situation seen to occur by the aid of the supernatural forces that were invoked by the Christian baptism of the money bill. Once activated in this way, money becomes interest-bearing capital. An inert medium of exchange becomes a self-breeding quantity, and in this sense becomes a fetish—a thing with lifelike powers.

This is truly a bizarre belief. But one has to consider that the system against which it is leveled is surely no less bizarre. We who have been accustomed to the laws of capitalist economics for several centuries have grown to accept complacently the manifestations of these laws as utterly natural and commonplace. The early prophets and analysts of capitalism, such as Benjamin Franklin, already regarded the operations of the economy as completely natural; hence, they could casually refer to interest as an inherent property of capital itself (see chapter 2).

As expressed in their folklore concerning the baptism of money, however, the peasantry of the southern Cauca Valley regard this as utterly unreal and supernatural. Moreover, the baptism of the bill is done at a terrible cost to the child: it denies him a legitimate place in the rites of the life cycle and the cosmological order and hence bears the same stigma as does the wage workers' contract with the devil. This immorality of the process distinguishes the baptized bill from a "pure" or capitalist commodity fetish.

In addition the baptism of the bill is still seen as the outcome of a chain of events that is *initiated by man*. It is true that the relationship is still mystified, since supernatural power is seen as necessary for the money to bear interest, but on the other hand, it is clearly understood that the money would not do this on its own. The multiplication of money as capital is not seen as a power inherent in money. Thus, it is not commodity fetishism, since these people do not consider it to be a *natural* property of money to reproduce. Indeed, it is seen as so unnatural that supernatural power has to be invoked by the most devious and destructive means. Although the true relationship of capital to labor is mystified, man is still seen as necessary to trigger off the magical cycles; this is in keeping with the fact that in a use-value economy the relations that persons enter into in their work appear to them as direct, reciprocal, personal relations and not as activities controlled by the relationships of their products. Indeed, the specific forms of precapitalist fetishism that here concern us arise precisely out of this consciousness of human interdependence and reciprocity, in which both persons and their products are seen as forming a unity. When people are confronted by the commodity market in its early stages of penetration, the warping and imbalancing of that interdependence cast the fetish into the realm of the unnatural and evil—the illicit baptism of money and the proletarians' devil contract.

Analogical Reason and the Philosophy of Use-Values

It is striking how similar the principles that underlie the belief in the baptized bill are to those of money and exchange in Aristotle's *Politics* and in the economic theory of the late Middle Ages. Basic to this outlook was the distinction Aristotle drew between what are today called use-value and exchange-value, a distinction that occupies a central place in Marxist theory as well. In book 1 of *The Politics* Aristotle writes:

> Every article or property has a double use; both uses are uses of the thing itself, but they are not similar uses; for one is the proper use of the article in question, the other is not. For example, a shoe may be used either to put on your foot or to offer in exchange. Both are uses of the shoe; for even he that gives a shoe to someone who requires a shoe, and receives in exchange cash or food, is making use of the shoe as shoe, but not the use proper to it, for a shoe is not expressly made for exchange purposes. The same is the case with other articles of property (1962:41).

Although the exchange function of any article could be legitimately utilized within a householding or subsistence economy, it was from this exchange function that money making or capitalism arose to the detriment of the householding or "natural economy." As Roll points out in *A History of Economic Thought*, this distinction between the two arts of money making "was not just an attempt to drive home an ethical distinction. It was also a true analysis of two different forms in which money acts in the economic process: as a medium of exchange whose function is completed by the acquisition of the good required for the satisfaction of a want; and in the shape of money capital leading men to the desire for limitless accumulation" (1973:33).

In his discussion of Aristotle, Roll emphasizes the idea that money as used in the circulation of use-values—Aristotle's householding, the natural economy—is barren. "Money is intended to be used in exchange, but not to increase at interest; it is by nature barren; through usury it breeds, and this must be the most unnatural of all the ways of making money" (1973:33). This information can be organized in tabular form (see Table 2).

Several analogies emerge from the set of contrasts depicted in the table, for instance:

Use-Value of Money	Exchange-Value of Money
(money)	(capital)
$\dfrac{\text{natural}}{\text{barren}}$:	$\dfrac{\text{unnatural}}{\text{fertile}}$

But in nature, in the biological world for example, things are naturally fertile. Aristotle writes: "Money was intended to be a means of exchange, interest represents an increase in the money itself. We speak of it as a yield, as of a crop or a litter; for each animal produces its like, and interest is money produced out of money. Hence of all ways of getting wealth this is the most contrary to nature" (1962:46).

Using the method propounded by Mary Hesse in her discussion of analogy, this can be expressed as a set of positive and negative analogies, in which there is explicit recognition of both similarity and difference between the paired terms that constitute the analogy (1963).

Biological Realm	Use-Value of Money	Exchange-Value of Money
(natural)	(natural)	(unnatural)
$\dfrac{\text{animal}}{\text{litter}}$:	$\dfrac{M}{M}$:	$\dfrac{M}{M'}$

TABLE 2:
Characteristics of Money

Type of Value	Use-Value	Exchange-Value
Aim of circulation	To satisfy natural wants	To gain money as an end in itself
Characteristics of money	Means of exchange	Means to make more money (means as ends; capital)
	C-M-C	M-C-M'
	Natural	Unnatural
	Barren	Fertile

Note: M = Money; M' = Money plus interest on that money, i.e., capital.

The analogy between animals and money as use-value expresses relationships both of similarity and of difference. They are similar in that both are part of the natural world and their properties function to ensure the original purpose of the ideal society: "to re-establish nature's own equilibrium of self-sufficiency," as Aristotle phrases the issue. They are different in that it is the natural property of animals to breed more of themselves, whereas money is by nature barren.

The analogies between animals and capital and between money and capital are also based on a set of similarities and differences. For instance, capital reproduces, just as animals do; but whereas one is natural, the other is unnatural. Likewise, money in the use-value paradigm is similar to money as capital, but whereas the former is barren, the latter is fertile.

Therefore, the task facing the inhabitants of the plantation zones in the southern Cauca Valley is how to explain, and in some cases actually effect, the transformation of properties of similarity into those of difference and those of difference into those of similarity. They must explain how characteristics that were once the exclusive property of animals are now ascribed to money, the natural property of which is to remain barren. They must explain the transformation of money into interest-bearing capital and the conversion of use-value into exchange-value.

This is done through the illicit rite of baptizing money. Unbaptized or natural money is not and should not be capital: it cannot and should not yield interest in the way capital or animals breed more of themselves. Money can achieve this unnatural property only if it is acted on ritually through baptism. Barren money can become unnaturally fertile when transferred to God's domain and stamped with his life-giving properties.

The efficacy and rationality of the magical act seem to be understood by means of a comparison between observed relationships of similarity and difference in separate spheres of existence, and the rite is utilized to manipulate and transmute relationships of difference into relationships of similarity:

<table>
<tr><td align="center">Natural</td><td></td><td align="center">Unnatural</td></tr>
<tr><td align="center">$\dfrac{\text{animal}}{\text{litter}}$</td><td align="center">:</td><td align="center">$\dfrac{M}{M'}$</td></tr>
</table>

The litter is the natural yield of the animal, whereas the increase on capital (M') is unnatural.

The negative analogy (the comparison of difference) can be overcome and harnessed to the comparison of similarity (positive analogy) by means of the baptismal rite:

<table>
<tr><td align="center">$\dfrac{\text{baptism of child}}{\text{legitimation and growth}}$</td><td align="center">:</td><td align="center">$\dfrac{\text{illicit baptism of money}}{\text{delegitimation and growth}}$</td></tr>
</table>

Nevertheless, that transferral is achieved by an illicit rite when applied to money, and that rite is a sacrilege, which deprives a human child from receiving the sanctification and endorsement that is necessary to the fulfillment of human potential. Thus, although money can be converted into interest-bearing capital, this is seen as both supernatural and antinatural. Money cannot do this on its own; for it is not an inherent property of money. It has to be supernaturally activated, and the only way of effecting such an activation is illegal and against the norms of the culture. Capital is thus explained in terms that reveal it to be unnatural and immoral. The analogical paradigms based on a use-value orientation can be restructured through supernatural means, but for all the restructuring, the original meaning of use-value economics is still upheld.

The Devil Contract and the Magic of Capitalist Production

In the case of the devil contract made by the plantation wage laborers in order to increase production, the money earned is understood to be barren. It can be spent only for luxury items, which must be consumed immediately. If the money is invested in land, the land will not bear fruit. If an animal is bought for fattening and future sale, that animal will die. Furthermore, the crop worked under a devil contract will also die: the ratoons of the sugarcane, for example, will cease to sprout and grow. Thus, in this case, although the proletarian's production may increase, the money is not fertile; in fact, it is redolent of infertility—the antithesis of baptized money.

What is the meaning of this? At one level this could be explained by the fact that the contract is made with God's antithesis—the devil. But one can dig deeper behind the symbols and explore Aristotle's and Marx's distinctions a little further. Aristotle makes the connection between production and the different forms of money in the following way: "Hence we seek to define wealth and money-making in different ways; and we are right in doing so, for they *are* different; on the one hand true wealth, in accordance with nature, belonging to household management, productive; on the other money-making, with no place in nature, belonging to trade and not productive of goods in the full sense" (1962:43). Here, the antithesis between money as a mere means of exchange and money as capital is paralleled by the contrast between productive and nonproductive goods and activities. Indeed, for Aristotle the contrast is even more stark than this since money making or capitalism is inherently *destructive* of the natural or householding economy: destructive of the reciprocal interplay of natural forces that are responsible for production and growth.

Thus, the initial reference to the barren and fertile characteristics of money as a medium of exchange is placed in the context of production and a more profound sense of fertility. The analogy between animals and their offspring on the one side and money breeding money on the other is a totally unnatural one in Aristotle's eyes: unnatural most especially in that the naturally barren form of money is grounded in productive activity—"in the full sense"—whereas the fertile form of money is not. Only in its naturally barren form does "money keep to its original purpose; to re-establish nature's own equilibrium of self-sufficiency." Hence, use-values, money as a neutral mediator of exchange, nature's equilibrium of self-sufficiency, and productivity in the full sense are all intrinsically related and necessary to one another.

A basic set of positive and negative analogies that can be derived from this view is as follows:

$$\frac{\text{money}}{\text{capital}} : \frac{\text{productive capacity}}{\text{destructive}}$$

The problem facing the people in this culture is, therefore, how to explain and effect the inversion of these natural analogies, since the empirical fact of the matter is that production can be maintained and increased within the sphere of capitalist production. On inversion we have the following:

$$\frac{\text{money}}{\text{capital}} : \frac{\text{destructive}}{\text{productive}}$$

This inversion is effected and explained in the devil contract: through the agency of this evil and destructive force, production within capitalist relations on the sugar plantations can be increased. At the same time, as the analogy so neatly displays, the money wage gained is nonproductive: it kills whatever it buys except for luxury articles consumed immediately. The natural set of relationships that should obtain according to the use-value paradigm can be transformed into capitalist relationships that defy the use-value analogies. But these capitalist relationships are viewed neither as natural nor as good since they necessitate the agency of the devil.

Conclusion

The superstitions with which we are concerned in the Cauca Valley, namely, the devil contract and the baptism of money, are thus revealed to be beliefs that endorse systematically the logic of the contradiction between use-values and exchange-values. In so doing, these beliefs are identical with the basic tenets of Aristotelian economics, the dominant doctrine of economics as postulated by Aquinas and others in the late Middle Ages, and one of the basic premises of Marxism. These superstitions are not confused vestiges deriving from a prior era when peasant life or Church influence was more intact but are precise formulations that entail a systematic critique of the encroachment of the capitalist mode of production. As manifested by these beliefs, the sensitivity to the distinction between use-values and exchange-values is not the result of nostalgia or mummified ideals retained from the days when the peasant mode of production was flourishing. Nor can it be explained solely as a result of the coexistence of some peasant production with the developing capitalist mode of production. It is also due to the fact that the "slum economy" of the recently urbanized peasants is similarly one based to a major degree on use-value practices.

The paradigm of rationality entailed in these formulations is heavily dependent on analogical reason. Analogical explanations involve an account of the unfamiliar in terms of the familiar, and the analogical mode of reasoning that is at issue here is inherently holistic and dependent on identifying things by their relationships to larger wholes. On the other hand, the causal paradigm that has so thoroughly permeated modern Western social science and the mainstream of what is loosely called Western thought since the seventeenth century is inherently atomistic and reductionist; it defines identity by the thing itself and not by the relation to the context of which the thing is a part.

The mode of analogical reason that is outlined above appears to be more prolific and consciously used in cultures that are guided by use-value economics, and as S. J. Tambiah has so elegantly displayed in his interpretation of Zande magic, an awareness of its logic and systematization dispels the pejorative confusions that are entailed when such beliefs are subjected to the canons of validity that are embodied in modern positivist methodology and utilitarian social philosophy (1973). Where Tambiah falls short, however, is in his failure to consider the underlying system of metaphysics from which the terms in such analogies draw their meaning. Although it is a great service to have demonstrated how apparently weird connections and influences between phenomena can be postulated and upheld in the purely formal properties of an analogical set, the indigenous ontology has to be considered as well. Placing the emphasis on the formal characteristics of analogical rationality gives us an understanding of the systematic precision that is entailed in modes of explanation that are not based on the cause and effect paradigm alone. But this takes us not much further than the nineteenth-century analyses of Tylor and Frazer, who exposed both the intellectual achievement of and also what they considered to be the fatal error entailed in the analogical formulas of magic: the error, that is, if these formulas were held to be instrumental means of achieving some concrete good. But if we do not subject these formulas to the

modern demand to explain such things by their utility, then not erroneous science but a statement about the meaning of the world
confronts us in these magical expressions. Evans-Pritchard argued
against the psychological reductionism and utilitarianism of Tylor
and Frazer by saying that magical formulas are not psychological but
social facts, the truth value of which lies in the language of social relationships and the inescapable legacy of culture (1933). To para-
phrase Durkheim's famous aphorism regarding religion, magic is
society casting spells on itself. Returning to the analogies that constitute magical beliefs, we have therefore to ask why certain properties and not others are considered to be analogically related in the
first place anyway? Although we can point to the analogical relationship between money and capital, for instance, and demonstrate
the problem and solution that such an analogy convey, we are still
doing no more than pointing to a set of givens the meaning of which
ultimately lies in a basis other than those given in the formal reasoning rules themselves. This basis is to be found in the metaphysics and the social philosophy of the group concerned, and in this specific case an important dimension of that philosophy is conveyed by
the paradigm of use-value economics as that paradigm conveys the
meaning of commoditization and reification.

The analogical mode of reasoning is compelling in use-value economies because things are seen not as their self-constituents but as
the embodiments of relational networks. Things interact because of
meanings they carry—sensuous, interactive, animate meanings of
transitiveness—and not because of meanings of physical force
locked in the privatized cell of self-enclosed thinghood.

The types of analogies that were considered in the examples taken
from the Cauca Valley are interesting in that the relationship of
cause and similarity between the separate terms that make up these
analogies depend upon the total set and are not given in the terms
themselves. The concept of "cause" herein entailed is not that of
mechanical causation but that of pattern, association, and purpose.
Nothing but immense confusion can result from subjecting this
concept to the mechanical paradigm of interacting forces, which is
akin to rebounding billiard balls or interlocking cog wheels; hence,
when presented with such forms of reason, the reifying optic sees
them as irrational. Describing the properties of the following type of
analogy, which is the same type as those considered above, Hesse
points out that the relations of similarity at the horizontal level are
contingent upon the particular meaning established by the vertical
relationships (1963).

$$\frac{\text{father}}{\text{child}} \quad : \quad \frac{\text{state}}{\text{citizens}}$$

Moreover, the vertical relationships themselves are not causal in any specific sense, and furthermore, if the individual terms are considered apart from the total analogical set, they each possess a *variety* of connotations. Thus, the specific meaning of any of the terms within the total structure is dependent on the total set of relationships. This is to say that the significance of the individual terms is *not* a result of their meaning as isolates, disconnected from other isolates. Rather, they are relational terms that embody the meaning established by the set of relationships of which any term is a part. Things are relationships, and these relationships are ontological rather than logical.

An analogy selects from a variety of possibilities in order to make one meaningful and persuasive. In the Cauca Valley examples, the meaning concerns the social preconditions of growth and exchange. This is not a science of things but a science of rhetoric, whose medium is social conditions and relations that are threatened with becoming things.

The individual terms are not viewed atomistically. They do not conform to the Newtonian corpuscular paradigm or what A. N. Whitehead calls a philosophy of external relations. Instead, they conform to an organic philosophy of internal relations, in which each of the separate terms embodies the total set of relationships of which it is a part (Whitehead, 1967: 111–18; Ollman, 1971: 27–42).

Put briefly, the metaphysical doctrine of external relations is the foundation of the analytic and reductive method; in this method, explanation analyzes any given phenomenon by its supposedly irreducible atomistic constituents and concludes by illustrating the mathematical laws of cause and effect that supposedly hold between these atoms, which in sum constitute the whole phenomenon. This doctrine is central to the Cartesian tradition and the view of nature with which Galileo, Descartes, and Newton propelled modern science and positivism on their successful course. Although discounted by theoretical physics since the early twentieth century, these ideas continue to provide the bases of modern social science and popular Western ideologies concerning society. Two properties concern us here. First, as Whitehead says: "The character of each of these ultimate things is thus conceived as its own private qualification. Such an existent is understandable in complete disconnection from any other such existent: the ultimate truth is that it requires nothing but itself in order to exist" (1967:113). In other words, the meaning or identity of a thing is given in itself alone, rather than in the context of which it is part. Second, as Whitehead also points out, by virtue of such decontextualization, relationships between things (and changes of things or their relationships) are conceived of as external to the things themselves. These concepts compel recourse to a type of deism and fetishism, which is how Newton himself conceptualized the cosmos of otherwise atomized things.

The fetishism that is inherent in the Cauca Valley beliefs arises from a quite contrary metaphysic and set of social preconditions. In the peasant and working-class epistemology individual terms or things are conceptualized as are Hegel's "moments": each expresses the totality of which it is the manifestation. Things contain the totality within themselves, so to speak, and can be seen causally, acting on and acted upon by other constituents. But they are of interest here primarily as ciphers and signs that echo the meaning of the system that society forms with them.

I, too, have chosen, and indeed felt forced, to interpret them in this sense, rather than see a world of atoms swimming mechanically in the ethereal vapors of time and space. Marxism itself rests on an acute appreciation of such a perspective (cf., Ollman, 1971), although this is commonly ignored because subsequent interpreters understood his notion of materialism to be the same as that of bourgeois science, mechanical and empirical.

In conclusion, it bears repeating that, although the analogical structures can be inverted and relationships can be transformed, in the examples drawn from the Cauca Valley, where one mode of production is displacing another, the ethics and reason of use-value are being maintained. The metaphysics that underlie the analogical mode have not been disowned even though the peasants now own little else than their abstract labor power. The analogies are not neutral, despite the neutralizing influence of the fact-value distinction that is intrinsic to modern science and economic theory, in which it is held that "economics is entirely neutral between ends; that in so far as the achievement of any end is dependent on scarce means, it is germane to the preoccupations of the economist. Economics is not concerned with ends as such" (Robbins, 1935:24).

Nothing could be further from the economic theory and behavior of the peasants and field hands in the southern Cauca Valley, for whom economics is totally concerned with ends. Whether it is economic or whatever, reason is for them far more than the narrow concern with the maximal coordination of scarce means to alternate ends. Rather, reason is that which embodies the conditions of objective existence. Their understanding of capitalist reason and the praxis that it embodies leads them to conclude that that system is contrary to the laws of nature, evil, and ultimately destructive of the conditions of objective existence.

To subject their reason to the instrumentality of means and ends and to the empty formality of analogies considered apart from their contents and purposes is merely to hasten the demise of those conditions. A peasant society or community can be involved in commodity production, but this need not constitute it as a reified culture. A community can in many ways be affected and controlled by the wider capitalist world, but this in itself does not necessarily make such a community a replica of the larger society and the global economy. Attempts to interpret precapitalist social formations by means of what Polyani called our obsolete market mentality are misguided exercises in an ingenuous ethnocentrism, which, in fact, is not even applicable to the market society itself, but is merely a replication of its appearance.

PART III

The Bolivian Tin Mines

They did not know the inflationary power of money. Their coin was the Sun which shines for everybody, the Sun that belongs to everybody and makes everything grow, the Sun without inflation and deflation: and not those dirty "soles" with which the peon is paid (who will show you his ruins for a Peruvian sol). And they ate twice a day throughout the Empire.

Financiers were not the creators of their myths

> Ernesto Cardenal, "The Economy of Tahuantinsuyu"

CHAPTER 8

The Devil in the Mines

I n the shafts of the tin mines in the mountains
around the city of Oruro, Bolivia, the miners have
statues representing the spirit who owns the mines
and tin. Known as the devil or as the uncle (Tio),
these icons may be as small as a hand or as large as a
full-sized human. They hold the power of life and death over the
mines and over the miners, who conduct rites of sacrifice and gift
exchange to the spirit represented by the icons—the contemporary
manifestation of the precolonial power of the mountain (Nash,
1976:27; Costas Arguedas, 1961, 2:303–4).

His body is sculptured from mineral. The hands, face, and legs are
made from clay. Often, bright pieces of metal or light bulbs from the
miners' helmets form his eyes. The teeth may be of glass or of crystal sharpened like nails, and the mouth gapes, awaiting offerings of
coca and cigarettes. The hands stretch out for liquor. In the Siglo XX
mine the icon has an enormous erect penis. The spirit can also appear as an apparition: a blond, bearded, red-faced *gringo* (foreigner)
wearing a cowboy hat, resembling the technicians and administrators who control the tens of thousands of miners who excavate the
tin that since the late nineteenth century has made Bolivia a satel-
lite of the world commodity market. He can also take the form of a
succubus offering riches in exchange for one's soul or life (Nash,
1972).

Without the goodwill of this spirit, effected through ritual, both
mineral production and the miners' lives are imperiled. To say the
least, this spirit owner of the mines is extraordinarily ambivalent,
representing the force of life and the force of death; as the political
and economic context changes, so does his ambivalence. Following
the revolutionary changes and state nationalization of the mines in
1952, personalistic private ownership by the tin barons was replaced

by stultifying bureaucratic control and military dictatorship, which, in some ways, has made the struggle over workers' control even more arduous and critical than it was in the days of the tin barons. Since the military takeover in 1964, the miners' rites to the spirit owner of the mine have been suppressed. Asserting that they impede progress, some miners think that these rites are better forgotten. Others claim the opposite and maintain that the management suppressed the rites because they sustain proletarian solidarity and the high level of revolutionary consciousness for which the mining areas are famous.

Each change in the mode of production and each new development of political struggle add new meanings and transformations to the symbolization and understanding of the spirit owner of nature. In the peasant communities of the Andean plateau, where, individually and communally, the tillers of the soil exercise a measure of real control over the means of production, the spirit owners of nature differ from those in the mines, where the capitalist mode of production reigns. In peasant communities, also, the spirit owners hold the power of life and death over people and over resources. Especially important are the mountain spirit owners, which are often personified, but never sculptured. But they do not bear the actively evil character of the spirit of the mines, and rites to them are far less frequent. In peasant life the mountain spirit owners are embodied in natural icons, such as crags or boulders, whose vitality and wholeness ensure the vitality and solidarity of the community residing on the mountain slopes. Rites of sacrifice and gift exchange with the mountain spirit owners exemplify and ratify these beliefs. They ensure the smooth flow of production, which is aimed mainly at self-subsistence and exists largely outside of capitalist market exchange. By feeding the mountain spirit, peasant producers ensure that the mountain spirits will feed them. Gift exchange with the spirits ensures that the spirits will reciprocate with gifts of life for the peasants. In communities that are relatively isolated from commercial trade and commercial culture, the understanding and representation of the mountain spirit owners respond more to Indian motifs and benevolence than they do in peasant communities that are not so isolated. The ambivalence of the spirit owners is always present. They can harm as much as help. But ritual gift exchange can channel this ambivalence into a favorable outcome.

Only in the mines, honeycombed mountains of capitalist organization, does the spirit owner seem predominantly and actively evil. There, rites to the spirit owner are necessary and frequent; yet, try as they might, the miners are constantly on the verge of failure despite their ritual propitiation. Up until the early 1950s, under the personalistic control of the tin barons like Simón Patiño the miners' rites had a great deal of legitimacy. Patiño himself participated in some. Following nationalization and the reorganization of the mines under the aegis of state capitalism, the miners were exposed to a different situation with new contradictions. As part of the Bolivian nation they theoretically shared in the ownership of the mines. In their left-wing unions they fought continuously for this right. Yet the real day-to-day management of the work process and the real claim to the distribution of the wealth of the mines have not passed into their hands, and bureaucratic domination may have in some ways worsened their situation. It certainly seems to have made their plight even more arbitrary and more anonymous, and bloody state violence against them has by no means ceased. With this recent historical development in mind, one becomes more keenly attuned to the transformations and ambivalence that mark the devil figure owner of the mines, the uncle or Tio. "Whoever plays with the Tio becomes like a demon," says a miner's wife in the late 1960s. Women were especially prejudiced by the organizational changes, mechanization, and strictures against their gleaning ores. She continues,

> Therefore, we don't consult with the Titito [dear little uncle] any more. He used to appear formerly, but now he can't. He is completely tired out and he can't. It is in vain that they *ch'alla* [perform ritual] for the Tio. We made him of great stones that had metal in it. He used to look like a person smoking a cigarette just like us. After he finished the cigarette he would chew coca, chewing with the women from their bags of coca. We used to enter before the Tio with our silk shawls. We used to consult him. We reached for the metal in his hands. It was beautiful, like raw sugar. [Nash, 1976:81]

As did miners in late medieval and early modern Europe, Bolivian miners today attribute organic and spiritual life to the mine. They have to understand the metabolism of this life and work with it, and to do this, they must above all exchange with it. This is attained through a ritual that dramatizes exchange and brings its specific meaning to a fine pitch of understanding.

Prior to nationalization, wages were shared between the ten to fifteen members of a work gang who were tied to contracts based on the amount of metal excavated. Following nationalization the gangs were dismembered into two-person units and wages were fixed by the cubic meter dug out rather than by the amount of mineral extracted. To some degree the intense solidarity of the small work group was replaced by the national Bolivian workers' union (the Central Obrero Boliviano). But after the military coup and takeover of the mines in 1964, the union lost much of its power. Now the workers have neither the strength of their old primary work groups nor that of the monolithic union.

In keeping with the structure of payment and work organization before nationalization, the miners' rites to the spirit owner of the mines and tin every Tuesday and Friday stressed the desire for mineral and for the alleviation of danger. Now the rites are generally prohibited by the management, but the miners persist in performing them (albeit on a greatly reduced scale), even though the primary work group no longer exists and they earn wages by volume excavated and not by the amount of tin. Notwithstanding this radical alteration in the calculation of payment, the miners and their persistent rites continue to be concerned with the life of the mine.

This concern transcends the narrow economism of the managers and of the truly alienated worker typical of modern industry. The miners regard themselves, and not the managers, as the people who understand and care for the mine. In the autobiography of the miner Juan Rojas, it is strikingly clear that the miners are preoccupied with the life of the mine as a living entity, so to speak. From Rojas's detailed account the reader sees and feels again and again how the miners' work is a process of empathy with the mine, nourishing it as much as excavating it. They are forced by the management hierarchy to struggle with the rock face and to hate the work that destroys their lungs and shortens their lives. Yet, at the same time they care for the mine. Their attitude is more than respect: it is reverential, stemming from the interaction on which miners depend. This sense of mutuality is a daily lived practice of coparticipation with other workers in a highly dangerous enterprise requiring common trust and fine coordination. It is also the sensibility of coparticipation with the ways of the mine itself. This sense of affiliation with the mine comes from the experience and skills that are painfully learned at the rock face as one gradually enters into the metabolism of the mine (Rojas and Nash, 1976).

Joseph W. Bastien describes a similar sensibility on the part of the peasants in northern Bolivia toward the mountain on which they live. These people say that they are united because their communities correspond to different but interlocked parts of the mountain, which they conceive as a human body. They work with the lands of the mountain; the mountain gives them life; they feed the mountain with ritual gifts and give it life and wholeness. While they sustain its life, the mountain sustains theirs (1978:190–91). It is this sense of living mutuality between work, between people, and between persons and nature that ritual enforces, even when modern commercial production and exchange oppose such mutuality. In fact, by threatening its integrity, commodity production and market exchange seem strangely to exacerbate this sense of living mutuality.

In accord with a vast series of meanings inscribed in mythology, magic, and the arousal of nature's sleeping powers, mineral ores are often spoken of as alive, resplendent with movement, color, and sound. They may be said to be flowing like water, moving, asleep, pure, beautiful, growing like a potato, like raw sugar, sweet, screaming below the ground. The miner's wife quoted above describes how the Virgin of the Mineshaft is on top of the gold in the shaft. Boiling water passes over this gold, whose beauty the wife compares to raw sugar. This gold cannot be moved, though it itself is moving. The Virgin hates to be moved. If she were moved, the city of Oruro would be lost because the water on which she walks would then carry her away. One propitiates the Virgin, who might otherwise eat people (Nash, 1976:77–78). Throughout Latin American highland Indian mythology the Virgin is commonly associated with fertility and water and contrasted with a leading male deity who is associated with destruction and heat. The antitheses of mobility and immobility correspond with the lust for gold and the dangers of removing it from its proper place. The same beliefs apply to the silver and gold in the mountain that is guarded by San Pedro. If he were moved, the mountain would burn and people with it. The coca sellers, it is said, carry a newborn baby there each Carnival and throw it alive into the hole. In exchange, the devil gives them silver. This contract was made by the same sort of sacrificial rite, the *k'araku*, that the tin miners make with a llama to the spirit owner of the tin mines, the Tio. The mountain of San Pedro is very rich with mineral, but people cannot move it in any way. The mine of San José also has good metal, but people say that it is sleeping and that they cannot now work it. Many enchanted spirits inhabit that mine.

The mine is enchanted, but it is the antithesis of a Christian enchantment. In fact, its very power seems to derive from that antithesis. It is opposed to the world of Christ; it is of the antichrist. At the entrance to the mine one may pray to God and make the sign of the cross. But inside one must never do this. One cannot even use the pick when working close to mineral because the pick has the form of the cross. Otherwise, one may lose the vein (Rojas and Nash, 1976:371). God reigns on the surface, but the Tio is king in the mine. "We do not kneel before him as we would before a saint," says a miner, "because that would be sacrilegious" (Nash, 1972:226). Father Monast, who worked in Bolivia, tells us that the bishop of Potosí was prevented by the miners from celebrating Mass inside the mine. Like any priest, the bishop is considered to be the enemy of the Tio, and his presence would cause the tin to disappear. The Tio is Lucifer, the devil, and the securing of tin depends on doing homage to him. Two icons stand at the entrance to the Siglo XX mine: on one side, St. Michael; on the other side, the Tio (Monast, 1969:100–101). "We would not say Jesus, Maria, and Joseph, and make the sign of the cross, because the metal would disappear," says the woman cited above (Nash, 1976:126).

Just as the mine lies opposed to the sacred power of Christianity and the Tio to God, so there is a further opposition between the Tio and the Pachamama (Earthmother). The Tio is a masculine figure, monstrously so, as represented with a giant penis. The dangers of mining can cause miners to lose their virility, and when this happens they ask the Tio to make them as potent as he. Throughout the Andes the Pachamama stands for fertility, and she receives ritual offerings of liquor sprinkled on the ground. Before offering liquor to the Tio, the miners sprinkle some on the ground for her. They say that when they *achamama* (chew coca), they ingest her spirit (Nash, 1972:226). Before entering the mine, miners greet her, "Good day old woman, don't let anything happen to me today"; when they leave, they thank her for their life. When they feel in danger, they ask her to intercede with the Tio, and when they set off dynamite, they ask her not to get angry.

Before suppression by management, rites to the Tio were regularly held on Tuesdays and Fridays, the days for rites of sorcery and its reversal throughout Latin America. "We begin to *ch'alla* in the working areas within the mines," describes a miner. "We bring in banners, confetti, and paper streamers, all those things. First we begin with the Tio. We put a cigarette in his mouth. After this we scatter alcohol on the ground for the Pachamama. I and my partner do it, we are 'politicos,' a kind of team. We scatter the alcohol and then give some to the Tio. Then we take out our coca and begin to chew, and we smoke. We serve liquor from the bottles each of us brings in. We light the Tio's cigarette and we say 'Tio, help us in our work. Don't let any accidents happen'" [Ibid.]. They drink liquor, talk, and sing about their work and political history. They wind streamers around the neck of the Tio and prepare an altar with offerings—herbs, a llama foetus, and cakes with pictures of desired objects, like houses, cars, or animals, or with pictures of monsters. These are burnt in front of the Tio. Then they drunkenly go to where they change their clothes, following which they make further offerings to the Tio, wrapping streamers around the other's neck.

Accidents are frequent, often lethal, and intimately bound to the malevolence of the Tio and his propitiation. Nash quotes a miner describing how when the miners are frightened they yell, "What are you doing, Tio?" Following a near accident, they offer coca and liquor to the Tio with thanks for saving them. When three men died in an accident the year before, the men were convinced, he says, that the Tio was thirsty for blood. They asked the administration for free time to conduct a rite. Three llamas were purchased and a shaman hired. The men offered blood to the Tio saying, "Take this! Don't eat my blood!" (Ibid.: 229–30).

Although in this instance a specific physical accident was the immediate cause for holding the rite, the miners pleaded with the Tio, not to rectify faulty mining practices, but to not eat their blood. There is constant danger in the mines. Tunnels may collapse, dynamite explode harmfully, and so on. To this terribly real danger is added the danger of the spirit owner who subsumes all these physical dangers because the Tio is basic to the life of the mine. Contact with the gods is always dangerous and marred by the threat of death. Sacrifice allows men to approach the gods through the mediation of the sacrificial victim. Peace can be purchased in this manner, but cannot be vouchsafed. The sacrificer can become the sacrificed. The appeal to the Tio "Take this! Don't eat my blood!" is an appeal that illustrates this ever present possibility. On another level this possibility is testimony to the ambivalence of the gods, the true owners of the mine's wealth. It is also testimony to the dangers that manifest imbalanced exchange and the fear that the exchange between miners and the mine is always unbalanced. When the miner Juan Rojas gives an account of a sacrificial rite to the Tio following an accident, he describes how the miners become happy (Rojas and Nash, 1976:366–69). They declare that they feed the Tio with all their heart so that the mine will prosper. The rite does not so much prevent accidents as follow them. Danger to miners is subsumed by concern with the prosperity of the mine.

A work mate of Rojas's was badly hurt in 1966. Rojas himself felt that his luck was out. He was refused permission by the engineer to resign as head of the gang. When his mate returned to work, he suggested to Rojas that they perform a rite to the Tio. They bought the offerings of sugar, hard corn, sweet corn, beer, white wine, red wine, pisco, and a sheep. A visiting shaman was contracted. Instead of allowing the shaman to puncture the heart with wire, which would dirty and kill it, the miners insisted on slitting the animal's throat and then sprinkling its blood over the rock face deep in the mine. Then they went to eat the sheep. The shaman had prepared the *mesa* (altar) by the fire with different forms of sugar sweets, grains, llama fat, and six miniature llamas made of llama fat, meaning that the sacrifice would be equivalent to six real llamas. The sugar, which is ritually opposed to salt, was for the Tio's female companion. After the small group ate the sheep, a man who worked elsewhere arrived unannounced. This was a good sign. He was given the name Mallku, which is also the term for sacred earth shrines on mountains, the shrines of the ancestor sites. In Quechua the group said, "The Condor has come to help us eat." (Mountain spirits can assume the form of the condor.) The man wanted to take the meat home and eat it there, but the shaman stopped him. "You have to eat," he said. "If you don't, the Tio's companion will eat you!" Frightened, the man ate. When they were finished, the bones were wrapped in red wool, and they made their way back to the mine. Ritual infusions were sprinkled at the mine's entrance. They were happy, saying that they were giving this meal with all their heart; the mine would prosper. They entered the site where they were going to place the heart and bones. The heart was placed in the center of the sugar sweets and flowers, and on top the bones were placed in the form of the complete skeleton, which was then covered with the hide. At the four corners they placed white wine, red wine, alcohol, beer, paw paw, and some little vases of clay. They drank a toast "to the memory of the sacrifice that we were making for the Tio." Then they left rapidly without daring to look behind. After staying two hours at the lift level, they ascended to the outside and continued drinking until night fell the following day (Rojas and Nash, 1976:366–69).

This rite is strikingly similar to the llama sacrifice recorded by Bastien in his account of the New Earth ceremonies performed by the peasants of Kaata prior to potato planting. The spirit owners of the field, of the agricultural cycle, of the crops, and of the territorial kinship group are fed with special gifts, coca, llama fat, flowers, incense, and blood. The llama is embraced and kissed—just as the miners were described in Bernabé Cobo's account written around 1653 as kissing the metal and smelting instruments. Its neck is deeply slit, and the heart is immediately removed. While the heart is still beating, blood is collected and sprinkled over the ground in all directions. The participants call out to the spirit owners of the llama, of the *ayllu* (social group), and of the agricultural cycle: "Receive this blood from the sacrificial llama. Give us an abundant harvest, grant increase to our flocks, and grant us good fortune in all.

Mother earth, drink of this blood." The llama's heart is cut into small pieces, and each spirit owner is fed a piece. Then, llama fat is fed to the major participants. Summarizing, Bastien writes, "The blood from the ayllu's most esteemed animal flowed to all parts of the ayllu body and vitalized its geographical layers to produce more life" (1978:51–83).

In the mining communities a special rite to the Tio is performed on two occasions: on the first of August (the month of the devil), which is when the rite described above took place, and on the first Friday of Carnival. Up until 1952, when the great tin barons were still in control, the miners offered them around one hundred pounds of the richest mineral as part of a rite in which they sacrificed a white llama to the Tio. In return, the tin baron reciprocated with gifts of coca, liquor, and clothing. It is highly probable that this descends from the rites that occurred prior to conquest between miners and their chief, the *curaca*, or with the Incan king himself. Today, the old miners say that Patiño, one of the most famous tin barons, firmly believed in the Tio and made large offerings to him (Nash, 1972:227). The brief description of this rite that was proffered by a veteran miner has themes that parallel those of rites recorded by the mid-seventeenth-century Spanish chronicler Berbabé Cobo (1890–95, 3:345).

During Carnival, when this public rite to the Tio and the tin barons occurred, two pageants dramatizing the history of conquest and mining also take place. These dramas present the meaning of mining and class relationships in a spectacular manner.

In one, Hahuari, who was the spirit of the mountain and is now identified with the Tio or devil of the tin mines, is depicted as seducing the virtuous peasants to abandon their fields and enter the mountain to find the rich minerals he holds inside. The people become dissolute drunkards paying their way with the riches of the mountain. Then monsters come to eat them but are halted by lightning that is sent by an Incan princess, who is later identified as the Virgin of the Mineshaft. These monsters can be seen today as natural icons surrounding Oruro, as rocky crags, sand dunes, stones, and lakes. According to Nash, they must be propitiated during Carnival (and in August), when hundreds of dancers take to the streets dressed as devils (1972:224).

The second pageant is *The Conquest of the Spanish* enacted on the Sunday and Monday of Carnival in Oruro. It is also part of the celebration of the Virgin of the Mineshaft, identified as an Incan princess. Nathan Wachtel considers it as a clear manifestation of Andean messianism (1977). The actors in this pageant have a written script, and this was recorded in its entirety in Quechua and Spanish by Ena Dargan in 1942 (Hernando Balmori, 1955). It vividly displays the drama of European conquest: its cruelty, deception, and greed for precious metals. The bewilderment and total miscomprehension of the Incan king confronted by the demands for gold and silver is emphasized. The Spaniards' chaplain tries to explain the mysteries of Christianity and to persuade the Incan king to submit to the king of Spain. The Inca responds by saying that he is the legitimate owner of his dominion and that neither this nor his religion will be abandoned. He asks the priest for some sign of his religion, and is shown a Bible, which he throws on the ground. In fury, the Spanish slaughter the Indians and take the Incan king prisoner. He is then decapitated, and the Andean people are conquered. A member of the Incan nobility curses all gold and silver so that it will disappear and so that the Spaniards will be forced to live by their work. An Incan princess prays: "Eternal Father let the young powerful Inca come. Resurrect him!" As Clemente Hernando Balmori notes at this point in the narrative, the cousin of Pizarro, the leading conquistador, wrote in 1571 that when the Incan king Atahualpa was killed his sisters and wives stated that he would return to this world (Ibid.:46). At the end of the pageant, Pizarro returns to Spain and offers the Inca's head and crown to the king of Spain. "Oh! General Pizarro," exclaims the king, "what are you saying? My orders were not to take the life of a great king, one who is perhaps greater than I!" Following a long discourse on the cruelty and hubris of Pizarro, the king orders him to die in the same way he killed the Inca, and with that all his descendants shall be destroyed too.

The calling for life is predominant in the miners' rites to the Tio, the devil spirit owner of the tin mines. The desire for mineral and the alleviation of physical danger are important components of this call, but only within a broader purpose. Try as they might, the miners are constantly on the verge of being destroyed. The Tio seems implacably bent on their demise. Yet, as the rites to him suggest and as the pageants make clear, he coexists with a symbolized history of conquest and mining, the evil of which is bountiful with the promise of reversal. The miners deserted the ways of the peasant to enter the unnatural economy of wage work; now, they gut the mountain of its precious metals. Their imminent destruction, however, is staved off by the action of the Incan princess whom they publicly celebrate. The Incan king and the Indian universe were destroyed by the Spanish for the sake of precious metals and Christianity. The Incan nobility placed a curse on precious metals causing them to disappear. Men and women who seek them out by means of sweat and ritual from their hidden places, entombed by layer upon layer of entrenched symbolism, colors, myths, movement, sounds, drugs, and sacrifice, must know why it is difficult and what it means to persist. Yet they are forced to do so. The Tio stands as a custodian of the meaning of Indian submission and loss of control over the life they constantly call for. Yet, by the same curse the Spaniards and, hence, all non-Indians are condemned to lose their power to exploit the Indians' labor, and they will have to live from their own sweat and toil. The prevailing world is not accepted as good or natural. The Inca will return, and Pizarro's legacy be destroyed.

This is a fantasy, of course. Yet it is one that permeates the Andean universe. In peasant communities, too, the messianic myth of the Inca's return exists. But nowhere in peasant society do the spirit owners of nature take on the same humanly sculptured reality or active malevolence as does the spirit owner who oversees the grueling life of wage workers in the mines. A new element not found in peasant life has been added to the dross image of the Spaniard and the glitter of precious metals: proletarianization of Indians, associated with a strange fetishization of commodities.

These strange fantasies do not so much escape from life as oppose the exploitative and fragmented form that it has taken. The elusive "subjective factor" of political consciousness is here kindled and rekindled in myths of creation and in rituals of work that oppose the form that modern production has taken to an earlier organic form. A mythic vision of the past lives on to contest the present, denying the latter's assertions of normality and claims to perpetuity.

Historical materialism, writes Benjamin, wishes to retain that image of the past that unexpectedly appears to man singled out by history at a moment of danger. This danger threatens the content of tradition and the people who bear it with becoming tools of the ruling class. Political struggle starts with the determination to resist this ideological encroachment. In every era, he went on to say, the attempt must be made anew to wrest tradition away from a conformism that is about to overpower it. It is this politically inspired memorization, this active historiography, that the miners carry out in their rites to the Tio and to the life of the mine. In the darkness of the honeycombed mountains, they present their history as they see it. A leader in the miners union asserts:

This tradition inside the mountain must be continued because there is no communication more intimate, more sincere, or more beautiful than the moment of the *ch'alla*, the moment when the workers chew coca together and offer it to the Tio.

There they give voice to their social problems, they give voice to their work problems, they give voice to all the problems they have, and there is born a new generation so revolutionary that the workers begin thinking of making structural change. This is their university. [Nash, 1972:231–32]

To make structural change, to change society, is to make history. To make history it is necessary to retain the empowered imagery of the past which condemns the distortions of humanity that are wrought normal by the objective pretensions of the present. It demands, as Benjamin says, to seize hold of a memory as it flashes up in a moment of danger. For as Herbert Marcuse reminds us, " 'All reification is a process of forgetting.' Art fights reification by making the petrified world speak, sing, perhaps dance" (1977:73).

At the end of his autobiography, the miner Juan Rojas says:

At the moment I know what I'm doing and I remember what I've done and I know what I'm going to do. But to speak truthfully a miner is de-memorized. The memory of the miner is lost. So when a miner speaks it's not with fidelity. The memory of a miner is not fixed. No it's not fixed. Many times he speaks and does not remember. If he remembers for an instant, most of the time he forgets thereafter. Why? Because the brain of the miner is perturbed by the crackling of the machinery, withered by the explosions of the dynamite and the gas of the tin. This is what I want to explain to you about my situation. [Rojas and Nash, 1976:478]

CHAPTER 9

The Worship of Nature

The mining rituals and the sculptures of the devil are forms of art. If we accept Marcuse's suggestion that art fights the amnesia of reification by making the petrified world speak and sing against a repressive reality, then we begin to sense how and why the miners' art is informed by their history extending back through peasant life to preconquest times. As art, these rites and statues dramatize and mold the meaning of the present in the hopes for liberation from it. Through ritual the spirits of nature are aligned with man and come to his aid. Proletarianization of peasants into miners and the modernization of Indians have led not to a disenchantment of the world but to a growing sense of its destructiveness and evil as figured in the devil. Mining rites embody and attempt to transcend this transformation; they act out history and are rituals of the oppressed. They do so under the spell of a magic that points to nature's complicity with liberated man.

To Andean Indians nature is animated, and persons and nature form an intricately organized unity. They are bound together through common origins, and they reciprocate with one another. This unity depends on a balance in the forces of nature and a complementary balance in social activities. These reciprocations are clearly visible in rituals such as those concerned with birth, death, marriage, misfortune, agriculture, and healing. These rituals simultaneously exemplify metaphysical principles, instruct people in these principles, and create these principles anew. If severe and sustained, distortions in either the natural or the social sphere will greatly modify the frequency, timing, content, and meaning of the rituals, without necessarily modifying the underlying metaphysical basis. This seems to be the case with the miners' bizarre rites to the devil. Nature and social relations have been and continue to be distorted. Both are alienated from the balance that should obtain in ideal conditions like those approximated in contemporary Andean peasant communities. The miners' rites of production and misfortune exemplify this alienation and the demand to transcend it. They can be seen as healing rites, both in a literal sense and in the metaphorical sense of their healing the wounds and contradictions inflicted on Andean culture.

The culture of conquest and the indigenous culture have fused to form an antagonistic structure of oppositions. This fusion is an active and dynamic process of juxtaposition, reflection, and creation, the ambiguities and dualisms of which manifest divisions deeply rooted in the soul of colonial and neocolonial society. Hence, the devil in the mines is not identical to the devil of late-medieval Christianity and can be an ally as much as a foe. By the same token, whereas the surface of the earth attracts Christian-like obeisance, the depths of the mine impel worship of the antichrist. The dark and treacherous interiors of the mines are best known to the workers, who feel that only they really know how to work the mines productively and that the managers are superfluous and exploitative.

The unification of person with nature which was the hallmark of Andean culture prior to the Spanish conquest as much as it is today, has two associated components that must not be overlooked: a specific type of political economy and a specific type of epistemology. The former is a system of production and exchange in which people engage with one another through communal principles of ownership and exchange: the material preconditions of livelihood are extensions of the person as much as of the communal body. This kinship of resources, person, and society finds its expression and ratification in a series of ideas that enliven nature with a social persona and a humanlike empathy. As Hans C. Buechler and J. M. Buechler observe, the Aymara peasants of the shores of Lake Titicaca understand the relationship of the spheres of the natural and the supernatural to be one of mutuality. An event in human life is reflected in nature. They go on to state that in the reckoning of the Aymara this reflection of human life in nature is not a relationship of cause and effect but one of analogy (1971). This mode of understanding connections is not to be confused with the epistemology underlying atomistic and mechanical paradigms of causal explanation. Instead, as Joseph Needham writes, it is an epistemology that tries to "systematize the universe of things and events into a pattern of structure, by which all the mutual influences of its parts were conditioned" (1956:285). This pattern of structure is the pattern of the universal organism, as inclusive of social as it is of natural relations. "The parallelisms of the human and natural spheres represent more than merely the identity or association of unequal elements," write the Buechlers. "What is related are not so much *characteristics* but *similar relationships*. For instance, abortion is related to normal birth as hail is related to propitious climatic conditions. Abortion does not cause hail, nor does normal birth cause fertile fields, but in order to attain balance in the forces of nature a complementary normality in human reproduction must be maintained" (1971:93).

To the Andean Indians residing on the slopes of Mount Kaata, the mountain is a human body. Their fields are used and their different products are exchanged in accord with the different functional parts of that body. The conception of nature and society as fused into the one organism is here most explicit. The land is understood in terms of the human body, and the human body is understood in terms of the culturally perceived configuration of the land. The land forms a gestalt, the gestalt of the human body. The people feed the mountain body with gifts and sacrifice, and the mountain reciprocates with food for all the people. The sacredness of the mountain is dependent on its wholeness: of nature, of the social group, of the person, and of all three together. Rituals provide the constant rekindling of the body gestalt, and this gestalt ensures the cycling of reciprocal economic exchange binding people to each other and to the land.

Corresponding to this cosmology, the Kaatan epistemology and ontology do not conceive of body and mind, matter and thought, as being dualistic. Kaatans are not Kantians. "The body includes the inner self," writes Bastien, "and experiences are not dualistically perceived as those of the psyche and those of the body" (1978:43). This is nicely illustrated by the meaning of *yachay* (to know) associated with ritualists and with the taking of coca. This is not the knowing of an exterior world by interior thought, as Cartesian epistemology and its legacy would have us understand. Instead, it is "the omniscience to understand the secrets of the mountain body in terms of the corporeal body. Earth and humans no longer exist as dichotomies but rather as endless reflections of differently shaped mirrors" (Ibid.:56). To know is to be associated with everything around one and to enter into and be part of the land.

From this it follows that rites of sacrifice and gift exchange with the spirits of the mountain are not seen as causing in any direct or mechanical way the fertility and prosperity of the fields. These rites awaken the sleeping power of the mountain, "not to control it, but to experience and be in exchange with it" (Ibid.:81). In this sense exchange with the spirits of nature is not an instrument of utility but a tautology and an end in itself, renewing the important meanings that ritual makes visible.

It would be equally mistaken to construct a dictionary of taxonomic properties of spirits without first establishing the total system of metaphorical kinship binding nature, society, and spirits. As the Buechlers stress, identity is inherent not in things themselves but in the similar relationships or analogies that constitute things. To adopt the atomistic view of identity as residing in things themselves can only incur the risk of portraying such cultures as confused miscellanies of jumbled statements from different informants. Faced with this inevitable result of the methodology of atomism, the ethnographer inevitably concludes, with an air of mournful realism, that a once intact traditional system now lies in heterogeneous disarray as a result of acculturation, modernization, and so forth (cf., Tshopik, 1968). This conclusion, which is dependent on the same edicts of methodological individualism that have driven conquest and oppression in the Andes, exaggerates the degree to which everybody thought the same prior to acculturation and, by the same token, equally exaggerates the inroads made by modernization in fragmenting Andean culture.

It is important to note that the analogies between the human body, the social body, and nature form a cultural system, that is like a language with its own autonomy and integrity. A single person can, and indeed must, speak that language; but his or her knowledge of that system is perforce incomplete and individualized. This is like the relation that Ferdinand de Saussure invoked between "language" and "speech" (*langue* and *parole*) or that Noam Chomsky coined between "competence" and "performance." Like a language system, culture is inherited from generation to generation and is inescapable. And like language, culture changes systematically, and people as social beings actively create with the legacy bequeathed them. In this dialectical manner the system of analogies obtaining between the human body, the social body, and nature is never completely fixed or isomorphic. Changes occur in all spheres. Andean culture proves its dynamism and imagination in the constant refurbishing of the associations that constitute this network of analogies, particularly when it has been distorted by intruding political and economic forces such as those that cause communities to cede land and resources to whites. As a result of such discrepancies between the mountain metaphor and the body metaphor, notes Bastien, "the struggle in the Andes is an attempt to remove the discrepancies between the analogous terms. This provides a cultural explanation for violence in the Andes" (1978:194). This constant violence is a symbol "of the tension within the metaphor, when the people and the land are not analogous" (Ibid.:197). John Earls had similarly analyzed resurgent Andean messianism. He saw this as a dialectical response to the antithesis struck between indigenous form and externally imposed content. The messianic response is a means to overcome that imposed content and restore indigenous forms with balance (1969). In this connection both Earls's and Bastien's finely textured accounts confirm the pioneering work of José Maria Arguedas, who devoted his life to the explication of the Quechua world of which he was part. As a novelist, ethnographer, and folklorist, he displayed the political implications of the crypto-paganism that has persisted in the Andes as a response to colonization by the West. Precisely because of their soul-destroying form of organization, capitalist and state capitalist attempts to subjugate the Indian open up new channels for the expression of Indian culture and the resistance of its participants. He was especially scornful of the argument that Indianist or pro-Indian ideologies of *indigenismo* could become tools for the benefit of the ruling classes. Both those who advocate and those who fear capitalist cultural imperialism, he asserted, err by forgetting "that man truly possesses a soul and that this is very rarely negotiable" (1975:188).

Crypto-Paganism

Despite four centuries of humiliation and vicious subjugation, preconquest institutions still flourish in the Andes. H. Castro Pozo (1924:156), José Carlos Mariategui (1971), and Luis E. Valcarcel (1967) support this when they write that while public performance of rites held in preconquest times has been suppressed, the Indians, who form the bulk of the population in Ecuador, Peru, and Bolivia, still carry out many of their ancient rites with great force, surreptiously or under the mask of Catholicism. Herman Trimborn states that much of the preconquest religion survives today (1968:146). R. T. Zuidema contends that the basic form of sociocultural organization today is the same as that prior to European colonization (1968). Bastien points out that because the thrust of academic research has been concerned with what has changed, he was quite unprepared to find that in 1972 the people of Kaata held the same idea of the mountain as a human body metaphor of their social organization as that described in the preconquest Huarochirí legends. He goes on to make the point that, retained as a vital organizing principle today, this ancient concept provided the fighting spirit behind their largely successful struggle against land appropriation (1978: xvii). In general terms preconquest institutions have survived because Indian communities managed to wall themselves off from intrusive cultural influences. But they have survived also because the force of cultural intrusion stimulated a culture of resistance.

In this regard Weston LaBarre writes of the hostility with which the Aymara of the Lake Titicaca region regard Christianity:

> Centuries of nominal Christianity have merely added another alien mythology to the body of Aymara belief. A brutally oppressed and bitterly exploited people, many of them have taken fanatically to the sado-masochistic symbols of the blood-dripping, thorn-crowned figure on the cross of the more extravagant Iberian iconography of colonial times, and to the tragic-faced all-merciful mother whom some of them identify with their own ancient earth-goddess. Although they are all accounted Christian, many of the Aymara, however, hate the religion with the same vehemence that they hate its representatives.[1948:171]

Juan Victor Nuñez del Prado B. has recently pointed to the culture of resistance formed by this crypto-paganism:

> We find that the supernatural world has characteristics very similar to those it had during the Inca empire, although the worship of some deities has died out and the veneration of others appeared. The surprising thing is not, however, that the supernatural world has changed, but rather that it has not disappeared entirely, considering that the culture under investigation has coexisted for 400 years with another that has constantly tried to eliminate native beliefs and replace them with its own. We can attribute the phenomenon of persistence to the fact that the pressure, discrimination and segregation applied to the Indians, first by the invaders and then by the dominant mestizo group, have generated a protective barrier behind which native tradition and rituals have been able to maintain themselves thanks to their clandestine practice. [1974:250]

Adolph F. Bandelier sees the intensity of paganism as directly related to attempts at its suppression, and its public emergence as related to rebellion: "The Indian of Bolivia is a Catholic; at least nominally. . . . But in case of a general uprising, I doubt very much (and in this I am confirmed by the opinion of reliable parish priests) whether the Indians would not return openly to a paganism which at heart they still profess and in secret actually practice" (1910:91).

Cosmology: Animated Structuralism

Although Andean metaphysics stresses the all-encompassing unity that exists between persons, spirits, and the land, this unity is most definitely not the mushy totality that phrases like "the oneness of the universe" or the "unity of all" might suggest. On the contrary, this unity is composed of a highly differentiated system of dualities the parts of which are united through the dialectical mesh of binary oppositions. As the result of extensive research, Javier Albo writes that a recurrent theme in the social organization and symbolic organization of the Aymara "is the union of contraries, with an internal coherence that would delight adherents of dialectical philosophy" (1974–76:92). In the Andes "almost everything is understood in juxtaposition to its opposite," observes Bastien whose monograph contains many illustrations of the importance of contrasting pairs (1975:58): communities have upper and lower "moieties"; shrines on Mount Kaata are divided into those associated with death and those associated with life; lineages are made whole by division into male and female kin groups; shrines are served in pairs—male/female, young/old, mountain/lake, helper/owner, and so forth. The dualism inherent to this scheme bears no resemblance to Cartesian dualism. Based on an underlying monism of dialectics, it is ontologically and epistemologically opposite. The cosmos is seen as a series of macrocosmic-microcosmic relationships. For instance, Bastien states that the *ayllu* or kinship-territorial social cell of Kaata "is formed by a continual process of matching terms and constituting separate parts into wholes; it is the mountain, the communities on three levels, and their bodies insofar as they reflect one another and come together to form the mountain/body metaphor" (1978:192). In this case the human body is the cosmos writ small, and vice versa. Neither idealist nor materialist as we commonly, and vaguely, understand these terms, the Andean formulation of the relationship between person and nature is one in which pattern and balance not only exist but have to be continuously preserved. The natural properties and existence of any one thing are the result of its place in a pattern. Rather than a philosophy of mechanistic atomism, which focuses on antecedent causes and subsequent effects to link chains of physical force between discrete things, position in structure, place in relation to the whole, serves as the focus for understanding. For example, as the Buechlers note, the spheres of the natural and the supernatural are seen in a relation of mutuality, rather than of causality, and balance is thus attained in the forces of nature (1971:90, 93). It is to this concept of circular motion with neither mechanical impulsion nor leadership by man or thing that the Andean cosmos corresponds. For example, in the fertility rite of the New Earth in Kaata, llama fat and blood are circulated from the center of the mountain body to its extremities. Community life and the energy present in all the parts have to be circulated and shared out. Political authority lies in the system of parts and whole and not in a leader, man, god, or thing. Needham describes this in Chinese Taoism, in which the natural and the political orders are isomorphic. The regularity of natural processes corresponds not to government by law but to the mutual adaptations of community life. The idea is that throughout human society, as well as in nature, he writes, "there is a constant give and take, a kind of mutual courtesy" (1956:283).

Such a scheme could be fitted into a hierarchical order like the Incan state only with difficulty. Incan rule was a tribute-paying social formation that was superimposed on communities. It was characterized by the contradiction between the continued existence of the autonomous community and the negation of the community by the state (cf., Baudin, 1961:xix; Murra, 1956:163; Katz, 1972:292). The concept of a supreme god was, in all likelihood, an artifice imposed by the Incan nobility. LaBarre cites the early-seventeenth-century part-Indian chronicler Garcilaso de la Vega for the Aymara: "The king Inca put a stop to all these things, but chiefly to the worship of many gods, persuading the people that the sun, for its beauty and excellence, and because it sustained all things, alone merited adoration" (1948:169). The Spanish conquest destroyed the hierarchy of the Incan state, but left the structure of Andean religion relatively intact, "whose foundation, of course, rested in the Quechua community" (Kubler, 1963:345).

Even though the Incan state created a hierarchy, the microcosm-macrocosm concept prevailed. According to Garcilaso de la Vega, the Incan king divided the empire into four parts; the name that he gave to the empire, Tawantinsuyo, means four distinct parts united into one. The center was Cuzco, which means the navel of the world. This name, Garcilaso de la Vega noted, was well chosen because Peru is long and narrow like a human body and Cuzco is situated in the middle of its belly. The residents of upper Cuzco were the elder brothers to the residents of lower Cuzco. Indeed, he went on to say, "it was as in the case of a living body, in which there always exists a difference between the right and the left hands. All the cities and villages in our empire were subsequently divided in this way" (Bastien, 1978:45). Likewise, Zuidema has dissected the intricate microcosm-macrocosm structure that is common to the empire's administrative and cosmological structure and to its community organization (1964, 1968).

Sexual union—male and female forming a whole—is a recurrent theme pertaining to the character of the relationship between part and whole. In his study of contemporary Aymara cosmology, Albo finds that the basis to its form is the dialectical union of contraries established with the marriage of man and woman. This dualism, he asserts, leaves its imprint on all Aymara symbolism (1974–76:92–94). We might add that marriage everywhere is held to be an especially favorable occasion for opening a cycle of reciprocal exchange (Lévi-Strauss, 1964:46). In other words, sexual union as expressed in marriage and in the structure underlying symbols is also expressive of the principle of reciprocity. This is also illustrated as a scheme of the macrocosmic order presented by Zuidema, taken from the early-seventeenth-century chronicle of Joan de Santacruz Pachacuti Yamqui, who discovered it in a Cuzco temple. In this scheme the universe is constituted by two symmetrical mirror images, male on the right, female on the left. These halves are combined into a circular form. The androgynous creator spirit connects the top. The productive activity of humans connects the bottom. Elements of the universe, such as sun and moon, the morning star and the evening star, land and sea, fit into either male or female lines and constitute dual oppositions, all connected within the scheme of circular motion. Zuidema has attempted to illustrate how this basic form underlies many different compositions and situations and has located an identical model noted by the chronicler Perez Bocanegra pertaining to Andean kinship structure (Zuidema, 1968:27).

Quite independent of scholars like Zuidema or Albo, Trimborn systematically rests his analysis of preconquest Andean religion on. the principle of paired oppositions of male and female. In his opinion worship of the sun and the moon was common to all Andeans. The two deities were thought of as a primeval pair created by a supreme being. This being embodied all dualities in the one unity, representing the pairing of sun and moon, male and female, morning and evening stars, and so on. These pairs formed a whole in which the creator and "the central theme everywhere was the sexual union between the sun god and the moon goddess" (1968:124). This dialectical unity underlies fertility. In certain archaeological sites the sun and the moon appear in human form emitting rays that end in serpent heads. Their union is consummated in a holy place, usually depicted as high on the mountain slopes and surrounded with specific plants and animals, symbols of fertility (Ibid.:124–26).

Inevitably, the conclusion must be made that the structuralism of Andean culture is not a static geometrical blueprint stamped out as a cognitive map on the blank space of the external world. Instead, it is a living and animated structuralism, which coordinates elements by embodying them as relationships in an organic universe. No element has existence, power, or meaning outside of its place in organic cycles of unity, reciprocity, growth, and death. Reciprocity and dialectics are the key principles of unity, both between elements and between individuals and the rest of the universe. Above all, it is reciprocal exchange and the experience of such exchange that Andeans strive for in coming to terms with life.

The Iconography of Nature

According to Bandelier, every conspicuous object in nature is believed by the Aymara to harbor its own spiritual nucleus that plays an active role in the life of its surroundings (1910:94). Such objects are often termed *achachilas* by the Aymara, synonymous with the *wamanis, apus, aukis,* and *huacas* found throughout Andean culture. All these terms can mean "grandfather" or forebears. The early chroniclers repeatedly mentioned that the Indians regarded the mountain peaks among their principal deities. It is salutary to point out that there is no hint of evil in the names given to such peaks prior to conquest, though the Spaniards referred to them as devils or demons (cf., Arriaga, 1968; Arguedas, 1966).

According to William Stein, the basic element in contemporary Hualcan religion "is its view of the world as permeated by supernatural powers. These forces radiate through the universe, but they can at the same time be more or less confined to objects which are 'charged' with them. Most of the time these powers are in equilibrium, but when someone breaks a rule a disequilibrium is created" (1961:295). Through these objects charged with power, particularly through places in nature, these supernatural forces are related closely to social activity and organization. So important is this pattern of interconnections that LaBarre writes, in reference to the Aymara, "Basically their religion was and is a worship and supplication of strongly localized, sometimes ancestral and totemic place-deities." Not the least important consequence or association of this is the Indians' strong attachment to their ancestral lands, as attested by the marked geographical localization of their *ayllus* or kin groups. "It is as if," the author continues, "the Aymara in their religion had projected into the outside world the marked localizing tendency present in their own internal social organization" (1948: 165). The pattern of nature is the pattern of society.

Both prior to conquest and today, the dead and the ancestors of lineages populate natural icons, such as mountain peaks. This cult of the dead caused much chagrin to missionaries in the seventeenth century, who were unable to convince the Indians that Christian burial in Christian graveyards was a suitable alternative (cf., Acosta, 1880:314–15). "In many places," wrote Jesuit Father Pablo José Arriaga in 1621, "they have removed the bodies of their dead from the church and taken them out to the fields to their *machays*, or burial places of their ancestors. The reason they give for this is expressed by the word *cuyaspa*, or the love they bear them" (1968:18). These *machays* were caves or niches that the Indians carved out of rock for their mummies or funeral offerings. They contained altars and imitation doors and windows for communication with ancestor spirits. The missionaries destroyed the mummies, but the shrines remain. Contemporary Quechua describe the mummies as still in existence—as tiny people dancing and playing flutes, eating inside the earth near the mummy sites. Moreover, there are cities for these people (Bastien, 1973:118). Lowland quechua and other *montaña* Indian societies describe the spirits of the hallucinogen *Banistereopsis caapi* the same way. They see them when they take the drug in rites held by their shamans and model their customs on these tiny spirit people.

Arriaga bitterly noted that the Indians worshiped high hills, mountains, and huge stones. Saying that these natural icons were once people, they had names for them and many fables concerning their metamorphoses. Since they could not be removed from sight, the Church could only try to root them from the Indians' hearts.

A myth of origin recorded by Cristobal de Molina de Cuzco (1943:9) (which Rowe states is an elaboration of earlier myths of the Colla—Aymara—whom the Incas conquered) relates that the creator made the first humans from clay. He painted them with different clothing for the different sexes, ages, and status grades, gave to each group its language, soul, and being, and placed them underground. Eventually, each one emerged in its proper and distinct place, some from caves, some from mountains, others from springs, lakes, trees, and so forth. From there they multiplied, and their descendants adored these sites as the beginnings of their lineages and of life. The first people to emerge were converted into stones, mountains, condors, falcons, and other animals and birds. All these things were called *huacas*. Garcilaso de la Vega noted, "This Cavina nation vainly believed and boasted that its forbears came out of a lake, to which they said that the souls of those who had died returned and came forth again to enter into the bodies of those who were born" (1966:52).

Arriaga observed that the rites to the dead were patterned by lineage principles. "They are grouped around the plaza by clans and factions and bring out the mummified bodies of their ancestors . . . together with the bodies taken from the church, and it looks like the living and the dead come to make judgement" (1968:19). In the Jesuit Francisco de Avila's account of the myths from Huarochirí it is clear that the *huacas* were patterned with one another in a systematic manner and that this pattern copied human social organization. This corpus of myths is important because Huarochirí had been conquered by the Incan state only a few generations before the arrival of the Spanish. In the myth of the settlement of the area pertaining to the pre-Inca epoch, each *ayllu* or kin group received in addition to lands a *huaca* as a new mythic ancestor or guardian (Spalding, 1967:72–73). Analogous to the fissioning of *ayllus*, there was a fissioning of *huacas* from a parent stem. Like the *ayllus*, these *huacas* were ranked into a widening and more inclusive system from the individual person up to the regional, ministate, and state level itself. Use of land and water was regulated in accordance with this ranking, and such usage was preceded by rites to the relevant *huaca* (cf., Arguedas, 1966:113). There was no supreme single deity in Huarochirí prior to the Incan conquest. There was a pair of *huacas*: Pariacaca, a snowcapped mountain, and his sister or sister-in-law Chaupiñamca, a large rock with five "wings." *Huacas* like these were seen not merely as creators of particular persons, households, or *ayllus* but as the creators and guardians of all persons and the world at large, including smaller mountains, trees, rivers, animals, and fields (cf., Gilmer, 1952:65). Specific rites to Pariacaca took place throughout the region every five years or so. Inhabitants from the entire area flocked to his mountain home. Some people claimed that both Pariacaca and Chaupiñamca were the offspring in ancient times of an earlier *huaca* and that Chaupiñamca was the creator of both sexes. Her fiesta, they said, was the fiesta of their mother (Gilmer, 1952:72). Special priests and priestesses attended these *huacas* and could marry them. Each *ayllu* had its corresponding *huaca*, and some community land was always reserved for the raising of the corn beer needed for their libation. Seventy years after the Spanish conquest, when the Incan state land tenure system was in ruins, these lands were still being secretly worked for the local *huacas*. Such lands were always the first to be planted, and nobody could sow his own plot until that was done (Murra, 1956:157–58).

As it did prior to the Spanish conquest, the worship of nature in the concrete configuration of the *huacas* gives testimony to the origins of life and civilization. It is also testimony to the constant recreation of life and society, in which the cycles of human birth and death circulate within the larger cycles of communal rites to the landscape and, beyond that, to the origin of mankind. The living emerge from nature, which perforce becomes a sacred geography of mountains, lakes, and slopes, and the lineage heads pass back into the *huacas*, thereby completing the circle in which individual autobiographies meet the biography of the community in the iconography of nature.

The structural isomorphism and the existential unity between person, social pattern, and the supernatural are perhaps nowhere more obvious than they are in the mountains. The mountains were and still are considered to be the caretakers of the regions that fall away from their peaks and of the people and natural resources of those regions. A definite kinship exists between the landscape of symbols and the humans who fit these symbols into their kinship system: a person is said to be "owned" by the nature-object that thereafter is his or her shrine (Bastien, 1978:91). In Kaata today it is believed that a person originates from the peak of the mountain and after death will return to it—not to heaven. The ancestors mediate the realms of nature and society, of the living and the dead. Despite the depredations of the missionaries, their grave sites remain today the shrines for rites that pay homage to those profound principles and ritual specialists are said to gain their power from these sites. The iconography of the mountain assumes the form of a human body in Kaata, as it did in ancient Huarochirí, whereas, according to Albo, the mountain in cougar form unifies the *ayllu* in villages near Tiahuanaco (1972).

Hence, the enchantment of nature and the alliance of its spirits with mankind form an organic resonance of orchestrated social representations. The organization of kith and kin, political organization, use of the ecosphere, healing, the rhythm of production and reproduction—all echo each other within the one living structure that is the language of the magical landscape. Organic forms, like the human body and the cougar, that are written into the landscape guide and energize this pattern of mental exchange which is nature's complicity with mankind. Through its system of empathetic exchanges, the magic of ritual illuminates this pattern of exchange and gives it its aura and authority. In this way, for peasants in control of their work and life and in some sort of harmony with the iconography of nature, to own the mountain is to be owned by it.

But for the miners, who neither control their work nor own the mountain, ritual illuminates a different pattern of exchange and carries a different aura. Here, the iconography of nature is wrought from the palette that is used by peasant ritual craftsmen, but the iconography has undergone a significant historical transformation in the emergence of the devil owner of the mines. The miners' art makes the petrified world speak and live, but the shadow of death and sterility constantly threatens to consume this flicker of life.

CHAPTER 10

The Problem of Evil

I n contrast to the religion and folklore of Spanish imperialism there was no almighty spirit of evil in the Andean figuration of the spirit world. Evil was neither reified nor fetishized, neither a thing opposed to good nor a thing spiritualized like the devil. Instead, moral philosophy partook of an organic relational quality that reflected the epistemology of transitive social relationships, mutuality, and reciprocity. Yet, insofar as Spanish Catholicism and Andean nature worship blended, the spirit of evil could emerge in Andean symbolic life as the sum of the contradictions that consumed the Spaniards' and the Indians' understandings of one another. This fetishization of evil in the form of the devil is born from the structure of caste and class oppression that was created by European conquest.

Along with their lust for gold and silver the Spaniards brought to the New World their fear of the devil—the Prince of Darkness, the active principle of all evil, cruelty, filthiness, and folly, whose triumph was unleashed in the witch craze of seventeenth-century Europe. For the Spaniards the world could be said to be divided into two opposed parts, the virtues and the vices. Christians cultivated virtue, and the infidels fomented evil—the servants of God and the agents of the devil, locked in a death struggle. Although the power of the Gospel had vanquished and disarmed the devil "in the most important and puissant places of his kingdom," yet "he hath retired himself into the most remote parts, and hath ruled in that other part of the world which, although it be much inferior in nobility, yet is not of less compass" (Acosta, 1880: 299). This cosmic scheme is anything but static. The dualism is frenetically animated and urgent. Under this aegis the spirit of evil in the Andes came to life.

The Spaniards equated the gods of the Indian religion with the devil of their own. They saw the Indians as the spawn of the devil and their rites as devil worship. Even the strange similarities between Christian sacraments of baptism and confession and Indian rites were explained as satanic inversions of divine truth, testimony to the devil's low cunning and overweening treason in imitating God. The credulous Spaniards were fearful, not scornful, of Indian deities. No doubt the Indians stood in awe of the Spaniards and perhaps regarded them as quasi-divine. But the Spaniards, too, were entranced by the power of the Indians' demons. In their remorseless extirpation of idolatry, as much as in their resort to Indian magic for healing and divination, the Spanish bestowed a strange power on their subjects. In conquering the Indians they granted them the power of their supernatural foe, the devil. For instance, the Jesuit Father Arriaga exhorted that the Indians be taught that the devil is a fallen angel taking vengeance on God through the idols of Indian worship (1968:109). The Manichaean fervor of the Spaniards' Christianity planted the seed for millenarian revolts on the part of the Indians.

In their efforts to stamp out idolatry, the Spanish credited Indian gods with power and invincibility. A further difficulty preventing the extirpation of indigenous religion was that it permeated everyday life, birth, death, agriculture, healing, and so on. Moreover, their icons were largely ineradicable since they were the mountains, rocks, lakes, and streams that composed the sacred geography of nature. Futhermore, the soul of their religion lay in the workings of the indigenous community, and after 1570 the Spaniards tried to reinvoke this communal form while the great campaign against idolatry got under way. Then, one century later, this intransigence toward Indian nature worship was relaxed. As long as the Indians held God paramount, their nature fetishism was considered a tolerable superstition.

Even though the followers of the old religion were cruelly persecuted, the authority of native ritualists did not necessarily diminish. Called *brujos*, witches, or sorcerers by the Spanish, such ritualists perforce led a secretive existence. Preconquest religion did not die out; it went underground in the form of "magic" and dissimulated itself in a variety of ways. Based on his personal experience during the last quarter of the sixteenth century in Peru, Father Joseph de Acosta observed, "Although the Indians forbear to sacrifice many beasts, or other things publicly which cannot be hidden from the Spaniards, yet do they still use many ceremonies that have their beginnings from these feasts and ancient superstitions" (1880: 377). He went on to say that it was the devil who organized them so as to counterfeit those things that are of God and obscure the difference between light and darkness. Some communities shielded their ritual specialists from paying tribute and labor services (Spalding, 1967), and Father Arriaga complained that the leaders of the Indian communities warned their followers against Christianity (1968:79). In some instances, such as in Huarochirí in the eighteenth century, the Indian mayor responsible for effecting Spanish rule was himself secretly serving as a ritualist.

The Jesuit Father Avila captured the powerful paradoxes concisely. According to him, the chief problem was that the devil had taught the Indians that they could worship in both the Christian religion and their own and that on no account should they forget their *huacas*, for fear of punishment or death (Gilmer, 1952:121). Thus, insofar as the Indians assimilated Christianity they also assimilated a spirit of evil, the devil, who ratified the nature spirits whom they persistently worshiped as their "owners" and as their source of identity. It followed, as Avila was quick to point out, that to desert these gods would have fearful consequences. Indeed, epidemics of disease were often blamed on Christianity. From this seething complex of contradictions the devil's ambiguities arose, ambiguities that could so easily be channeled into a promise of Indian victory over their oppressors.

Father Arriaga cites a letter to this effect from a contemporary recording his tour of extirpation in the provinces in the early seventeenth century. Following Christian instruction some Indians confessed that although they had desisted from worshiping the *huacas* as before, they had persisted in worshiping them in their hearts, fields, and houses, with both "inward and outward" signs. By the urging of the devil "they had been persuaded that after this time another would come when they could safely return to their ancient ways" (1968:81). This dialectic of submission and resurgence restlessly surged within the unstable syncretism of Christianity and indigenous religion. A new culture of resistance had already surfaced only three decades after conquest in the massive Taqui Onqoy (Dance Sickness) millenarian cult. This was nothing less than a cult of reconquest, which predicted the overthrow of God and Spaniard, and it spread quickly through the old heartland of the Incan empire. In the middle of its ten-year course, from 1560 to 1570, a pan-Andean armed uprising from Quito to Chile was planned by the rebel Incan king. This stormy period of Andean history was bloodily ended with the punishment of some eight thousand Indians and the execution of their king, Tupac Amaru, in 1572.

The Dance Sickness cult invoked the passion that accompanied the return to life of the *huacas*, united to defeat the Christian's God.

Their return coincided with the end of the world and the birth of a new order as predicted in long-established legends of the cosmos. The *huacas* were resuscitated by traveling ritualists, and rites of initiation for cultists were established. Traditional understandings of the universe were mobilized to make sense of the meaning of conquest and the inevitability of its demise. It was said that the Christian God had created the Spanish and all the animals and things necessary for their sustenance. But the *huacas*, who had created the Indians and their means of livelihood, now also supported the Spaniards, which was testimony to the huacas' greater worth (Millones Santa Gadea, 1964:136). In this way, said the eyewitness Molina, the Indians quit God of his power, and the world was to be turned upside down (1943:80; cf., Duviols, 1971:112–22).

A further illustration of the force with which traditional religion could interpret and defy Christianity was the widely held belief that the *huacas* were wandering in the air, thirsty and dying of neglect, because the Indians were foregoing their ritual exchanges with them. As Mauss points out in his work on gift exchange and reciprocity, to deny reciprocity with the gods, the true owners of the world's wealth, is to invite death and ruin (1967). It was said that the *huacas* were angry with the Indians who had adopted Spanish ways and would have to kill them unless they gave these up, but that those who believed in the *huacas* would live in prosperity, grace, and health. The *huacas* prohibited the eating of Spanish food, the wearing of Spanish clothes, and the entering of the Christian Church, praying, and waiting on the priests. Sickness and misfortune were attributed to the wrath of the *huacas*; Molina believed that the healing rites of offerings to the *huacas* were a result of this millenarian movement: "To all the *huacas* and *vilcas* of the four parts of this land, and to my grandparents and ancestors, receive this sacrifice wherever you are and grant me health." These offerings would be placed in sea shells on the grave sites of the ancestors "because the sorcerers told them that the ancestors were dying of hunger and that was why they created sickness." To complete the healing the victim had to walk to the junction of two rivers and there wash with the flour of white corn, leaving the sickness there, removing it from the house (1943:82–83). Almost identical rituals for curing ancestor sickness and alleviating misfortune are described by Bastien for contemporary Andeans (1978).

The belief of this revivalist cult that the *huacas*, emerging from stones, mountains, rocks, and clouds, were incarnated in the bodies of Indians, causing them to shake and dance, attested to the fearful tension implied in the threatened loss of the old gods. Moreover, Indians sometimes sacrificed themselves to the *huacas*. The explosive forces of destructuration that accompanied conquest created an opposite reaction: the ancient structure of person and gods imploded, becoming embodied in humans.

As Wachtel (1977) and George Kubler (1963) point out, this millenarian movement also illustrated how acculturation provided weapons for contesting Christianity. For example, the two female Indian assistants to the chief prophet were named Santa Maria and Maria Magdalena. The power of the Christian gods could also be utilized, although submerged in Indian religion. This was also obvious in the forms that magic took following conquest. Father Acosta called its practictioners ministers of the devil and observed how very frequently the Indians made use of their services for divination and success (1880:367). Typically, he stressed supposed similarities with the witch cults of Europe, emphasizing the role played by old women, the use of unctions smeared on the body, the taking of hallucinatory purgatives, and the induction of trance. Kubler asserts that so-called sorcery proliferated wildly after conquest, due partly to the spread of poverty. The rites assimilated Christian elements into indigenous forms. It was said that God's goodness was, in fact, finite and that the Christian remission of sin was not accorded great sinners; natural events, however, were governed by the *huacas*. Indeed, the Christian saints were *huacas*, too, and Jesus and the devil were brothers (Kubler, 1963:398).

In this way Christianity was blended with indigenous belief and subordinated to it. However, the blending was more a juxtaposition than a seamless fusion. For example, Arriaga describes Indian sorcery that was aimed at burning the soul of a crown inspector. Since this sorcery was directed at a Spaniard, a figurine of pork was used rather than the llama fat that was used in ritual affecting Indians. Furthermore, the fat in the figurine was mixed with flour of wheat, the cereal introduced and eaten by the Spanish; for an Indian it would be mixed with the flour of corn, the indigenous staple (1968: 44).

Huacas and mummies were often secretly buried beneath the Christian crosses implanted by the Church. When the Catholic priests discovered them they were broken up, but the Indians patched them together again. This series of movements and collation of images in which the Christian cross is placed over secretly buried indigenous icons vividly illuminates the structure of syncretism. And in the grim determination of the Catholic priests to dismember and destroy native icons, "so that the devil might not join them together again," we find the key metaphor (Ibid.:84). The image of the devil joining the dismembered parts together is a graphic illustration of the structured tension caused by colonization, on the one hand, and the indigenous formulation of how their survival and revitalization was bound to maintaining the integrity of structural forms, on the other. This theme abounds in Andean legend and myth, nowhere more than in the myths concerning the origin and messianic return of the Incan king who was decapitated and quartered by the Spanish. In the contemporary myths recorded by Arguedas, for instance, this dialectical tension of dismemberment and eventual restoration to wholeness of the king's body is the motif standing for the eventual triumph of the dismembered Indian world over Spanish dominion (1975). Likewise, the various parts of the *huacas* and mummies may lie broken and scattered by the Spanish, but the potential for reunification lives on within this structure of hysteresis: though torn from the whole, the parts persist as relationships in tension-filled space. In Arriaga's formulation the devil oversees this tensed pattern the inner force of which predetermines resolution. Spanish and Indian understandings had to cope with one another on points such as these, forming a complex language of cross-cultural communication and dissension that constituted the new culture of imperialism.

In this regard it is salutary to remember that Christianity had history and myths to work out concerning its own pagan roots. The early Christians in Europe were branded as disbelievers and heretics; yet, far from denying their gods, their opponents classed them as evil spirits, thus increasing the possibility of magic (Thorndike, 1936: 661). But from the fifteenth through the seventeenth centuries, with its power consolidated, European Christianity mounted a rigorous attack against paganism to try to eliminate its hold on popular feeling, while the spread of the market and the development of modern class society altered social morality (Hill, 1969: 116). Jules Michelet went so far as to argue that the European devil of the early modern period was a figure emerging from popular paganism who was seen as an ally of the poor in their struggle against landlord and Church.

There is one further significant connection between Indian nature worship and Christian views of the devil. In the Gnostic view of the medieval Church the world of matter and objective reality was created by the devil, and in this sense much of nature was regarded as the incarnation of the evil spirit (Rudwin, 1959: 122). Because demons were thoroughly acquainted with the secrets of nature, magicians and sorcerers could perform marvels by enlisting their aid.

The Christian Fathers in the Andes had the supremely difficult task of supplanting pagan views of nature with Church-derived doctrines. They had to effect a revolution in the moral basis of cognition itself. Many of the *huacas* populating and coordinating nature could not be removed. The Church, as the Fathers said, had therefore to root them from the Indians' hearts. If the signs could not be eradicated, then their signification had to be. A new semiotic had to be written, as large and as all-encompassing as the universe itself. The Indians had to be "properly taught the sources of springs and rivers, how the lightning is forged in the sky, how the waters freeze, and other natural phenomena, which their teacher will have to know well" (Arriaga, 1968:24). Two issues stood out: the implications of the regularity of nature and ontogeny.

The Christian Fathers sought to demonstrate to the Indians that natural phenomena could not be gods, because of their regularity. The sun, for instance, could not stop its motion when and as it wished. It was therefore natural and subservient to the supernatural. Arriaga makes much of this, as does Acosta, who commended the teaching of a "discreet captain" who had persuaded the Indians that the sun was no god. The captain asked an Indian chief to order an Indian runner to carry a letter. Then he asked, "Tell me who is Lord and chief, either this Indian that carries the letter, or thou that sends him?" The chief answered that he was, because the runner did what he ordered. So it is with the sun, taught the captain: the sun is but a servant to the most high lord, who commands it to run swiftly giving light to all nations, and it is therefore against reason to yield to the sun that honor which is due the creator and lord of all (Acosta, 1880:310). This illustrates how a conception of a self-organized system of mutually supportive things was transformed into a conception of a different sort of organic unity that was dominated and orchestrated by a single leader, God—the celestial engineer, the unmoved mover. Christianity sought to supplant the system of mutually conditioning parts with one that wrote the master-servant relationship into nature.

The Church also had to dispute the Indians' concept of social and human origins. Arriaga wrote that the Indians' belief in the origin of different "clans" from separate ancestors and from different origin sites (*pacarinas*), such as mountains, caves, springs, and so on, had to be replaced by the notion of one common ancestor. Moreover, this new conception had to include the notion of original sin. All of this was tantamount to denying the essential links in Andean cosmology, which bound persons to their origins through the icons of nature. It was also a vain attempt to substitute a hierarchical scheme for the framework of dual oppositions bound to one another as reciprocating parts in a segmented totality. Such a substitution called for a radically new logic, a different notion of relationships, and a different notion of the relation between part and whole. Moreover, the Christian scheme inevitably foundered on the problem of theodicy, which, bound to the idea of original sin, evoked the idea of the devil. None of these tortured contradictions easily entered in the structure of preconquest Andean religion, which, with the conquest, found itself cast in the devil's domain.

Morality and Duality

The patterned dualism that composed Andean cosmology was tied to a series of reciprocal relationships that effected a unity of the ethical and the cosmic order. The antagonistic dualism of the Christianity that was forced on the Andeans saw the cosmos as constantly threatened with rupture, and the primary markers of this dualism, God and the devil, embodied pure good and pure evil. Andean ethics, however, was not registered in the forms and symbols of pure moral essences in contest with each other. These ethics reposed on the principle of balance, not between good and bad deities, but between an enormous variety of spirits embodied in natural icons. Furthermore, the Andean concept of sin was quite different from the individualistic Christian notion. Many infractions and crimes were seen as disturbances in the universe at large. Today, in the community of Hualcan in the Peruvian highlands, for example, certain misdemeanors are felt to imperil the whole community, the future of the crops, and other natural phenomena (Stein, 1961). Concerning the Aymara communities in which they lived, the Buechlers write, "Any transgression of the natural flow of events [like hail] was considered an affliction or grief-bringing act involving suffering for the person in question and for the community as well" (1971:92–93).

The Andean pantheon of deities was not structured into a dual hierarchy of good gods and bad gods. Even the principle of a supreme god, such as the sun, was an artifice imposed by the Incan state. Deities existed as paired opposites, like male and female companions, sun and moon, sky and earth, and so on. Although the Supay, or a similar evil spirit such as the Hahuari, did exist in Andean religion prior to the conquest, it was but one of several earth demons, and the concept of a pervasive and all-powerful spirit of evil did not exist. Christian distinctions between good and evil were difficult to make. Trimborn states that in preconquest religion the distinction between good and evil spirits was based on what he calls utilitarian and not ethical criteria. John Rowe asserts that the supernatural beings were almost entirely protectors and friends of man, worshiped in the hope of gaining practical benefits (1963:298). He stresses that evil spirits were of far less importance and seem not to have been worshiped or respected except by sorcerers, of whom, so he says, there were few. Prayers contained no terms suggesting fear (Rowe, 1960:416).

Although the Indians had a practice similar to Christian confession, it struck the Spaniards as a hideous parody of their own (Métraux, 1969:138), and according to the chronicler Cobo (1890–95, 4:89–90), the Indians "were much in error in their judgement of sin . . . because they never took account of internal desires and sensibilities." Their conception of "sin" was normative rather than moral; it applied to murder outside of war, carelessness in the veneration of the gods, disloyalty to the Incan king, incest, and adultery. Perhaps by referring to that other great Indian empire, we can grasp the nature of the difference that confused observers like Cobo. William Madsen writes that the Aztec "did not believe that he sinned in eating, drinking, laughing, playing, mocking, or in failure to better his life. He did not believe that the world, the flesh and the devil were enemies of the soul nor did he believe that memory and understanding and will were powers of the soul" (1960:131). Needless to say, Indian beliefs also differed from the Spanish concerning the relation of the soul's final resting place to one's behavior in this world. The Indians failed to distinguish between good and evil, admonished Cobo, and held that it was the caste difference (that is, ascriptive social relations) between nobles and commoners that determined the soul's destiny (Cobo, 1890–95, 3:319–20). Arriaga asserted, "They say that at death they go to the beyond to work their farms and sow their seeds. They do not believe there will be punishment there for the wicked, nor glory for the good" (1968:64). Trimborn suggests that any interpretations to the effect that the fate of the soul was determined by ethical criteria is a product of Christian misinterpretation (1968:93), and in Bastien's report on contemporary religion it is made adamantly clear that, even today, heaven is not seen as a desirable goal. The people of Kaata want to remain on the mountain when they die (1978:171–87).

The idea of a pervasive spirit of evil was an import of imperialism, and practically all the commentaries concerning Andean religion prior to the conquest and during the colonial period fail to appreciate the importance of this fact. The nineteenth-century anthropologist Daniel Brinton expressed this forcefully. He claimed that the idea of the devil is foreign to all primitive religions and challenged interpreters who classified the deities of native Americans as either good or bad, thereby distorting native creeds into a static dualistic form. "What has been reported to be the evil divinity," he wrote in 1876, "is in reality the highest power they recognize." He gave many examples such as the Aka-kanet of the Araucanian Indians of Chile, whom the Christian commentators regarded as the father of evil but who was actually the "benign power appealed to by their priests, who is throned in the Pleiadaes, who sends fruit and flowers to the earth and is addressed as Grandfather." As for the Andean Supay, this "never was as Prescott would have us believe, 'the shadowy embodiement of evil,' but simply and solely their god of the dead." Brinton's view is that with European conquest the Indians "caught the notion of a bad and good spirit, pitted one against the other in external warfare, and engrafted it onto their ancient traditions. Writers anxious to discover Jewish or Christian analogies, forcibly construed myths to suit their pet theories, and to indolent observers it was convenient to catalogue their gods into antithetical classes" (1968: 79).

Instead of cataloging their gods into antithetical moral classes, native Americans generally seem to have regarded them as morally neutral, or as good and bad at the same time. In reference to Mayan deities, Donald Thompson asserts that they were inherently neither malevolent nor benevolent, and he sharply distinguishes this from Christianity (1960:7). The only reference to a god of evil in J. Eric Thompson's *Maya History and Religion* is to Mam, who holds power during the five unlucky days of the end of the year, only to be joyfully spurned with the arrival of the new year (1970:297–300). However, the Spaniards appropriated the name of the Mayan god of the dead, Cizin, to denote the devil, and they did this also with the corresponding gods of other indigenous groups (Correa, 1960). The situation must have been most puzzling to Europeans because these mesoamerican deities had dual natures: they could be both malevolent and benevolent, young and old, female and male, human and animal—at one and the same time (J. Eric Thompson, 1970:198–200). There also existed a quadraplicity of gods, four in one and one in four, which J. Eric Thompson regards as similar to the Christian doctrine of the Holy Trinity. Based on his fieldwork among Guatemalan villagers (Kanhobel linguistic group) in 1932, Oliver LaFarge also refers to the Trinity, which "here is reduced to a duality, the concept of the Holy Ghost being almost entirely lost. The duality, however, is far more clearly understood by the ordinary Indian than is the Trinity by most North Americans" (1947: 103). Writing about the Chorti Maya in the 1930s, Charles Wisdom says that they believe in a god of evil that is a whirlwind, whom in the Spanish language they call the devil (*diablo*) or King Lucifer, but he believes that this deity may be entirely a Catholic concept (1940:405). Similarly, in the Andes the Supay is supposedly synonymous with the devil, but LaBarre, Duviols, and Bandelier all say that the Supay is not truly equivalent to the Christian devil and that it is a "specialization along Christian lines of what was originally perhaps only one amongst many earth demons" (LaBarre, 1948:168).

Wisdom states that among the Chorti all supernatural beings have the following characteristics: moral neutrality or duality, sexual duality, multiplicity, bilocality in sky and earth, and dual personality as expressed in native and Catholic counterparts. The notion of duality is so compelling that an Indian will ascribe it with little hesitation to any being. In what Wisdom refers to as 'moral dualism' either the supernatural being has two aspects, good and bad, or else it has only one of these corresponding to another supernatural being that possesses the opposite quality. In "sexual dualism" there are again two forms: an entire group of deities of the one sex is paired with another group of the opposite sex. Another group includes spirits of dual gender, the male element dealing with or affecting women, whereas the female element affects men. In many cases the being is a single entity that assumes either gender or either moral attribute at will, according to the situation (1940:410).

Most of the Chorti deities have their counterparts among the Catholic saints. The Virgin becomes the female consort of native gods associated with planting, soil, fruit trees, family life, childbirth, and other activities in which the ideas of fertilization and growth are paramount. In fact, life and growth are believed to depend on the union between the Virgin and the native deity concerned. However, Catholicization has meant that those native deities that have counterparts among the saints have only their benevolent aspect thus represented; thus, whereas the saint signifies the benevolent side, the native deity signifies the malevolent side of the same supernatural being. With its attendant acculturation, colonization has severed a unified whole into separate good and bad figures, saints and native deities, respectively. This startling development suggests how European influence could produce a spirit of evil in native American religion and confirms Brinton's view. Nevertheless, it is also obvious from Wisdom's ethnography that the native propensity to dualize is preponderant and that although fission into good and bad deities, Christian and indigenous, has occurred, even these figures are far from being clear-cut ethically homogenous essences. Saints may wreak misfortune on one's enemies, or on their devotees if improperly treated, whereas the devil figure is also capable of worthy deeds.

Albo well captures the implications of this moral dualism among the contemporary Aymara when he notes, "They suppose that good and evil coexist in everything and they avoid excessive manifestations of extremes because this would bring on its contrary; 'You shouldn't laugh too much, so that later you won't cry too much'" (1974–76:94). Unlike the devil of the Christians, who tempts mankind into evil ways and widens the cleavage in an all-or-nothing cosmic drama, the spirits (*chicchans*) who assist the devil in Chorti belief frighten people out of their immorality. Their malevolence is seen as serving to maintain, not to split, the moral sphere. Whereas Christian confession served to ally the individual with the good side in the cosmic duel, Andean Indian confession was an indigenous rite aimed at restoring the balance of nature, as Métraux puts it (1969: 138).

In the Christian doctrine opposed forces of pure good and of pure evil structure the moral field, reflecting an ontology and epistemology that sunders totalities into static dualities incapable of flux and synthesis. But a dialectical logic cannot oppose so much as encompass good with evil and matter with mind. Andean culture is a specific manifestation of such a logic, in which reciprocity of meanings established through an intricately patterned system of dual oppositions is the hallmark. These, rather than causation through the medium of physical forces, are the principles that comprehension and understanding turn on. As the Buechlers emphasize in their discussion of Aymara epistemology, connections between different spheres, such as the human world and the world of nature, are connections established in terms of similar relationships and not in terms of similar characteristics. Neither particulate things in themselves nor pure moral essences stake out the organic picture of the world's structure and function that forms Andean epistemology. Instead, there is a kinship of person and group with the iconic powers of nature. This kinship effects a unity of the cosmic and ethical orders that is antipathetic to moral dualism and to the animation of moral essences. This unity is also expressed in communitarian economic structures that are opposed to the alienation of land and labor. It is also a unity which makes a fetish of nature by attributing to it spiritual powers. This fetishism animates nature, not moral essences. Christianity did the latter when it made a fetish of the almighty spirit of evil. This was a profoundly self-alienating act, identical to man's creating God only to deny authorship and to credit

God with creating man. Subsequent to that fetishization of evil in the shape of the devil in early modern Europe, the commodity fetishism of capitalist cosmography arose and man, the creator of commodities, came to see and speak of commodities as ruling him. This type of fetishism is the antithesis of the andean fetishism of nature, for it evolves not from unity but from the alienation of persons from one another, from nature, and from their products.

The devil in the Bolivian tin mines offers spellbinding testimony to the fidelity with which people can capture this transformation of fetishization while subjecting it to a paganism that will capture it. The problem lies not in their worship of evil but in the problem of evil itself.

CHAPTER II

The Iconography of Nature and Conquest

The Spanish conquest brought a spirit of evil to the Indians of the New World, initiating a process of destruction which that spirit could symbolize. Beyond that, the conquest also entered the iconography of nature. The landscape of symbols came to include the Indians' experience of Spanish greed, mastery, and violence.

Harry Tschopik, Jr., relates that the Aymara of the Bolivian province of Chucuito believe that gold and silver are owned by an evil supernatural being who causes sickness and death; he is often seen as an old dwarf dressed as a Spanish soldier surrounded by his treasures. Given the grief that precious metals have caused the Aymara from the time of the conquest, he adds, it is not surprising that gold and silver should be associated with evil and danger (1968:135). But prior to the conquest, precious metals were revered and do not seem to have been associated with either evil or danger. Mining was then essentially under local, not national, control, and gold and silver were exchanged as gifts, especially between local *curacas* (chieftans) and the Incan king.

As the principles of reciprocity and redistribution, which guided and gave meaning to life under the Incas and legitimized their control, gave way to colonial oppression, the icons of nature came to embody this history, its constant tension, and the possibility of its eventual transcendence. Nowhere was this more evident than in the character of the spirit owners of nature, the ineradicable fetishes basic to folk religion, which oversaw local resource usage and were capable of surviving the intensive colonial campaign against idolatry. These fetishes came to embody the conflictful juxtaposition of Spanish and Indian societies, and the ambiguity inherent in these collective representations was vastly magnified by this juxtaposition.

The supernatural lord or owner of the mountain in Mesoamerican communities was a figure of great importance throughout highland Latin America. He was the absolute owner of nature and had the power of life and death over people. Gustavo Correa asserts that although his preconquest character of benevolence still exists in a few regions, his secondary character of malevolence has been extended everywhere (1960:59). In other words, history has heightened the ambiguous character of sacred things by accentuating the evil and dangerous potential in them. The lord of the mountain is thought to own and regulate the resources that lie under him, as he did in preconquest times. But today much of the land formerly controlled by Indians has been expropriated by non-Indians, while some of the resources that the Indians still do manage have acquired a new significance as the Indians enter into the web of the new economic system organized by market principles and commodity exchange. Because the Indians can claim some control, both individual and communal, over the resources that skirt the mountains and because their internal economy is not, strictly speaking, organized into capitalist institutions, their political and economic situation has a peculiarly dual character that is animated by a systematic tension. On the one hand, these communities are becoming increasingly integrated into the juggernaut of capitalist trade and labor relationships which is converting the domain of the mountains into increasingly scarce and alienable commodities, while social relationships between the Indians themselves are being threatened with atomization. On the other hand, an institutionalized defensive reaction against commercial encroachment is occurring, motivating Eric Wolf to type them as "closed corporate communities" (1955). Encysted by a capitalist economy, the communities supervised by the mountain spirit owners are not capitalist in themselves. These communities are functional cogs within a national and even international capitalist system, but they are not replicas of that system. Inevitably, their internal institutions and practices will reflect this peculiar duality, as will the spirit owners of nature. In short, the argument I wish to advance is that the spirit owners of nature have come to reflect a new system of ownership, which was superimposed on an earlier model in which ownership corresponded to nonmarket principles of reciprocity and redistribution. With some regional variations, since the conquest the spirit owners have come to embody the contradiction that finds reciprocity coexisting with commodity exchange and exploitation by whites and mestizos, whom the Indians generally regard with hate, fear, and awe.

Today, in highland Mesoamerica the supernatural lord of the mountain is commonly regarded as an evil and dangerous figure of European extraction: rich, foreign, and urban, a *patrón*, a missionary, and even, sometimes, an anthropologist. Morris Siegel states that outstanding among the supernatural beings in northwest highland Guatemala is the *wits akal*. Dressed in European garb, this spirit is thoroughly evil and bent on the destruction of Indians, whom he lures to his abode to eat. Strangers, foreigners, and missionaries are commonly condemned as *wits akals* and greatly feared (1941:67). Richard N. Adams found that the spirit owner of the mountain in a highland community near the capital of Guatemala is frequently described as a blond person from the city, a rich outsider occupying the position of a local *patrón* (1952:31). Adams, an anthropologist, was himself characterized in this way as the "administrator" of the mountains, just as an estate has its administrator. It is said that pacts (like the devil pacts of late medieval Europe) can be made with the owner of the mountain for hunting success and for money, in exchange for which the person making the pact has to live in the home of the mountain spirit after death. In Zinacantan, Chiapas, the Earth Lord who owns and cares for the earth is envisioned as a fat and greedy mestizo (*ladino*) in constant need of human workers and pack animals for his enterprises. He possesses piles of money, herds of horses, mules, and cattle, and flocks of chickens. He controls the water holes on which the Zinacantecos depend, the clouds that emerge from caves and produce rain for crops, and all the useful products of the earth. One cannot use the land or its products without compensating the Earth Lord with appropriate ceremonies and offerings (Vogt, 1969:302).

The situation is similar in the Andes. Rowe states that mountain worship is a very important element of modern Quechua religion, as it was prior to the conquest (1963:296). Bastien found that the mountain of Kaata was not so much an "element" as the very basis of religion; it was conceived of as a human body writ large over the landscape, which "owned" people and resources alike (1978). Oscar Nuñez del Prado describes the spirits of the mountains as occupying the chief level in the religion of the Indians of Q'ero in the department of Cuzco (1968). These spirits are organized into a hierarchy capped by the spirit of the largest mountain, El Roal, who is also the creator spirit. He controls smaller peaks, such as Wamanripa, to whom El Roal has entrusted the day-to-day care of the people of

Q'ero. Like other natural objects, rocks and trees have spirits that converse with one another as the mountain spirits do with humans, especially through shamans. The annual rite for El Roal is attended by thousands of Indians from almost all the Cuzco region, including the people from Q'ero, who climb passes around sixteen thousand feet high in order to reach his shrine. There is also a Catholic chapel in the village of Q'ero built by a *hacienda* owner a few generations ago, but the Indians are indifferent toward it.

In the department of Ayacucho, Peru, the mountain spirits are the lineage ancestors. They are described as "living beings like ourselves . . . with the same needs and same organization as the mortals, and they live in villages and marvellous palaces within the mountains as absolute owners of nature" (Palomino, 1970:119). Known as *wamanis*, they are by far the most important deities and have the power of life and death over the Indians, their crops, and their animals. The various *wamanis* are thought to be organized in the same hierarchical form as are the community's own political offices; at the same time they are said to be directly engaged in the service of the government of Peru (Earls, 1969:69) in order to solicit favors for the community (Isbell, 1974:118). They are very wealthy; inside their mountains they possess much livestock, gold, and silver. These riches are obtained from the ritual offerings bestowed by the Indians. Sacrificed llamas, for instance, are converted by the *wamanis* into gold and silver, which is annually handed over to the government on the coast. In return for ritual offerings the *wamanis* grant personal security and the fertility of livestock. If annoyed, as can happen because of the incorrect execution of ritual or the lack of reverence, the *wamanis* may kill livestock, ruin families, and cause sickness and even death; they may even eat the hearts of their victims. Sometimes described as tall bearded white men dressed in expensive Western clothes and, at other times, as lawyers, priests, policemen, or wealthy white landowners, they can also appear as condors, as fire that erupts from stones, or simply as lakes or the peaks of mountains. Their power, writes Earls is the power that is generally ascribed to whites or mestizos (*mistis*) (1969:67). But they are also the lineage ancestors, worshiped and revered as such! Small wonder, then, that great ambiguity is expressed toward them: although they are the owners and protectors of life, they are also thought of as devils and associated with filth.

Bernard Mishkin asserts that it is a widespread belief in the Andes that mountain peaks known as *apus* (lords) or *aukis* (shamans) have concealed within them great palaces and *haciendas*, together with

herds of livestock that are guarded by the servants of these mountain spirits. Among these helpers is the Ccoa, a cat with the power
to kill and to destroy crops; he is the most active, feared, and important spirit in the daily life of the people. The Ccoa is the sponsor of
sorcerers. Moreover, people are said to be divided into two classes:
those who serve him and those who fight against him. Whereas the
former are rich and their agriculture successful, the latter are poor,
their harvests are small, and their households are plagued by sickness (1963:463–64). In other places, such as the village of Hualcan,
Peru, malevolent spirits may also appear as animals or as mestizos
and *gringos*, who are the tutelary spirits of sorcerers and are notable
for having a lot of hair and tremendous teeth (Stein, 1961:323). In
this connection it is noteworthy that the Tio or devil figure who is
seen as the true owner in the contemporary Bolivian mines is also
described as *gringo*, tall, red-faced, fair haired, bearded, and wearing
a cowboy hat. Following fatal accidents in the mines, miners say
that the Tio is eating the miners because he has not had the necessary ritual offerings; he prefers the juicy flesh of young miners
(Nash, 1972). Like the mountain spirit described by Mishkin, the
Tio too has an animal familiar, a bull, which assists miners who
make a compact with him.

The identification of the spirit owners with the new legal owners
and managers of Andean resources is striking, to say the least. Icons,
fetishes, and mental images have been cast in the likeness of the
conquerors and of the small class of men who claim dominion down
to the present day; therewith, the icons register the evil and aggression that the Indians associate with the rulers of land and minerals.
Iconography is popular historiography. Conquest and the encroachment of a new economy have led to a dazzling self-portrayal in the
iconographics of nature, but it is an elusive portrait with contradictory dimensions. Its symbols manifest the powerful tensions of Andean history and society. The spirit owners do not merely reflect the
power of the oppressor. They also reflect the yearning of the oppressed.

> Now
> the pottery is faded and sad
> the carmine of the *achiote*
>> no longer laughs in the textiles
> the textiles became poor
>> have lost their style
>> fewer threads per inch
>>> and they do not spin the "perfect thread" any longer

Llacta mama [the soil] belongs to the landowners
the golden butterfly is imprisoned in the Bank
the dictator is rich in money and not in virtues
    and how gloomy
    how gloomy the music of the *yaravies*
The Inca Empire confined forever
    to the unreal kingdoms of the *coca*
    or the *chicha*
(then only are they free and gay
    and speak loudly
and exist again in the Inca Empire)

        Ernesto Cardenal, "The Economy of Tahuantinsuyu"

Messianism

Messianic rebellions invoking the Golden Age of the Incas have been a fixture in Andean history since the conquest. This messianism has commonly centered on the idea that the Incan king who was killed by the Spanish would return to life (Ossio, A., 1973; Wachtel, 1977). In myths collected by Arguedas in the 1950s, the Incan king Inkarrí is seen as having been decapitated by the Spanish. Although he is in constant suffering, he is bound to return to completeness, which will signify the restoration of Indian society and dominion.

Analyzing such myths from the community of Puquio in the department of Ayacucho, in which monolingual Quechua speakers predominate, Arguedas concludes that they give "a necessary explanation of the origin of man and the universe, of history and of the actual situation of the Indian, and of his final destiny up till the initiation of the revolutionary process of change" (1975:44). Here, the mountain spirits or *wamanis* are held to have been created by the first god, Inkarrí. He created all Indian things, which the *wamanis* then give and regulate, such as pasture, water, and the power to divine and cure sickness. *Mistis* or whites cannot acquire these powers to divine or cure, because they do not have the resistance necessary to sustain the punishments and tests demanded by the *wamanis*. Furthermore, these secrets can be acquired only by living for long periods inside the mountain. Yet, on occasions *mistis* may seek out shamans who are thus trained when they suffer from strange or incurable illnesses, and the Indians say that the *mistis* would die without their aid.

In the community of Quinua in the same department, the majority of the Indians are bilingual in Quechua and Spanish, indicating a greater degree of intercultural contact than in Puquio. Here, the myth of Inkarrí and his return is similar to those found in Puquio, but the Catholic imagery is stronger. In comparison with that in Puquio the messianism in this myth is more conditional: it exists only as a possibility.

In the *hacienda* of Vicos in the department of Ancash, where Indians long existed as serfs and had frequent contact with Catholic missionaries, the creator god of humanity has been described as the son of the creator of ancient humanity who impregnated the Virgin. This son destroyed the ancient people with a rain of fire, but they are not completely dead, and their protesting voices may be heard by hunters of pumas and foxes, which were the cattle of the ancient people. He also made the world of today, divided into two classes of people: the Indians and their dominators, the *mistis*. The Indians are thus obliged to work for the *mistis*, but in heaven, which is exactly the same as earth, class position is totally reversed: the Indians become *mistis* and make all those who were *mistis* on earth work for them like Indians.

Finally, in the community of Q'ero (department of Cuzco), which is even more isolated than Puquio and less exposed to non-Indian influences, there is no messianic element in the myth of Inkarrí. Moreover, the myth says nothing about the Spanish and their killing of Inkarrí nor has it any Catholic imagery or reference to the Catholic god. Instead, it proclaims the undiluted divine descent of the people of Q'ero, who are integrated with the icons of nature and oblivious to the history of conquest and the far-off non-Indian authorities. It is of great interest that in this version of the myth of Inkarrí he is said to have been created by the largest mountain spirit of the region, El Roal, who also had the power to dominate the sun, which in other myths from other regions is seen as the father of the Inca (cf., Nuñez del Prado B., 1974 : 240).

Comparing these myths and asking ourselves what social experience they interpret and why certain forms recur or change, it is striking how all of them recapitulate essential themes in pre-Hispanic myths of the origin of the Incan empire. Equally striking are the adaptations and promise of restoration that are displayed by these myths according to the degree of foreign contact and oppression suffered by the different communities. The role of the mountain spirit owners of nature is integrally connected with the promise of Indian restoration, except in the two opposed and extreme cases of Q'ero, the least acculturated, and Vicos, the most affected by outside domination. In Vicos we hear nothing of the mountain spirits, except perhaps in the protesting voices of the ancient people when their "cattle" are being hunted. In Q'ero, relatively secure in its isolation from outsiders, not only is there no sign of a messianic strain but the mountain spirit is seen as actually creating the Incan king, as well as continuing to control all natural resources and people. If the myths from Puquio and Quinua, which stand between these two extremes, are any guide, we see how the ambivalence of the mountain spirit owners of nature comes to the fore and how it stands in relation to the promise of eventual Indian restoration. Their ambivalence derives from two distinct types of mediation. On the one hand, they mediate between the common people and the mighty Incan king-god. On the other hand, they mediate the possibility of Indian messianism.

Evil and Social Control

A great deal more needs to be said about the attribution of evil to important spirit owners of nature. It should first be pointed out that such an attribution can defend Indian society against the detrimental effects of money and stratification by wealth. Both money and wealth can be obtained through illicit compacts with the spirits. However, such pacts are said to mean disaster, like illness and crop failures, for the rest of the community. Mishkin's account of the Ccoa familiar of the mountain spirit is a case in point, and Pedro Carrasco relates a somewhat similar belief among Tarascan Indians in Mexico concerning people who sell their soul to the devil in order to acquire money or to oppose natural law and accelerate growth or return on livestock. In exchange for one's soul a person may obtain a snake that excretes coins or a bull or a sheep that grows faster than normal. "In their defense of poverty," writes Carrasco in a theme that parallels one developed by Wolf (1955) in his analysis of Indian "closed corporate communities" throughout highland Latin America, "can be seen a defense of the Indian way of life. The money economy imposed from the outside is a disruptive influence in the village community, creating conflict within it or the loss of land to outsiders" (1957:48). Evon Vogt details similar functions of sorcery accusations involving the earth lord which serve to diminish social stratification and to oppose money (1969).

White Gods?

Regarding the identification of their spirit owners with whites and mestizos, it is salutary to note how much the Indians hate these outsiders and that their great and consuming hostility reflects an underlying sense of pan-Indian solidarity. With reference to Guatemala, LaFarge writes, "The Indians as a whole, are clearly conscious of themselves forming a vast body under special conditions within the nation. The feeling may not be strong enough to bring about any lasting cooperation between tribes, but it is none the less present. They seem to regard themselves even to this day as a conquered people and the true natives of the soil" (1947 : 15). Writing in 1870, David Forbes stated that the Aymara cherished a deeply rooted, inveterate hatred toward the whites and consoled themselves with the idea that one day they would obtain the country of their ancestors. In the course of his field research among the Aymara in the 1940s, LaBarre came to the same conclusion; he stressed the hostility toward whites, who were very rarely allowed to stay overnight in Indian villages. The quarters of the U.S. engineers in Corocoro, he noted, were a high-walled compound that was defended by a machine gun, and in his opinion, the already mobilized aggression of the Indians was kept down by the whites only with the "usual terroristic methods of an upper caste" (1948 : 158).

Given this, we obtain a deeper sense of the vehemence and also of the rationale with which Indians attribute to certain spirit owners the characteristics of whites when the interests of those spirits fuse with or pertain to property, enterprises, or motifs of white control. Yet it is perplexing, to say the least, that the Indians may also revere these spirits as, for example, lineage ancestors and protectors of life: in Bolivia, where the spirit of the mines inside the mountain is described and feared in no uncertain terms as a white, he is also, in Nash's words, a projection of the miners' hopes for the future and their ally (1972 : 233).

Variations

The attribution of evil or non-Indian characteristics to spirit owners is not found in all Indian communities. Nor does it include all spirit owners, even in those communities in which one or more spirits are so designated. In communities far removed from commercial life or in communities that have successfully held the outsider at bay, such as Q'ero in the department of Cuzco and the Bolivian Qollayuaya *ayllu* of Kaata, the mountain spirit is not described as evil or non-Indian. Bastien repeatedly notes that the sense of completeness given to the community by its connection to the mountain spirit provides a firm basis to *ayllu* solidarity and the morale and rationale for fighting off outside usurpation of the mountain's body—very much including attempts by non-Indians to appropriate Indian lands (1978). In communities where a particular spirit owner is credited with non-Indian features and evil, as is the owner of gold and silver among the Aymara of Chucuito described by Tschopik, there also exist other spirit owners who are regarded as benevolent, such as the owner of llamas, who bears an Indian name and lives in a mountain (1968:135). Other spirit owners of nature are identified with mountains bearing the names of Christian saints and are thus designated in ritual. It is true that if offended they will withdraw their support, but they are not seen as actively evil, and hence propitiatory rites to these spirit owners tend to be cyclical or seasonal in frequency, except in emergencies. The spirit owner of the lake's fish, however, receives constant propitiation; the spines of cooked fish are burnt ritually and the wind is asked to carry the smoke to the lake so that other fish will know that the caught fish has been well treated. The primary objective of this rite is to convince the owner of the fish that his subjects have been treated with respect. If this is not done, no more fish will be caught and the nets will tear.

Spirit owners with non-Indian features may coexist with Indian ones who represent Indian interests. In Zinacantan, Chiapas, Indian identity is most definitely not present in the figure of the Earth Lord, but it is present and most remarkably so in the twelve ancestral gods who inhabit the twelve sacred mountains with the permission of the Earth Lord (represented as a greedy fat *ladino*). Unlike the Earth Lord, these twelve gods are prototypes of all that is proper and correct for Zinacantecos, whose basic rites replicate those models, transferring by analogy properties from the realm of the gods to the sphere of the Indians. By contrast, in an exchange with the Earth Lord for money, the transfer of properties occurs through sale like a commodity transaction with the fat *ladinos* that he symbolizes. Whereas the Earth Lord controls nature and has the power to grant money for souls in an exchange that threatens the remainder of the community, the twelve ancestral mountain gods, which are subordinate to him, regulate Indian social relationships.

In neighboring Indian societies these gods are even more structured, belonging to specific patrilineages, and this may well have been the case in Zinacantan earlier (Vogt, 1969).

Even when the mountain spirit owner has the features of a rich white exploiter, he can also have characteristics that associate him with Indians and preconquest imagery, as in the description recorded by Earls of the Ayacucho *wamani* who often appears in human form riding "on a beautiful white horse, luxuriously appareled with a fine saddle, and San Pedrano saddle cloth, with silver reins, blinkers—all complete. He wears a beautiful poncho, *pallay* poncho of the ancient ones, very fine with spurs; he dresses as these rich ranchers[*hacendados*]" (1969:67).

Reciprocation and Mediation

In this respect the *wamani* evokes the ambiguous figure of the *curaca*, the local chieftan who mediated between the community and the center of authority—with the Incan king prior to conquest and with Spanish officialdom thereafter. Indeed, the seventeenth-century Indian chronicler Poma de Ayala mentions that the local chiefs in the Ayacucho region during the time of the Incan empire were called *wamanis* (Earls, 1969:77). In examining this analogy between *curaca* and mountain spirit owner of nature, it is necessary to analyze the changing role of the *curaca* under Spanish rule as well as the ambiguous properties inherent in reciprocity as a mode of exchange.

It has been claimed that toward the end of the period of the Incan empire the *curacas* were absorbing ever greater powers, not unlike those of feudal lords, and that this process was predetermined by the structure of Incan government, which sowed the seeds, so to speak, of its self-destruction (Wachtel, 1977). Following the conquest this process accelerated. *Curacas* tended to become Spanish stooges in the new system of racist exploitation, and although their overall powers decreased, the despotic nature of their control increased. Instead of mediating reciprocal gift exchanges as the society's means for distributing economic goods, the *curacas* now mediated opposed systems of exchange, each with radically different implications for the definitions of man, the cosmos, and meaning of social intercourse. On the one hand, the *curaca* embodied the hub of the reciprocal interaction of gift exchange, while on the other hand, he now also mediated forced tribute exaction together with commodity exchange for profit. Hence, three layers of ambiguity were superimposed on one another: the ambiguity inherent in reciprocity; the ambiguity in the *curacas'* status toward the end of the Incan empire; and the final ambiguity, which began under Spanish rule and continues to the present day—the mediation of opposed exchange systems of gift exchange with commodity exchange based on profit and violence.

Before the conquest a finely balanced system of exchange determined the efficiency and stability of the economy, without money, private property, market principles, or commodity exchange. This economic equilibrium was composed of reciprocal exchanges among peasant producers at the base of society; they gave tribute, which was viewed as a gift, to their immediate chieftans, who, in turn, were responsible for redistributing the largesse; much of it went back to the producers and some went, of course, to the Incan king. To a large extent, this economic system functioned well because of the punctilious bureaucratic regulation established by the Incan nobility; yet religion and ritual circumscription of exchange was mandatory for its successful operation too.

The singularly important feature to note is that the exchanges that play the determining role in the economy of premarket societies are not so much economic exchanges as reciprocal gift exchanges. Therefore, as Lévi-Strauss writes, the goods exchanged are, in addition to their utilitarian value, "instruments for realities of another order," marking events that are more than economic (1964: 38). They are "total social facts," simultaneously social, moral, religious, magical, economic, sentimental, and legal. This implies that the evaluation of the worth of the goods exchanged is highly subjective, situationally specific, and more a function of the relationship established than value supposedly inherent in the thing exchanged. Reciprocal gift exchange also implies and creates social amity by making individuals partners; thereby, it adds a new quality to the value exchanged. Such a system accents generosity and distribution as well as stimulates the need for cooperation and work. There must also be a deeper principle at work—namely, the reflection in exchange of the human capacity and need to identify with others; through this identification with the other, one knows oneself. Reciprocal exchange is a type of empathy that invigorates a social mode of production, the aim of which is to render the foreign familiar and the indifferent different. To deny such exchange is to deny amity and the system of differences that sustains identity, and the wrath of the gods in this instance is as merciless as the war with men that also follows.

In a market system of commodity exchange mediated by the abstract and general equivalent of money, however, possessive individualism is accented, as is competitive profit seeking. Here, the pitiless spur of self-responsibility and private accumulation encourages work and transforms cooperation from an end in itself into a utility for private gain. Exchange reflects social relationships that subordinate empathy to self-interest and men to things, and it is here that value appears objective, precise, and general as established in prices.

Under the mediation of Incan sovereignty by the *curacas*, land worked by commoners was set aside for the king and the cult of the sun, while local control was implicitly acknowledged in the leaving of the remainder to the community, which partitioned it on a more or less annual basis to satisfy changing household needs. The produce from the fields of the state went in part to the state granaries to be used in times of famine. Corvée labor or *mita* requirements were organized so as to imperil neither community nor household self-sufficiency, and the workers were paid at the expense of the king. Generosity was the keynote in defining the tenor of exchanges and was obligatory. This brings to mind Mauss's statement regarding economies based on gift-type exchanges: "Generosity is necessary because otherwise Nemesis will take vengeance upon the excessive wealth and happiness of the rich by giving to the poor and the gods" (1976:15). In 1567 an inspector of the Spanish crown noted that the Aymara lord gave his vassals plenty to eat because otherwise they were offended, and this appeared to the inspector as less than adequate compensation, founded on a kind of "superstitious abuse" (Murra, 1968:135). But it is precisely this "superstitious abuse" that lay at the heart of the economic system, making what appeared as unequal exchange to outsiders appear as equal exchange to its participants, thus cementing the icons of nature, labor, lords, and vassals into the one meaningful and legitimate whole. For instance, no distinction was made in Aymara lexicon between a llama sacrificed to the spirit owners of nature and one sacrificed to the *curaca*.

In an exchange system that is organized by reciprocity of a multitude of use-values, both the religious sentiment and the semiotic system constituting value will be circumscribed by the play and structure of social relationships, which channel exchanges and are ratified by them. In this sense not only is the "economy" subordinate to "society" but exchange will persistently have a propensity to uncertainty, the giver presupposing the good faith of the receiver, and vice versa. The circumspect and ritualistic nature of exchange in nonmarket contexts is testimony to this uncertainty. Exchange is no guarantee of reciprocation either with the gods to whom one offers sacrifices in the hope of greater return or with one's lords or neighbors; one does not demand so much as hope, pledge oneself, magically facilitate, and wait for it. One is as likely to be eaten by the gods as to be fed by them; and in exchange with other men, festival and warfare lie close together. In a market system, on the other hand, the situation is very different. The peace of the market and the stability of society require far less trust and far more cold utilitarian calculation in which the pursuit of individual gain is paramount. Uncertainty here is seen as a function of an abstract economic mechanism, the market, and not as a function of trust.

The quality of ambiguity that is basic to reciprocity in good part explains the blended tones of trust and fear that are found both in Andean nature worship and in the relationship between lord and peasant, in which men meet in peace but "in a curious state of mind with exaggerated fear and an equally exaggerated generosity which appears stupid in no one's eyes but our own" (Mauss, 1967:79). Through their collective participation in ritual, the theatrical organization and dramatic embellishment of all that is essential to gift exchange, people consolidate these antinomic propensities into a balanced form. The necessity for this increases as the relationship between the partners to an exchange becomes more ambiguous, as the social distance widens between commoners and their chiefs or gods. This will be all the more challenging when history captures the chiefs and the gods and makes the familiar foreign and the different indifferent. At that point reciprocity as a process of empathy will be prone to the wildest of perturbations.

The Incan king built his dominion on the reciprocity existing in the local community. He transformed its tenets in his function of absorbing and redistributing tribute through the agency of the *curacas*. The *curaca*, therefore, most acutely embodied the tension of the Incan state—the contradiction between the continued existence of the community and the negation of the community by the state. Of the chroniclers, Blas Valera saw this most clearly, writes John Murra: "Mutual help, reciprocity in private and communal tasks was an age-old custom; 'The Inca approved it and reaffirmed it by a law they issued about it.' It was this age-old custom which was at the base of the state revenue system; the rest was an ideological attempt which probably convinced very few beyond some European Chroniclers" (1956:163). There is no doubt that the Inca's empire was built on the exploitation of the peasantry and that his redistribution was an ideological construction that was erected on the basis of reciprocity and buttressed by the appeal to the divinity of the ruling class, but it is also essential to understand, as Wachtel asserts, "that this exploitation was not experienced as such by those who were subject to it; on the contrary it made sense in a coherent vision of the world" (1977:83).

Following the conquest, the factors conditioning this invisibility of exploitation largely disappeared. The Incan king, the ritual head of the entire system, was killed, and Cuzco was no longer the sacred center of the empire. The figureheads of Incan religion were extirpated, leaving the peasants with their local *huacas*, whom they continued to worship in secret rites. Much Indian land was confiscated by the Spaniards, and the ecological pattern of usage was disrupted. The *mita* system of corvée labor under the Inca became a terrible parody of its former self; combined with heavy tribute exactions by the Spanish, it resulted in compulsory wage labor. This new system of exploitation decisively weakened the legitimacy that had formerly bound subjects to their rulers. "The unfavorable ratio of labor to its rewards was gradually worsened during the eighteenth century," writes Kubler, "finding expression, in the fulminating rebellions of the last quarter of the eighteenth century" (1963:350). The self-sufficiency of the Incan economy was destroyed, for in addition to the usurpation of lands and the disruption of eco-usage the economic equilibrium that had prevailed was upset by the introduction of a mercantile economy based on exports and imports that enormously raised the demand on Indian productive capacity (Ibid. :370). In many ways the linchpin in this new system continued to be the *curaca*, who mediated Spanish dominion and Indian hostility and who found it necessary to exploit his subjects in order to comply with his own tribute obligations. According to Kubler, this seriously affected the social morality of Indian life. Under these circumstances, write Giorgio Alberti and Enrique Mayer, "the *curaca* falsified the ancient notion of reciprocity in order to constitute a vast personal following that had a profound effect on communitarian ties and on the traditional system of reciprocity" (1974:20). The *curaca* immediately controlled the Indian communities; he mobilized corvée labor for the mines and elsewhere and delivered communally organized tribute to the Spaniards, just as the *wamanis* today in Ayacucho are said to convert the offerings made to them by Indians into gold and silver, which is then passed on to the white rulers in Lima (Earls, 1969:70). He and only he was allowed and eagerly adopted the prestige symbols of Spanish dress and horse; in this too he is like the *wamani* who, with his poncho of the ancient ones and his white man's clothes, represents the hybrid form and flamboyant contradictions that assail the Indian economy, society, and religious life.

To better understand this it is necessary to grasp the historical tension embodied in the figures of the *curaca* and the spirit owner of nature, through whom the opposed currents of conquest and Indian resistance coursed within juxtaposed Spanish and Indian cosmologies. Conquest and colonization destroyed much of Indian society, it is true. But it is also true that, reworked into a theme of defense, Indian tradition triumphed over acculturation, as Wachtel and many others have pointed out (1977). The internal logic of the pre-Hispanic economic system, which was based on reciprocity and redistribution, was subordinated to Spanish hegemony, which was maintained more by brute force, wage slavery, and market mechanisms (cf., Lockhart, 1968 : 27–33). But as Alberti and Mayer have asserted, even given their displacement, proletarianization, and exploitation, the Indians maintained the economy of reciprocity, above all, in the form of mutual aid in relations of production (1974:20). Most significantly, as Wachtel has illustrated, Indians continued to evaluate their relationships to their new masters, white or Indian, by the criteria of reciprocity, despite its being constantly abused or denied (1977 : 115). So long as this principle of reciprocity was a living force in the minds of the Indians it meant trouble. To recapitulate Mauss, to deny reciprocity is to invoke war and the wrath of the gods.

This leads me to suggest that the malice of the spirit owners of nature, from the conquest to the present day, corresponds to this denial of reciprocity as it had to be denied by the overarching system of commodity exchange. The spirits of the dead and the gods are the real owners of the wealth of the Andes. With them, it was and is necessary to exchange—and dangerous not to. As written into the aesthetics and morality of gift exchange, reciprocity aims to buy peace. In this manner the potential for evil, which can kill one, is kept at bay. The Indians persist in seeing their world in this way, and not without reason. Although muted, the old economy coexisted with the form of the new. A dual economy was established, and opposition to conquest not only persisted but became, in an important sense, the very culture itself. Yet this world otherwise failed to correspond to the dictates of reciprocity. The circuits of exchange between nature and producers, as mediated by the spirit owners, were gravely threatened by the exactions of the Spanish.

Precisely because of the assault on their coherent vision of the world, the universe of the conquered is far from being meaningless. Instead, it has a frightening plethora of significance in which the old gods must be fed so as to stave off evil—as so painfully illustrated in the Taqui Onqoy movement shortly after the conquest and in the rites to the devillike spirit owner in the Bolivian mines today. Conquest and commodity exchange may have exacerbated the spirit owner's ambiguity, but ritual, which perforce expresses this ambiguity, serves to bind him to the miners' hearts. It also serves to bind his propensities for production and destruction into a transcendent synthesis—a reciprocal affirmation of reciprocity itself.

CHAPTER 12

The Transformation of Mining and Mining Mythology

Preconquest Mining

Under the Incas, mining was a rather small-scale activity. It was run as a state monopoly and labor was provided by a rotating corvée, the aforementioned *mita*, which was not particularly burdensome to the miners (Rowe, 1957:52). John Leddy Phelan echoes the prevailing opinion when he says that mining was a minor economic activity because the Incas valued silver and gold only as a form of ornamentation and not as currency or as a depository of wealth (1967). The essential difference between preconquest and postconquest mining was that the former was a tiny part of a self-sufficient economy, whereas the latter became the mainstay of the burgeoning world capitalist economy, in which precious metals from the New World played a vital part in the early stages of capital accumulation.

Garcilaso de la Vega, who was not loath to identify enforced tribute when it occurred in other spheres of the Incan economy, was adamant in saying that precious metals were mined prior to conquest not as part of forced tribute but as gifts to the divine ruler.

The gold, silver, and precious stones which the Inca kings possessed in such great quantities, as is well known, were not produced by any enforced tribute that the Indians were obliged to pay, nor were they demanded by the rulers, because such objects were not regarded as necessary either for war or for peace, or prized as property or treasure. As we have said, nothing was bought or sold, for gold or silver, and these metals were not used to pay soldiers or expended to supply any wants whatsoever. Consequently they were considered to be something superfluous since they were not good to eat or useful in obtaining food. They were only esteemed for their brilliance and beauty, to adorn the royal palaces, the temples of the Sun, and the houses of the Virgins. [1966:253]

These metals had a sacred status, as befitted their status as gifts to the king. The *curacas*, who visited the king at the times of the great festivals celebrating the sun, the shearing of the llamas, the great victories, and the naming of the heir to the throne as well as when they were engaged in consulting with the king on more mundane matters of administration, would never do so without presenting him some gold and silver.

> On all these occasions they never kissed the Inca's hands without bringing him all the gold, silver, and precious stones that their Indians extracted when they had no work to do, for as the occupation of mining was not necessary to sustain life they only engaged in it when they had no other business to attend to. But as they saw that these articles were used to adorn the royal palaces and temples, places which they valued so highly, they employed their spare time in seeking for gold, silver, and precious stones to present to the Inca and the Sun, their gods. [Ibid.:254]

Cobo tells us that the miners worshiped the mountains above the mines and the mines themselves, asking them to give forth their mineral. One of Pizarro's secretaries describes mines of 60 to 240 feet deep, which were worked by a few score miners, both men and women—twenty from one chief, fifty from another. He was told that the miners worked only four months of the year, and Murra interprets this to be a result of their having to return to their villages in order to resume their agricultural responsibilities (1956:189). Murra also cites Cieza De Leon to the effect that when villagers were away in the mines, their lands were worked for them by the rest of the community, and that single men could not be miners. Only able-bodied heads of households were eligible. Other sources state that each unit of one hundred families had to supply one miner on a rotating basis (Ibid.). Writing in 1588, Acosta stated that the Inca entertained the miners with all they needed for their expenses and that mining "was no servitude unto them, but rather a pleasing life" (1880:418).

Colonial Mining

With the arrival of the Spanish, mining became a large and voracious industry, the keystone of the colonial economy. La-Barre is of the opinion that, at any one time, slightly over 14 percent of the Aymara population was occupied in forced labor in the mines and that the mortality among these Indians was exceedingly high. He states that some eight million Andeans, the majority of them Aymara, died in the mines over the whole colonial period (1948 : 31).

Mining was an important cause of the disintegration of communities and the destruction of kinship ties. This occurred as a direct consequence of the forced labor drafts and as an indirect consequence of the flight of Indians from their communities of origin in order to avoid the draft. Other Indians were attracted to the mines as free wage laborers in order to obtain money with which to pay the royal taxes. Still others seem to have preferred the mines to an even worse situation back home—which could occur with a tyrannical *curaca* who lorded it over trapped peasants.

With the changing composition of people in and around the mines, the old *ayllu* organization changed. Married couples were rarely from the same village of origin and "in the absence of kin ties through which traditional reciprocity and exchange were articulated, standards and patterns of wealth and social prestige were altered" (Spalding, 1967 : 114). Sex ratios were grossly imbalanced. In Yauli, a mining region close to Huarochirí, 24 percent of the adult male population in 1751 was composed of single men, excluding widowers (Ibid. : 121).

But something was retained of the old *ayllu* form. Karen Spalding speaks of its being "reconstructed," and refers us to the institutionalization of economic cooperation and mutual aid among the miners. Indeed, this was as much to the Spaniards' advantage as the Indians'. How could such a mammoth enterprise be sustained under such inhospitable conditions without allowing the Indians some measure of control over their own activities? Here as elsewhere in the Andes the Spanish strategy was to integrate the indigenous society with the new economic forms. If correctly guided from above, Indian patterns of social organization, which were derived in great part from the principles of *aine* (reciprocity), could help the Spanish to maintain their control. For instance, it was precisely through *ayllu* or quasi-*ayllu* forms that the Spanish allocated the lands that adjoined the mines to the Indian miners. The Spanish were unable to develop modern principles of labor organization. They did not possess the resources to develop, much less to sustain, a completely specialized mining class; thus, some elements of reciprocity and redistribution were incorporated into the base of the evolving capitalist framework. Social relations among the lower class were as beholden to the pre-Hispanic past as they were to the exigencies of the new mode of exploitation.

Work in the mines was exceedingly oppressive. Miners were paid wages both when they worked under the *mita* system and when they worked as free wage laborers, although the pay of the former was less than that of the latter. The *mita* workers were responsible for their own transport. Rowe cites distances of one hundred leagues or so, which required two to three months to traverse. Workers often made the trip in enormous pack trains. For example, the departure of the *mita* from Chucuito to Potosí in the 1590s included seven thousand women, men, and children and over forty thousand llamas and alpacas for food and transport (Rowe, 1957:174).

At the end of the sixteenth century a double-shift system was introduced at Potosí, and workers were kept underground from Monday evening to Saturday evening in the dank, polluted mine shafts. They timed their shifts by candle lengths and swung picks weighing between twenty-five and thirty pounds against the usually flint-hard rock. In the eighteenth century, work was regulated by a quota system rather than by time. The pick work was done by free laborers, while the *mita* workers carried the ore up long ladders to the surface. The sacks that were used contained one hundred pounds of ore, and each worker was expected to carry up twenty-five sacks within twelve hours, or else the wage was cut proportionally. One way of meeting the quota was for the worker to subcontract with other Indians, paying them out of his wages. In such conditions many *mita* workers ended their service heavily in debt, which forced them to flee to some region other than their communities of origin or else stay on in the mines as free laborers. Each escape from the community further increased the burden on those who remained at home. The *mita* quotas decreased far more slowly than did the number of *originarios* available to satisfy the draft, and "the proprietors of Potosí were merciless in their insistence that the quotas be met to the last man" (Rowe, 1957:174–76).

Small wonder then that even some of the Spanish referred to Potosí, which annually consumed thousands of innocent and peaceful natives, as a "mouth to hell" and observed that "what is carried to Spain from Peru is not silver but the blood and sweat of Indians" (Hanke, 1956:25). The mines spewed forth a class of homeless and masterless people—a colonial lumpenproletariat—whose presence and energy were to become very noticeable in swelling the mass of discontent and rebellion, particularly in the great Tupac Amaru Indian nationalist uprising of 1780 (Cornblitt, 1970).

Religion and the Change to Colonial Mining

Mining always involved ritual and magic. But only after the conquest did this involve the spirit of evil. Referring to preconquest customs, Bernabé Cobo wrote: "Those who went to the mines worshipped the mountains over the mines, as well as the mines themselves. They called the mines *Coya*, imploring them for their metal. In order to achieve this they drank and danced in reverence of these mountains. Similarly they worshipped the metals, which they called *Mama*, and the stones containing those metals which they called *Corpas*, kissing them and performing other ceremonies" (1890–95, 3:345). The mining city of Potosí was adored as a sacred place (Kubler, 1963:397). Martin de Morúa, another contemporary source, describes fertility rites, predating the conquest, common to agriculture, house-building, *and* mining. In these rites two figures were propitiated: the Pachamama or Earthmother, and the *huaca* pertaining to the enterprise in question (1946:278–81). Nowhere in these accounts is there even a hint of a figure of evil like the contemporary devil in the Bolivian tin mines. To the contrary, it is the feminine figure of fecundity that holds the stage.

The mining centers, such as Potosí, were great hubs of Spanish civilization and programs of religious indoctrination. "The Indians of these provinces, due to the frequent trade and communication of the Spanish, are more cultivated in human niceties, and instructed, and have profited by the Christian religion more than the Indians of other parts where there are not so many Spaniards" (Cobo, 1890–95, 1:292). However, such proximity and density of intercourse with the Spanish need not have had the effects so blithely claimed. A priest writing in the seventeenth century at roughly the same time as Cobo said: "The infirmity of these unfortunate people is general, though more pronounced in Potosí, where this accursed pestilence of idolatry rages at its height. . . . From this country to Charcas (a distance of more than 100 leagues and one of the most populated and well-frequented regions of all Peru) the faith has not been planted, for the ways of the people reflect indifference and haughtiness, with no hint of devotion. They seem rather to feel hatred and enmity and have a bad attitude towards God." He considered that the Indians were almost justified in this because "we who teach them appear to demonstrate that growing rich quickly is our principal aim," and that the Church barely provided any sort of answer for specifically Indian problems of colonization (Arriaga, 1968:78).

If the Church was unable to provide an answer, it should come as no surprise that Indians had to promulgate their own answers and to persist in "idolatry." It is logical to assume that in the mining settlements, where exploitation and commodity development were most prevalent and the cultural barrage mounted by the Spanish was most intense, the most extreme manifestations of that idolatry would prevail. If ever the devil were to emerge, he would appear here in these mines. Here, we would expect to find him at his fiercest and clearest. The amounts extracted from the earth by far exceeded anything under the Inca; yet at the top of the ladder the Indians met only further indebtedness, while the ore was removed to Spanish coffers. There was neither the material nor the spiritual repayment necessary to overcome the traumas inflicted on the mountain gods, traumas that by their sheer and senseless size would overtax the resynthesizing capacity of any traditional ritual. Virtually nothing returned to the miners, or to their gods, to whom the Indians, as much as all of surrounding nature, were beholden. The indigenous world was riddled by the destructive powers of the universe that had been unleashed from their protective moorings in the earlier cycles of exchange. The original totality was split at every point. The preexisting cyclical regeneration of mortals and nature was madly unscrambled to form a one-way linear movement, which was far more magically conceived as being endless.

At the same time the Spaniards brought their own peculiar metaphysics concerning mining and precious metals. We see this in Acosta's account of natural history: precious metals were thought of as plants, which were engendered in the bowels of the earth by the virtues of the sun and other planets. In late-sixteenth-century Europe, according to Paul Sébillot, miners believed the earth to be the female depository of rare metals, which were generated by the action of the masculine firmament interacting with the earth below. The moving planets acted on the open veins in the earth: gold was the offspring of the sun, silver of the moon, tin of Jupiter, and so forth. The earth exuded humid emanations of sulphur and mercury which united under the action of the planets to create the different metals. Sulphur vapor was thought to act as semen, the father, while mercury vapor was the female seed or mother. The veins were thought of as uteri, their inclination and physical orientation connecting them more with one set of astral influence than with another. Furthermore, being organic, minerals could regenerate: when a mine was worked to exhaustion, it could be allowed to rest for a few years; the influences would interact once again with the depleted veins to produce more mineral. Verification of this principle of refertilization came not only from European mines but also from the mines of Potosí (1894:392–99).

This microcosm-macrocosm model of animated structuralism was not very dissimilar in some essentials to that of the Indians, thus allowing for a great deal of acculturation and continuity of Indian mining metaphysics. However, the European concept emphasized a single force—God—while the Indian concept stressed the spontaneous cooperation of the different parts of the world organism and the harmony of the whole, not dependent on the authority of an external force. Acosta, for example, outlines a clear hierarchy of statuses and functions in which inferior natures are ordered by God to serve superior ones. Plants and minerals exist to serve the happiness of man, who is himself subject to God, the author and creator of all matters. And of all the uses of precious metals the outstanding one is their use as money, "the measure of all things"; indeed, "it is all things." By the same doctrine God has planted mineral riches in the Indies, where men do not understand this nor covet riches as do the Europeans, thus inviting the Church to seek out these lands and to possess them in return for planting the true religion (Acosta, 1880, 1:183–87).

Nineteenth-Century Peruvian Mines

Johann J. von Tschudi, who visited the Cerro de Pasco silver mines in highland Peru around 1840, has left us with some insightful observations. Nothing but the pursuit of wealth could reconcile anyone to live there, he wrote. The cold and stormy climate raged around an inhospitable region, where the soil produced nothing. Nature had buried all her treasure in the bowels of the earth, and the incessant hammering of the Indian miners burrowing through those bowels kept the traveler awake at night. The majority of the mine owners were descendants of the old Spanish families, and although at times they gained enormous wealth, they were mostly in great debt to the usurers in Lima who charged 100 to 120 percent interest. Any money gained from a strike was soon dissipated in paying off interest, searching for new mines, and gambling. "The preserving ardor of persons engaged in mining is truly remarkable," he wrote. "Unchecked by disappointment they pursue the career in which they have embarked. Even when ruin appears inevitable, the love of money subdues the warnings of reason, and hope conjures up, from year to year, visionary pictures of riches yet to come" (1852:236–37). In few other places were such vast sums staked at the gambling tables. Cards and dice were played from the very earliest hours of the morning until the next day, and men frequently gambled away their shares in future strikes.

To liquidate his debts the mine owner would make the Indian wage laborers dig out as much ore as possible without taking any precautions against accidents. Galleries frequently collapsed, and many miners died each year. The dangerous parts of the shafts were not shored up. "Rotten blocks of wood and loose stones serve for steps, and, where these cannot be placed, the shaft, which in most instances runs nearly perpendicular, is descended by the help of rusty chains and ropes, whilst loose fragments of rubbish are continually falling from the damp walls" (Ibid.:231). The loaders (*hapires*), whose job it was to carry the ore up the shafts, worked twelve-hour shifts, and the mining continued uninterruptedly throughout the twenty-four-hour cycle. Each load weighed from fifty to seventy-five pounds, and the *hapires* worked nude despite the coldness of the climate since they became so heated by their strenuous labor.

The silver was separated from the ore through the use of mercury. Although in some places this was done by the trampling of horses, in other places it was performed by barefoot Indians stamping on the mixture for several hours. The mercury quickly and irreparably damaged the hooves of the horses, which soon became unfit for further work; in the Indians it caused paralysis and other diseases.

Silver was the only item produced in the immediate region, and all the necessities of life, including housing, were exceedingly expensive. The warehouses were stocked with the choicest luxuries, and the market was equal in goods to that of the capital city of Lima. Although the Indians worked with a degree of patient industry that von Tschudi thought it would be vain to expect from European workmen, they were very prodigal with their wages, which they quickly spent on all manner of luxuries and alcohol at the end of the week. The Indian miner never thought of saving money, and "in the enjoyment of the present moment they [lost] sight of all considerations for the future." Even the Indians who migrated from distant parts invariably returned home as poor as when they had left. European goods, which they had bought at vastly inflated prices, were quickly spurned. Expensive goods (which were bought only when miners were working on a high-yielding mine and hence paid on piecework rates) were thrown away after they showed the slightest defect or satisfied immediate curiosity. Von Tschudi relates how an Indian bought a gold watch for 204 dollars (the average weekly wage was one dollar) and, after examining the watch for a few minutes and observing that the thing was of no use to him, dashed it to the ground.

Prodigal as they were with wages that they earned in the mines of the whites, the Indians exhibited quite different behavior when it came to the extraction of silver from sources that were kept secret from the whites and that they worked according to their own ideals. They mined only when they had an immediate and dire need for a specific purchase and extracted only the specific amount necessary to meet the cash obligation involved. Von Tschudi assures us that this was a general phenomenon, and he was very taken with what he terms the Indians' indifference toward obtaining wealth for themselves—an attitude so strikingly opposite to that of the white mine owners. The British mining engineer Robert Blake White described similar behavior on the part of Pasto Indians in southwestern Colombia in the late nineteenth century. "They only go to seek gold in the rivers when they want to purchase some special thing which can only be bought with money. But if they extract more gold than they actually want, they throw the surplus back in the river. Nothing will persuade them to sell or barter it, for they say that if they borrow more than they really need, the river-god will not lend them any more" (1884:245).

Significantly, von Tschudi was most surprised to hear that the Indians thought that frightening spirits and apparitions haunted white-owned mines. He thought this to be quite unusual behavior on the part of the Indians, whose imaginations he said, were not "very fertile in the creation of this sort of terrors."

The Devil, the Virgin, and Salvation in Contemporary Bolivian Mining

The mountains that overlie the contemporary Bolivian tin mines are believed to have been inhabited by a spirit called Hahuari, who is today the devil or the Tio (uncle), the spirit owner of the mines. "It was he who persuaded the people to leave their work in the fields and enter the caves to find the riches he had in store. They abandoned the virtuous life of tilling the soil and turned to drinking and midnight revels paid for by their ill-gained wealth from the mines" (Nash, 1972:224).

In contrast to peasant agriculture, mining is considered bad. It is a mistake. The peasants were lured there by the promise of wealth, but it is wealth that lacks virtue. It is the Andean version of the story of Faustus, and as there was for him, there was a great price to pay. "Then in turn came a monstrous snake, a lizard, a toad and an army of ants to devour them, but each of these was struck by lightning as it advanced upon the town when one of the frightened inhabitants called upon *Nusta,* the Incan maiden, later identified with the Virgin of the mines" (Ibid.).

A female informant described the Virgin to Nash as follows: "Señora, I am going to tell you of the Virgin of the mineshaft. She is on top of the metal, on top of the gold that is still there in the mineshaft, under the church and the *pulpería.* Boiling water passes over this metal, crystalline water that is bubbling and boiling. The Virgin is miraculous. The metal is liquid. It comes in very clean, and you can't move it at all. We went into the shaft under the *pulpería* once. . . . How beautiful it [the metal] was! It was like raw sugar." The Virgin must not be moved. "If she were to be moved, the Pueblo of Oruro could lose her. The water could carry her away because the Virgin is walking on water. The Pueblo of Oruro could be lost. . . . This hill would burn and we would lose ourselves in it" (1976:77).

So the Virgin of the mineshaft halted the march of destruction. The various monsters can be seen today in the forms of rocks, dunes, and lakes. The miners were thus saved, if only momentarily, from ultimate destruction. This is as much historical as persistent. It is a structure of forces that the situation maintains unremittingly. The petrified monsters engraved in the surrounding landscape are now conceived of as mute witnesses, but ones invested with the potential to return to life and continue their march.

It is believed that the excavation of silver and other minerals would inevitably lead to destruction, were it not for the intercession of the Virgin in the mines. But this macrocosmic drama of salvation is reenacted not only once a year at Carnival time. Essentially the same ritual is enacted inside the mines and whenever danger is imminent or accidents have occurred. This miners' rite is also a recurrent drama of salvation from a persistent threat of destruction; here also the role of intercessor is pitched against the destructive power of the devil. The intercessor is the Pachamama or Earthmother. The miners ask her to intercede with the Tio when they feel in danger, and when they set off dynamite they ask her not to get angry. A miner says: "The miner, particularly in August buys his wool, grease, *coca,* and other things that he offers, saying, 'Pachamama is not going to punish me.' With this he internally believes he has fulfilled a proposal to the Pachamama and from that moment he can arrive at a point of forgetting an accident. Then he can continue working with tranquility. It is a custom that the priests have not forced upon us" (Nash, 1972:229).

The Battle of the Gods and the Struggle for Fertility

What lies behind this antagonism between the male devil and the Earthmother, the one being the owner of the mine and the other being the spirit of the earth and fertility? Scanning the long history of colonization and acculturation in highland Latin America, one realizes that the characteristics ascribed to the Tio (devil) and the Earthmother (or Virgin) in the Bolivian mines are but particular expressions of a very general outlook and a common historical experience. The social effects of European colonization on indigenous ways of life appear to have distorted the idealized character of the relationship between male and female to the point at which it has now become transformed into a relationship of antagonism, most noticeably in those Indian communities where alienation is most extreme. Whereas the female divinity—the Virgin or the Earthmother—can be seen as the embodiment of Indian interests and the consciousness of the oppressed, the male god is often seen as the embodiment of alien forces that are bent on the destruction of those people whom the female nourishes and protects.

In both Mesoamerica and the Andes there is a deeply seated belief in cycles of destruction of the universe by God—the Christian God—which are averted or modified by a female saint, usually the Virgin—the Indian Virgin—who pleads for the life of her people. In the southern part of the valley of Mexico in the village of San Francisco Tecospa, it is said that man's sins turned the soil black. When God saw this, he became so angry that he decided to exterminate the human race. However, the Virgin of Guadelupe, the mother of all Mexicans, still loved her children, and she begged God, who is also her son, to spare them. But later she agreed with his judgment, and he caused the great flood. God still wants to destroy the world, but the Virgin protects mankind from his terrible anger, although, as before, she will let him have his way when she decides that people are too sinful to live any more. There will be omens when this is about to happen: mint will bloom, bamboo will blossom, and males will bear children (Madsen, 1960:143–44).

In the village of Santa Eulalia in northeastern Guatemala there is a similar concept. The patron saint of the village, Santa Eulalia, is equated with the Virgin, and she is seen as continally interceding on behalf of her people against the wrathful might of God. The First World War, which threatened to wipe out mankind but spared the inhabitants of this village, was one occasion of this sort. In the village of Hualcan in Peru, Santa Ursula is the main religious figure, and it is she who looks after the health and the harvests. She is called, affectionately, Mama Ursula, and it is to her that the villagers turn when they are in trouble. She is also seen as the protectress of warriors, and she is a great warrior herself. Moreover, she is implicitly identified with the Virgin, who is referred to as the mother of God.

In Mexico the dark-skinned Virgin of Guadelupe is the Indians' national saint. She symbolized the revolutionary movements of Morelos and Hidalgo in the Wars of Independence in the early nineteenth century, just as she adorned the apparel of the Zapatistas in their struggle to regain their traditional lands in the opening decades of the twentieth century. In fact, she is the Christian mask concealing the pre-Hispanic earth and fertility goddess, Tonantzin—a satanic device to mask idolatry, according to one prominent sixteenth-century Church Father. It has been suggested that this Virgin is identified with the promise of successful rebellion against power figures and is equated with the promise of life and salvation, whereas Christ is identified with the crucifixion, death, and defeat. Ultimately, the image of the Virgin extends to the promise of life and the promise of Indian independence, and although the Virgin is now pictured as subordinate in many ways to the male god, she is still capable of fighting for the Indians' salvation and the return to the "pristine state in which hunger and unsatisfactory social relations are minimized" (Wolf, 1958).

Similarly, in the European Middle Ages the Blessed Virgin was the chief protectress against the devil. Maximilian Rudwin describes her as a sort of Valkyrie or Amazon, always at war with the demons in order to snatch the pacts and the souls of the repentant sinners from them. He endorses the speculation that she was the vindication of the right of the common folk to a goddess of their own kind (1958:178–79).

Thus, the confrontation between the Earthmother (or Virgin) and the devil figure in the Bolivian mines is basically similar to a drama of threatened destruction and salvation that is played out in many, if not all, highland Indian areas in Latin America. A masculine power, embodied in an alien symbol drawn from the culture of conquest, is seen as bent on the destruction of the Indian community, while a female power, which embodies Indian concerns, is seen to be holding him at bay.

In the mining communities, however, the intensity of the ritual dramatization of this confrontation is markedly greater than it is in communities of peasant producers. In the mines the drama runs at a high pitch, and the frequency of the ritual is astounding. Before the national government suppressed the miners' *ch'alla* in the mid-1960s, it was held twice a week, and it still appears to be held frequently. In attributing support to the Earthmother, the miners' culture would similarly seem to be appealing for the maintenance and restoration of the principles of fertility that she embodies—namely, reciprocity and harmony in social relations and with nature in general. Although the drama of salvation that is played out in the miners' rites includes a concern with the salvation of the individual, it also includes a concern with the salvation of a way of life—enmeshed in class struggle.

Furthermore, whereas God and the Virgin feature in the accounts above that were drawn from peasant communities, in the Bolivian mines the principal male figure is not God but the devil, and a fearsomely male devil at that. With his giant phallus erect as though engorged with the blood of dead miners and animal sacrifice, he stands over miners and Earthmother as a grotesque symbol of male dominance. If the accounts concerning the Virgin of Guadelupe, the village of San Francisco Tecospa, Santa Eulalia, and Hualcan demonstrate a dramatic shift in supernatural symbolism in which changes in sex roles mirror analogous changes in community dynamics, how much more decisively and powerfully is this expressed in the Bolivian miners' *ch'alla*. This last occurs in a situation that is a further stage removed from the indigenous glorification of the preconquest past and from the ideal forms of socioeconomic organization. The replacement of the male deity by the male devil is surely a response to that.

From the Spirit of the Mountains to the Devil in the Mines

Hahuari lives on in the mineral-laden mountains around Oruro, Bolivia; yet he is venerated in the form of the Tio or devil as the owner of the wealth of the mines. What is the connection?

The name Hahuari is an older version of the term Supay, which was used in the colonial era, as much as today, to signify the devil. Supay was the term that was commonly used by the chroniclers and the friars to refer to the devil, just as Hahuari could refer to a "bad phantom." According to LaBarre, the devil is still called Supay by the Aymara Indians, who "spit on the ground in malediction when they use this word." But what sort of devil? LaBarre firmly believes that although the Supay is indisputably an earth demon, it is nothing more than what he calls "the specialization along Christian lines of what was originally perhaps only one among many earth demons" (1948:168). Bandelier curtly dismisses any notion that the Supay is truly the same as the Christian devil. "Supay is a Quechua term for evil spirits collectively, but any demon or fiend is Supay also. As little as the Indians had any conception of a supreme God, as little did they have a notion of a supreme devil" (1910:150).

In the opinion of the chronicler Bernabé Cobo, the Indians were ardent believers in the Supay as the malevolent spirit and corrupter of mankind, whom Cobo translated as the devil. It was his conviction that the Supay had gained such authority over the Indians that they served and obeyed him with great respect, and this, according to Cobo, stemmed from their fear of the Supay's power to do harm (Cobo, 1890–95, 2:229).

But the Supay was far from being the only figure of evil. Nor was he purely evil. Pierre Duviols cites the existence of many other such figures: the *achacalla,* the *hapiñuñu,* the *visscocho,* the *humapurick,* and still more (1971:37–38). He became the supreme figure of evil only by the efforts of the Christians. The Bolivian author M. Rigoberto Paredes has suggested that the evolution of the spirit of evil among that country's Indians followed this logic: "Step by step in proportion to their cruel victimization at the hands of the Spanish and the mestizos, and with the insistent sermonizing of the missionaries and priests to the effect that their cults were of the devil, the Supay became congenial and more firmly fixed in their understanding" (1920:57). The contemporary indigenous evaluation of the Supay, according to the same author, has achieved such extraordinary dimensions that the term is used to denote any bad or perverse person. Furthermore, the Supay is called upon to destroy one's enemies and to satisfy one's hates. Such a compact with the Supay requires the selling of one's soul, which Paredes dismisses with the offhand remark: "To the Indian it does not matter to gain glory in the after-life so long as the sufferings that weigh on him in this world are alleviated" (Ibid.:59).

This conception of the Supay is identical to Michelet's concerning the rise of the devil in early modern Europe (1971). One of many pagan spirits was promoted as the Prince of Darkness in the campaign by the Church to suppress paganism in a society that was beginning to feel the impact of commodity production and market exchange. However, the counterdefinition imposed by the authorities rebounded. The Supay became more congenial, possibly even an ally. His power to destroy could be channeled to suit one's desires. This is important to remember as we consider the role of Hahuari (read Supay) transformed into the devil of the mines.

The cosmic struggle to which this ideological evolution corresponds is analogous to the earthly struggle over competing systems of material production and exchange. This was, it should be stressed, not only a struggle for materials or resources, but was, and still is, a struggle over entirely different systems of organization of the economy. Two distinct modes of production and principles of fertility were set into conflict with one another by the conquest, a conflict that was later exacerbated by the rise of laissez-faire in the nineteenth century. Whereas the mountain spirits presided over a reciprocating system that ensured redistribution and a basic minimum of social insurance, the more abstract Christian deity was part of the ritual regulation and codification of unequal exchange, which was most transparent in situations like that of proletarian labor in the mining industry. To further delineate these two systems, we now turn to the peasants' mode of production and their so-called fertility rites.

CHAPTER 13

Peasant Rites of Production

To overlook individualism and conflict in Andean peasant life would be naive. Yet it would be even more erroneous not to emphasize the force exerted by reciprocity and communality. Peasant rites of production mediate the interplay of individuality with community, and in so doing they reflect the principle of inalienability in the constitution of rural life. Miners either come directly from this life or have a background in its dictates and sentiments. Yet the situation that they encounter in the mines is one predicated on alienation and the denial of reciprocity. Their rites of labor and of production reflect this contrast.

Reciprocal labor is one of the most frequent modes of organizing work on the Andean plateau, and communal forms of land tenure and work management are common (Nuñez del Prado, 1965:109; Albo, 1974–76:68–69), although this may be less true than it was in the nineteenth century (Klein, 1969:7; Forbes, 1870:200). In his monograph on the Aymara published in 1948, LaBarre states that peasant land is generally inalienable and that a rotational and communal pattern of tenure is practiced. Individual households have usufruct rights, which are apportioned by the headman (*hilacata*) each year or so. The headman is elected by the community, and he is responsible for the payment of the community's tax burden as a lump sum to the government. It has been claimed that the headmen tend to be chosen from among the wealthier men because they can assume the responsibility for the poorer members. This follows an informal and illegal procedure that is buttressed by centuries of custom. In Bolivian law, at least up until 1952, the state owns the land; individual Indians are supposed to rent it as private property. Likewise, the headman is usually supposed to be a government appointee or, in the *haciendas*, is supposed to be selected by the estate owner. In practice, the community generally selects the headman, who is endorsed later on by the central authority, and the concept of land ownership remains one of inalienability. As Bandelier notes: "Today the owners of *haciendas* believe that *they* appoint the Indian functionaries without consulting the wishes of their Indians. . . . On the island these two principal officers are accepted rather than appointed by the proprietor on or about the first of January each year. . . . The natives of Challa told me emphatically that there existed a council of old men, and this council *proposed* the *hilacata*, *alcade* and *campos*, to be appointed each year. The existence of such a body of men was denied by the owners" (1910:82–83).

LaBarre writes that although each household plot is, in legal theory, supposed to be the private property of the individual, this does not hold in practice. In fact, the whole community will turn out to prevent any part of the lands it considers to be its own from falling into individual ownership if a person refuses to use the allotment. The only personal private property of a family is its hut and the immediate small piece of land on which it stands (1948:156–57). Furthermore, ownership is very much bound up with productive activity. For instance, a house belongs to the person who built it. What is more, all weapons, utensils, pottery, textiles, houses, and other such property are destroyed at the death of the owner (Ibid.:145–46). Even precious livestock may be so destroyed. At the same time, the principle of mutual aid and reciprocity between community members, often called *aine*, regulates social relationships. This principle is enacted in ritual, such as in the *ch'alla*.

The practice of the *ch'alla* is ubiquitous in peasant life. Whenever an Aymara does anything of importance, writes LaBarre, it is always preceded by a propitiatory offering or sacrifice called a *ch'alla* or *tinka*. Literally, "the sprinkling," it usually consists in making a libation to the earth of a few drops of liquor, with perhaps the addition of some coca and other substances as well. It can be made to the Earthmother alone or to the ancestral spirits of the mountain peaks, or both. Typically, the *ch'alla* is made before fishing, hunting, building a house, making a journey, or making a purchase (1948:172).

Paredes describes the peasant's *ch'alla* as the clinching of a deal over a drink. In his view the ceremony gives thanks, at the time of exchange of some important item, such as a house or livestock, primarily to the Pachamama, the Earthmother, and secondarily to the human participants to the transaction. The new possessor invites the bestower or seller, friends, and kin to drink liquor. But before anybody is served, a portion is sprinkled on the ground to solicit the Pachamama's goodwill for the success of the exchange. Without this ritual, "effected with all pomp and enthusiasm, they suppose that the exchange will neither last nor be happy, and that the Pachamama will not display benevolence to the new proprietor" (1920:118).

During his archaeological work at the turn of this century in Aymara territory which involved the use of local labor, Bandelier came across some vivid examples of the *ch'alla*, which he summarized by saying that "the idea here is to give to the earth a remuneration or compensation for its favours." Without it, no work is expected to be successful (1910:96).

Bandelier relates that house building could not begin without a *ch'alla*. In ignorance of this, the archaeologist proceeded to instruct the Indians that he had hired from the local community to begin building, but he was interrupted by one of the leading shamans, who insisted that a *tinka* or *ch'alla* had to be performed to prevent disaster. Special bundles were prepared for the corners of the foundations, each bundle containing the foetus of a llama, the foetus of a pig, a piece of llama tallow, a plant unobtainable in the region, and coca leaves. When all the workmen were gathered at the site, the chief builder laid out a special cloth on which each laborer placed a trefoil of coca leaves, while the builder spoke the following prayer: "Children, with all your heart, put coca in your mouths. We must give to the virgin earth, but not with two hearts but with one alone." They then began to work, and in the afternoon gathered together once more and placed the bundles in the corners of the foundations with the head builder saying, "Children, we shall ask of God (*Dius-at*) and of the *Achachila* (Mountain Spirit) and of the grandmother, that no evil may befall us." Then, when the bundles had been buried he went on: "Let all of you together take coca, throw coca on the ground, give them their dues."

Prior to any archaeological excavation, similar rites had to be performed. These began with a shaman giving notice to the mountain spirits (*achachilas*) that a *ch'alla* was about to occur. The preliminary notification required that the shaman elicit the most favorable site for the propitiation, usually as a result of dream vision, and place two bundles in the ground at that spot. The contents of the bundles were much the same as those described above, and before placing them in the ground the shaman said: "Good afternoon, *Achachilas: Kasapata Achachila, Llak'aylli Achachila, Chincana Achachila, Calvario Achachila, Santa Maria Achachila, Ciriapata Achachila*. We have greeted all of you whom a white stranger has sent me to greet; for him I have come as he cannot speak to thee. Forgive me for asking of thee a favour." In the evening, in the company of several men, the same rite was performed but on a larger scale with twenty-two bundles and the use of brandy and wine. The shaman repeated the formulas used in the afternoon and sprinkled wine and brandy in the direction of the five *achachilas* saying, "All thy presents I have now brought, Thou has to give me with all thy heart." At this point he began to count out twenty of the bundles one by one, designating each one as a *quintal*. (A *quintal* is a Spanish measure of fifty kilograms, but, as used in this region, it is also taken to mean an undetermined but very large quantity—a fact of importance since it is for these that the *achachilas* are meant to reciprocate with their large favors.) The twenty bundles were then placed on a fire, which began to crackle. The people ran away saying, "The *Achachilas* are eating." When the fire had died down they returned, covered it over, and then took the two remaining and largest bundles to another spot, where the shaman dug a hole, declaring, "The virgin earth is now invited. Here is thy burial of treasure." He then put them into the hole, and continued, "The very things of the Inca thou hast to bring forth. Now with thy permission, we will take leave. Forgive me."

The following afternoon, during the lunch recess, another shaman appeared among the workers, and after the latter had all taken some coca, he sprinkled wine and brandy in the direction of the five *achachilas* and said: "*Achachila* do not make me suffer much work, we are those who work under pay; to this *viracocha* [lord] thou hast to return what he paid to us; for this thou are beckoned and invited"— a most striking verification of the persistence of the notion of reciprocity in wage-labor conditions (Bandelier, 1910:95–99).

Nuñez del Prado describes a similar rite for the fertility of the llamas in the community of Q'ero near Cuzco. He understands these rites to be the most important in the social life of that community because (like the miners and ore) the people are not owners of the land they occupy; hence, their animals, rather than the earth, serve as the focus for the maintenance of communal and familial solidarity. The members of the extended family gather together in the evening to invoke the chief mountain spirit of the region, El Roal, as well as the lesser mountain deities. A special cloth is laid in the center of which is placed a wide vessel. Within that vessel is placed a stone figurine that represents the type of animal whose fertility is desired. Coca is sprinkled over the cloth, and the wide vessel is filled with *chicha* (corn beer). Then, they make an invocation to the mountain spirits, inviting them to take the offering, accompanied by a prayer: "Make the flocks grow and multiply." The assembled people then drink the chicha from the vessel, the remains of which are then poured over the animals collected in the corral.

This is followed by a branding ceremony of the animals, which are adorned with colored woolen streamers (1968:252).

Before planting potatoes they make an invocation to the Pachamama. They dig a hole in the ground, into which they place some seed and selected leaves of coca, and then they say: "*Pachamama*, I place these seeds in your heart so that you may cover them, and in doing so, may you let them multiply and produce in abundance" (Ibid.:252–54). The Buechlers witnessed potato-sowing rites among the Aymara on the shores of Lake Titicaca. Led by a flute player, the Indians offered libations to the Earthmother and to a few potatoes that were wrapped in a cloth with earth. If on opening the cloth, earth stuck to the potatoes, then the future harvest would be good. These potatoes were the first to be planted, after they had had coca leaves and sheep fat inserted into them and after the people had chewed coca and drunk liquor. A month or two later the headman called the community to weed. Families raced one another to finish their furrows first, sometimes returning to aid the slower families. Then all began the next set of furrows. The families displayed the same spirit of cooperation and work when harvesting and drying the crop, cleaning the irrigation canals, and so on (1971:11).

Steven Webster also has described the Q'ero llama rituals. The structure of the rituals comprises persons, llamas, mountain spirits, and the earth. Such rites occur on an annual basis as well as when animals are sick. As he expresses it, the aim is to reestablish rapport among the components of a triad—family, herd, and the pantheon of extraordinary powers that affect the well-being of both. Throughout the various stages of the rite, the *ch'alla* is frequent and essential. As in the other fertility rites described above, although the mountain spirits are solicited frequently, they are never personified or represented in figures or statues as they are in the mines (1972:190).

The synergistic role of the Pachamama in such llama rituals is again brought out in Horst Nachtigall's description, in which the Earthmother occupies an important place. The *irantas*, or incense torches, that are burnt in great numbers on these occasions are conceived of as honoring either the Pachamama or the sacred mountains. Although Nachtigall is not entirely clear, it appears that the fertility rites that he observed involved the burial of a llama foetus as a sacrifice to the Pachamama. The burial of the skeleton of a sacrificed llama is done to ensure the rebirth of another llama through the powers of the Pachamama (1966:194–95).

In the Rio Pampas area in the department of Ayacucho, Peru, the cattle-branding rituals illustrate once again the importance of the local mountain gods (here called *wamanis*) in maintaining the herd.

The mountain spirit is considered to be the guardian of the animals, and he is constantly propitiated throughout the complex steps of the annual branding ceremony. If this is not done correctly, there is very great fear that his anger will burst forth. Apart from alcoholic libations to the mountain spirit, alcohol which is also consumed by the participants, there is the use of *llampu*, which is offered to the spirit, the human participants, and the animals. This *llampu* is described as a sacred substance composed of clay and corn ground together in a special rite. It is used mainly to "smooth over or calm the adversities that result from disturbing the harmony of the relations with the mountain spirit" (Quispe M., 1968:39; cf., Tschopik, 1968:297–99, 382).

Bastien's account of ritual in Kaata, in northern Bolivia, complements and transcends all of the aforementioned because he and his wife were able to see the total form within which different rites occurred, and, conversely, the way in which any particular rite served as a moment in time expressing that totality. The land of the *ayllu* is Mount Kaata. The mountain is conceived of as a living human body that is isomorphic with the human body and with the pattern formed by the social subgroupings resident on the mountain. The cycle of the sun and the life-cycle of the human being are complementary, and both cycles are centered on the mountain. At dawn the sun climbs the mountain. It grows in size and power to reach its zenith just above the mountain peak where the ancestors live. Then it descends into the mountain, shrinking to the size of an orange. Human beings originate near the peak, then travel down the slopes to die and be buried in the mountain. Then they swim upwards, as miniature people, to return to the summit, where the cycle begins again. Birth rites enact the mountain's ownership of the person.

The different eco-zones of the mountain favor different types of farming and livestock production. The subgroups that occupy the different eco-zones exchange their different products with one another. Women are married across the three levels of the mountain in accord with rules of exogamy and patrilocality.

Rites of production dramatize the meaning of these patterns of integration and exchange. The earth-breaking rite of New Earth is a fine example of this. This rite consists of two pulsating movements, centrifugal and centripetal. Ritualists are sent out from the center of the mountain to circulate blood and fat to the earth shrines at the periphery, the highlands and the lowlands. Then the people from the periphery come to the center with their gifts to feed the mountain shrine there and sacrifice a llama. From the lowlands they bring lilies, roses, carnations, and corn beer; from the center come snapdragons, buttercups, and other flowers; while from the highlands come the llama and plants that grow only there. Plates of seashells are prepared to feed to the spirit lords of the seasons and crops, the lords of the *ayllu,* and the field shrine. On each shell the ritualist places coca, llama fat, carnations, incense, and blood. While these are being prepared, the earth is broken into furrows by a man and woman, who are accompanied by the playing of flutes and drum. Guinea pigs are dissected to divine the future of the crops, and their blood is sprinkled onto the earth. The participants stand in a circle around the hobbled llama, receive the seashell plates, hold them up to the shrine of the birth of the sun, and then walk in a spiral around the llama to face the different major shrines of the mountain, inviting them to eat. A fire is lit at the mouth of the field shrine, and the participants are led in fours to it, while the ritualist says, "Ayllu men and only ayllu men, in so much as you constitute one ayllu feed this shrine." They place their ritual foods into the fire saying, "Serve yourself field shrine. With all our heart and sweat receive this and serve yourself." The llama is held down by his tearful attendants, kissed, and bid a farewell for his journey to the highlands. A prayer is made to the shrines, to the agricultural year and the crops, and to the spirit lords of the *ayllu,* inviting them to eat the llama and drink his blood. People embrace and kiss the llama. Others are drinking liquor and sprinkling him with it. The llama is slit open at the neck. His heart is immediately removed and, while the heart is still beating, his blood is sprinkled in all directions over the ground. People call out: "Lord of the sacrificial llama, lords of the ayllu, lords of the agricultural year and the crops, receive this blood from the llama. Give us an abundant harvest, grant us good fortune in all. Mother earth, drink of this blood." The blood from the *ayllu*'s most esteemed animal, writes Bastien, "flowed to all parts of the ayllu body and vitalized its geographical layers to produce more life" (1978:74–76).

All these rites express the totality of meaning that lies latent in the spirits of the mountain. Their central theme is the feeding of the mountain so that the mountain will give people food. Exchange awakens organic life, reconstituting form and revitalizing circuits of power. Control derives from experience, and experience comes from exchange.

Misfortune manifests the disintegration of the mountain body, and misfortune rituals aim at recomposing dissolution. In this context, exchange is the vehicle for reconstructing the body after it has been torn apart by misfortune. Unlike other rites, misfortune rituals in Kaata can occur only on Tuesdays or Fridays—the only days on which the Bolivian miners perform their rites to the devil figure, the owner of the mineral, source of wealth, and creator of misfortune.

Asked about the magic of plants, especially hallucinogens, a folk healer (*curandero*) who was interviewed by Douglas Sharon in the 1960s in northern Peru explained that the healer imposes his personal spiritual force over the plants, thereby arousing their innate potential to cure. It is this idea of sharing and exchanging that is essential. In his words the healer said that he gives the plants

> that magical power which becomes, let us say, the power that plants contain as a result of having been rooted in the earth and partaken of its magnetic force. And since man is an element of the earth, with the power of his intelligence . . . he emits that potentiality over the plants. The plants receive this influence and return it toward man. . . . In other words, all of the spirit of the plants is . . . fortified by the influences—intellectual, spiritual, and human—of man. He is the one who forms the magic potentiality of the plants. Because of the fact that they are in an isolated place, a place untouched by strange hands, by foreign elements, the plants together with water produce the magic power by virtue of their duality. [1972:123]

The "magnetic" power of the earth is immanent throughout the plant and the human world, and plants and humans energize each other in a dialectical interchange. This magical energy is inseparable from the consciousness that the healer describes as "seeing"—the same seeing that must be at work uniting people to ancestor spirits and mountain spirits. He describes the sensation of detachment and telepathy that carries one through time and matter. One can see very distant things clearly; one sees the past, or the present, or the immediate future; one "jumps" out of one's conscious mind, he says, and the subconscious is "opened like a flower. All by itself it tells things. A very practical manner . . . which was known to the ancients of Peru" (Ibid.:131). Indeed, the metaphor of the mountains unifying people with their origins and constant reincarnation is not forgotten. "I called certain saints, hills, ancient shrines; and I disappeared. There was an unfolding of my personality . . . my personality had departed to other places. . . . During my sessions at times I have been looking for a certain force, for example an ancient shrine or a hill, and suddenly while I was whistling and singing, the account was activated, and I felt myself enter the hill which opened all its passages, all its labyrinths. And suddenly I returned again. I had seen and I had visualized with all my spirit" (Ibid.).

In this exchange there is illumination: an "account" is activated. In exchanges that we have termed reciprocal there would seem to be a desire, if not a pressing need, for exchange as an end in itself, and the illumination that follows, the account that is activated, is the blending of differences to form a whole. But in another form of exchange a different sort of account is activated; here, exchanges are not ends in themselves but instruments of gain or loss. These are the exchanges wrought to perfection by the capitalist market, in which the social texture appears to the individual as merely a means to private ambition. This exchange system confronts the Indians when they enter the mine. Their confrontation with the devil stands as testimony to the confrontation of these two systems of exchange and illuminates the account that government repression has so far prevented them from settling with society itself.

CHAPTER 14

Mining Magic: The Mediation of
Commodity Fetishism

Let us briefly review the salient contrasts between the magic of peasant production and that of mining. Peasants own their means of production; miners do not. Peasants control the organization of work; miners are in constant conflict with managers over job control and wage levels. Peasants combine production for subsistence with some sale of produce; miners are totally dependent on the labor market: the buying and selling of their labor power. Peasant rites associated with production and the means of production are sacrificial exchanges to the mountain spirits. These exchanges secure the right to use the land and ensure its fertility; moreover, these rites sustain peasant social organization, its specific pattern, its solidarity, and its meaning. In Ayacucho the mountain spirits are said to convert these sacrifices into gold and silver tribute and transport it to the national government on the coast. Exchange between peasants and mountain spirits is essential. Yet these spirits are neither as destructive nor as evil as the spirit of the mines; nor does ritual appeasement have to be carried out at such a frenetic rate: it is only to overcome misfortune that peasants propitiate the spirits on the days that the miners regularly carry out theirs. Miners' rites are intimately concerned with production, and they are also like rites of misfortune.

It is said that llama herders in the vicinity of the mines have seen Hahuari (the devil figure owner of the mines) carrying mineral ore on teams of llamas and vicunas into the mines at night. The ore is deposited there and found later by the miners, who then excavate and exchange it with their bosses for wages (Nash, 1972). Every night, the Tio works indefatigably in this manner, accumulating vast quantities of mineral so that the wealth of the mines will not be exhausted by the miners (Costas Arguedas, 1961, 2:38–41, 303–4). This is a significant transformation of the exchange circuits outlined above. In those the peasants give gifts to the mountain spirit owner, who converts those gifts into precious metals and hands them over to the government in exchange for feudallike control over the peasants and their resources. This circuit ensures fertility and prosperity; it is based on an ideology of reciprocal gift exchange.

In the mines, however, the miners stand between the spirit owners of nature and the legal owners of the mines, which before the early 1950s were private capitalist enterprises and are now state owned. In effect the extended chain of exchanges in the Andes is this: peasants exchange gifts with the spirit owner; the spirit owner converts these gifts into precious metal; the miners excavate this metal, which they "find" so long as they perform rites of gift exchange with spirit; the miners' labor, which is embodied in the tin ore, is sold as a commodity to the legal owners and employers; these last sell the ore on the international commodity market. Thus, reciprocal gift exchanges end as commodity exchanges; standing between the devil and the state, the miners mediate this transformation. This circuit ensures barrenness and death instead of fertility and prosperity. It is based on the transformation of reciprocity into commodity exchange.

The spirit owner of the mines may be grotesquely virile, sometimes sculptured with a giant penis. He is greedy and grasping. The miners, however, are exposed to loss of virility and to death from the ire of the spirit, which seems beyond appeasement. It is impossible to keep or save wages, just as it is impossible for the legal owners not to accumulate capital. There is a fundamental dispute over who owns the mines, the devil figure or the legal owners, yet in important ways they represent one another.

The miners may so fetishize their oppressive situation that they take out their hostility on the devil statues that so graphically embody their despair. Some miners may even try to destroy him. Nash cites the history of a novice miner who worked exceptionally hard for seven months only to lose all his savings. He became terribly tired and disconsolate, began falling down often, and said that he was tired of life and could no longer work as before. During a work break he suddenly tore apart a statue of the devil and threw its head against a rock. His coworkers took fright. They told him that he could die, to which he replied, "No, no. I'm not going to die now. These are illusions. I do not believe in these things. It's not going to happen to me. I have destroyed the Tio many times and nothing happened." That afternoon he was killed in an elevator accident (1972: 227–28).

In the peasant community of Kaata blood is a symbol of claim to land. An important part of agricultural ritual is the sprinkling of the earth with blood, which invigorates the land with the principle of life as well as registers kinship with it. The gods in pre-Hispanic times provided the fruits of the earth, writes Trimborn, but not without active propitiation which most commonly took the form of sacrifice. Where fertility was desired, the most favored offering was blood (1969:126). A Bolivian miner told Nash what happened when three men died in the mine of San José: "The men were convinced that the Tio [the spirit of the mines] was thirsty for blood. A delegation requested the administration to give them free time for a *ch'alla*, a collection was taken and three llamas were purchased. A *yatiri* [shaman] was hired to conduct the ceremony. All the miners offered blood to the Tio, saying, 'Take this! Don't eat my blood'" (1972:229–30). The ultimate sacrifice is the miner himself. To deny reciprocity is to admit the specter of being consumed by the gods, yet what can the miners do, given the structure of exchange in which they are inserted? How can they successfully mediate the transformation of reciprocity into commodity exchange, the account books of which are balanced by one party only, the legal owners, and are written in blood and capital?

Whereas the ultimate sacrifice is the miner himself, the spirit owner of the mines is the commodity that the miners excavate: he is the tin. In the peasant situation the spirit owners are not sculptured, and they are sharply differentiated from the products the fertility of which is desired. These products, such as the llamas in Q'ero, may be represented by small stone figurines, but these figurines are tiny and not fearsome. In the mines the spirit owner is at the same time both the product and the fetishized, often larger than human, figure that stands sculptured in the clay of the mines, with lumps of tin ore for eyes, crystal or glass for teeth, and a gaping hole for a mouth. The mountain spirits in peasant communities are alive with movement; they appear as riders on horseback, as condors, or as lightning that flashes from stones, and so on. They appear and disappear. In the mines the spirit owner is not only personified but also actually sculptured, immobile, embedded in clay rock. Entombed in the mine, he is, for all his lifelike appearance, redolent of the message of death. Expressed in the humanoid appearance, his reality presages the end to all reality as he steps forth in the status of commodity.

Commmodity exchange and gift exchange cannot easily be mediated, for they are utterly opposed. The market, not ritual, mediates the exchange by the miners of tin ore for wages; the rhythm of that exchange is that, not of flutes and drums, but of the fluctuations in the struggle for profit in the world commodity markets. In a gift exchange the giver remains embodied in the good transferred, and the exchange is not for profit. But on receiving his wage, the miner must, by law, forfeit all control of and claim to the ore. Alienability and profitability take over, and the commodity rises transcendent, freed from the strictures that in a use-value economy bind goods to people, ritual, and cosmology. As a liberated object, the commodity stands over its subjects, evolving its own rites and its own cosmology.

Yet there is more than enough ambiguity in the miners' rites to indicate that their culture is far from being completely molded by the impetus of commodity production. The Indians have entered the mines, but they remain as foreign bodies within the capitalist framework. Capitalist hegemony is incomplete, and the continuity of production requires violence and compulsion. The working class has not as yet acquired the tradition or education that looks upon capitalism as a self-evident law of nature. As Georg Lukács points out, there is an enormous difference between the situation in which the commodity has become the universal structuring principle and the situation in which the commodity exists as but one form among many that regulate the metabolism of human society. This difference, he notes, has repercussions on the nature and validity of the category of the commodity itself: the commodity as a universal principle has different manifestations from those of the commodity as a particular, isolated, nondominant phenomenon (1971:85). Although the rise of the commodity implies the decomposition of Indian structuring principles, in the mines, at least, it has not as yet achieved more than a strange antithesis to itself. Moreover, the miners are very far from decreeing their state as a natural one: instead, they see it as totally abnormal. "Every entry into the mines," says the miner Juan Rojas, "is like a burial. And every leaving into fresh air is like a rebirth" (Rojas and Nash, 1976:110). All the gestures of sacred communion, which are appropriate to life outside of the workplace, are taboo inside it; there, the symbols of evil and sorcery have preeminence.

The devil is also the Tio, the uncle; as Paredes and others maintain, the Hahuari or Supay is as much a congenial as a frightening figure. The Earthmother is still on the side of the miners; she struggles with them to preserve new life within the old metaphysical system of dialectical dualities. The very fear that the miners have of the devil, as well as the symbolic context that he occupies, indicates the persistence of the belief that humans and nature are one. In order to preserve fecundity no single element can profit at the expense of the rest by converting the totality into a means to something other than itself. Many miners, including political militants, insist that the rites in the mines must be continued; they serve as forums for the development of critical consciousness and socialist transformation (Nash, 1971:231–32).

With the conquest, Indian culture absorbed but also transformed Christian mythology. The image of the spirit of evil and the mythology of redemption were refashioned to give poetic expression to the needs of the oppressed. Christian symbols came to mediate the conflict between opposed civilizations and between conflicting ways of apprehending reality. With the advance of capitalist production, as in the mines today, the contested terrain has expanded to include the meaning of work and things promoted by the capitalist vision of the world, especially its fetishization of commodities and devitalization of persons.

Against this mythic structure the miners have developed their rites of production. These rites refashion the symbolism of comodity production so that a distinct form of poetic wisdom and political insight comes to bear. They bear testimony to a consciousness that creatively resists the reification that capitalism imposes, just as the miners' trade union and twentieth-century political history furnish ample proof of their socialist militance.

The miners' rites bear the legacy of tradition: a preestablished way of seeing the world that structures new experiences. These new experiences transform tradition; yet, even so, this very transformation registers the meaning of the present in terms of history. The miners' rites serve, therefore, as the condensed expression of mythological history, composed of tensions transcending that history. "Is it not the character of myths," queries Lévi-Strauss, "to evoke a suppressed past and to apply it, like a grid, upon the present in the hope of discovering a sense in which the two aspects of his own reality man is confronted with—the historic and the structural—coincide?" (1967b:7).

The *ch'alla* in the mines is not merely a carry-over from peasant rites of production. Although the miners envisage tin ore as though it were responsive to peasant principles of fertility, production, and exchange, the fact is that the ore is located in a vastly different set of social relations and social meanings. Therefore the miners' *ch'alla* cannot reflect the principle of reciprocal exchange as it occurs in peasant communities. Nevertheless, the miners' *ch'alla* represents the ethical imperative of reciprocity, which is denied by the ideology of commodity exchange. The consciousness that is expressed indicates the tension that is imposed by this denial—and the need to overturn the history of conquest. The contrasting images of the Earthmother and the devil and the transformation of the *ch'alla* from peasant to proletarian production stand as keys to the unlocking of that dialectic, the tension of which will be resolved only when a truly reciprocal praxis allows mankind to control the products of its labor as much as those of its imagination.

In the mines, the apotheosis of commodities engenders the apotheosis of evil in the fetish of the spirit owner of the mine. With this reaction to capitalist development, indigenous iconography and ritual portray the human significance of market exchange as an evil distortion of gift exchange and not as a self-evident law of nature—bearing witness to Arguedas's rejoinder to the culture of imperialism that man truly possesses a soul, and that this is very rarely negotiable.

Conclusion

To interpret the social experience reflected in folk magic as that experience changes with a group's loss of control over its means of production is the hazardous task that I have set out to do. It is also a necessary task; no matter how painstaking we are in charting the chronology of history's great events, demography, the network of trade, and the transparent facticity of material infrastructures, we will remain blind to history's great lesson both for society and for the future unless we include the imagination of power as well as the power of the collective imagination.

As people make history, so it is made within a historically shaped imagination seized with the human significance given to otherwise mute things. Marxists, especially, cannot forget the crucial subtitle to *Capital*—namely, *A Critique of Political Economy*. With this focus, Marx's work strategically opposes the objectivist categories and culturally naive self-acceptance of the reified world that capitalism creates, a world in which economic goods known as commodities and, indeed, objects themselves appear not merely as things in themselves but as determinants of the reciprocating human relations that form them. Read this way, the commodity labor-time and value itself become not merely historically relative categories but social constructions (and deceptions) of reality. The critique of political economy demands the deconstruction of that reality and the critique of that deception.

Impugning reification and the fetishism of commodities, the beliefs and rites discussed in this book facilitate this task of critical deconstruction because they unmask something crucial about the human reality that is concealed by the mysticism of commodity culture. But insight of this order is merely a beginning; as a stage in historical development it can quickly be devoured by the intensification of commodity production, and idealism cannot be fought by ideals alone, although without ideals there is no hope at all. Furthermore, because a nonfetishized mode of understanding human relations and society is necessary for human liberation, both precommodity and commodity fetishism stand condemned.

Between the art of the imagination and the art of politics intervenes a vast range of practices, especially political organizing, and the conjuncture in which the collective imagination ferments with the appropriate social circumstance to give rise to liberating practice is notoriously rare. Yet only with this conjuncture can the multiple ambiguities in the collective mentality acquire a socially creative and clear expression, and the forces of repression are vigilant and almost always too powerful. Until that conjuncture takes place, the politics implied in the culture of folk magic works in several directions simultaneously.

If the phantoms of the spirit world sustain solidarity and uphold the ideal of equality among the oppressed, they can also create divisions or a crippling conformism. Frantz Fanon writes:

> The atmosphere of myth and magic frightens me and so takes on an undoubted reality. By terrifying me, it integrates me in the traditions and the history of my district or of my tribe, and at the same time it reassures me, it gives me a status, as it were an identification paper. In under-developed countries the occult sphere is a sphere belonging to the community which is entirely under magical jurisdiction. By entangling myself in this inextricable network where actions are repeated with crystalline inevitability, I find the everlasting world which belongs to me, and the perenniality which is thereby affirmed of the world belonging to us. Believe me, the zombies are more terrifying than the settlers. [1967:43]

Yet surely this is exaggerated—a blind belief in the blind belief of the primitive. The atmosphere of myth and magic takes on a reality, to be sure, but what sort of reality? It is not as much an actual reality as a possible and hypothetical one. It is a reality in which faith and skepticism easily coexist. Ritual endorses the truth of this hypothetical reality; but outside of ritual other realities intervene and the mind finds no tension between spiritual and secular explanations.

The gods and spirits are always and everywhere ambivalent, and the devil is the archsymbol of ambivalence. He does not so much determine specific actions as provide the shadows and patterns with which people create interpretations. As we have seen, these creations by no means spell conformity to the status quo. Furthermore, in the colonial situation the zombies or spirits change to reflect the new situation rather than the precolonial spirit world. They are as dynamic and as everchanging as the network of social relations that encompasses the believers, and their meaning mediates those changes. The devil in the Cauca plantations as much as in the Bolivian mines grew out of precolonial indigenous systems of belief, West African and (preincaic) Andean, as those systems responded to conquest, Christianity, and capitalist development. This devil is not unambiguously terrifying. He is not more terrifying than the settlers.

The religion of the oppressed can assuage that oppression and adapt people to it, but it can also provide resistance to that oppression. In trying to comprehend the coexistence of those opposed tendencies, we must again return to the social significance of precapitalist fetishism, which for all its fantasies does not disguise economic relations as relations between things in themselves, with their roots concealed in human reciprocity. The originality of the colonial context, Fanon notes, "is that economic reality, inequality and the immense difference of ways of life never come to mask the human realities" (1967:30). In the political and the armed struggle, to confuse the realities of the phantasmic and the corporeal is to court disaster. But the former illuminates the latter, giving voice and direction to the course of struggle. "The native discovers reality and transforms it into the pattern of his customs, into the practice of violence and into his plan for freedom" (Ibid.:45). The plantation workers in the southern Cauca Valley no longer believe that their bosses believe in sorcery, whereas the serfs and peons in the *haciendas* in the surrounding mountains correctly perceive the credulity of their masters on this issue. The plantation workers learn to conduct the class struggle in modern terms rather than through sorcery, but they do so within a vision that is informed by the fantastic creations that emerge from the clash between use-value and exchange-value orientations. The rites to the devil figure by the Bolivian miners manifest this same clash, and these same miners are in the forefront of the class struggle. Their magical rites stimulate the vision and sustain the morale upon which that struggle depends. "This tradition inside the mountain must be continued," says a union leader, "because there is no communication more intimate, more sincere, or more beautiful that the moment of the *ch'alla*, the moment when the workers chew coca together and it is offered to the Tio" (Nash, 1972:231–32). In this communion, both as intense human interexperience and as a pointed statement about injustice and the actual political situation, critical consciousness acquires its form and vigor. "There they give voice to all the problems they have, and there is born a new generation so revolutionary that the workers begin thinking of making structural change. This is their university" (Ibid.).

In a myriad of improbable ways, magic and rite can strengthen the critical consciousness that a devastatingly hostile reality forces on the people laboring in the plantations and mines. Without the legacy of culture and without its rhetorical figures, images, fables, metaphors, and other imaginative creations, this consciousness cannot function. Yet it can be made aware of its creative power instead of ascribing that power to its products. Social progress and critical thought are bound to this dialectical task of defetishization. To this end labor exerts itself: to control its material as much as its poetic products, and not be controlled by them. To falter in this struggle is to become enthralled by the fetishes of a patently false consciousness, whose material signs sustain an incomprehensible and mysterious reality—a void, bereft of humanity and of living people engaged in their daily livelihood. The beliefs and rites of the miners and plantation workers regarding the meaning of production defy this reality and fill this void with human concerns, and in this they have inspired some of the mightiest class struggles and poets of our times. In what was virtually his last testament, Pablo Neruda wrote;

> As far as we in particular are concerned, we writers within the tremendously far-flung American region, we listen unceasingly to the call to fill this mighty void with beings of flesh and blood. We are conscious of our duty as fulfillers—at the same time we are faced with the unavoidable task of critical communication within a world which is empty but which is no less full of injustices, punishments, and sufferings because it is empty—and we feel also the responsibility for reawakening the old dreams which sleep in statues of stone in the ruined ancient monuments, in the wide-stretching silence in planetary plains, in dense primeval forests, in rivers which roar like thunder. We must fill with words the most distant places in a dumb continent and we are intoxicated by this task of making

fables and giving names. This is perhaps what is decisive in my own humble case, and if so, my exaggerations or my abundance or my rhetoric would not be anything other than the simplest of events in the daily work of an American. [1974:27–28]

Bibliography

Acosta, Father Joseph de
1880   *The Natural and Moral History of the Indies.* (Published, 1588.) Reprinted from the English edition, 1604. Translated by Edward Grimston. Edited by C. R. Markham. 2 vols. London: Hakluyt Society.

Acosta Saignes, Miguel
1962   *Estudios de folklore Venezolano.* Estudios de etnología de Venezuela. Caracas: Ediciones de la Biblioteca Hespérides.

1967   *Vida de los esclavos negros en Venezuela.* Caracas: Ediciones de la Biblioteca Hespérides.

Adams, Richard N.
1952   *Un analisis de las creencias y prácticas médicas en un pueblo indigena de Guatemala.* Guatemala: Editorial del Ministerio de Educación Pública.

Alberti, Giorgio, and Mayer, Enrique
1974   Reciprocidad andina: ayer y hoy. In *Reciprocidad e intercambio en los andes peruanos,* edited by Giorgio Alberti and Enrique Mayer, pp. 13–36. Lima: Instituto de Estudios Peruanos.

Albo, Javier
1972   Dimánica en la estructura inter-comunitaria de Jesús de Machaca. *América Indigena* 32:773–816.

1974–76 La paradoja aymara: solidaridad y faccionalismo? *Estudios Andinos* 4:67–110.

Arboleda, Gustavo
1956   *Historia de Cali.* 3 vols. Cali, Colombia: Biblioteca de la Universidad del Valle.

Arboleda, J. R.
1950   The Ethnohistory of the Colombian Negroes. M.A. thesis, Northwestern University.

Arboleda, Sergio
1972   *La republica en américa española.* Bogotá: Biblioteca Banco Popular.

Ardener, Edwin
1970   Witchcraft, Economics, and the Continuity of Belief. In *Witchcraft, Confessions and Accusations,* edited by Mary Douglas, pp. 141–60. London: Tavistock.

Arguedas, José María
1966   *Dioses y hombres de Huarochirí: narración quechua recogida por Francisco de Avila.* Translated by J. M. Arguedas. Lima.

1975   *Formación de una cultura nacional indoamericana.* Mexico, D.F.: Siglo Veintiuno.

Aristotle
1962   *The Politics.* Translated by T. A. Sinclair. Harmondsworth: Penguin Books.

Arriaga, Pablo José
1968   *The Extirpation of Idolatry in Peru.* (Published, 1621.) Translated by L. Clark Keating. Lexington: University of Kentucky Press.

ASOCAÑA (Associación Nacional de Cultivadores de Cana de Azúcar)
1965   *Development of the Colombian Sugar Industry.* Cali, Colombia.

Bandelier, Adolph F.
1910   *The Islands of Titicaca and Koati.* New York: Hispanic Society of America.

Bastide, Roger
1971   *African Civilizations in the New World.* Translated by P. Green. New York: Harper and Row.

Bastien, Joseph W.
1978   *Mountain of the Condor: Metaphor and Ritual in an
        Andean Ayllu.* American Ethnological Society. Mono-
        graph 64. St. Paul: West Publishing.

Baudin, Louis
1961   *A Socialist Empire: The Incas of Peru.* Princeton: D. Van
        Nostrand.

Benjamin, Walter
1969   Theses on the Philosophy of History. In *Illuminations.*
        Edited by Hannah Arendt, pp. 253–64. New York:
        Schocken Books.

Bergquist, Charles
1976   The Political Economy of the Colombian Presidential
        Election of 1897. *Hispanic American Historical Review*
        56:1–30.

Berlin, Isaiah
1977   *Vico and Herder: Two Studies in the History of Ideas.*
        New York: Vintage Books.

Blake, William
1968   *The Poetry and Prose of William Blake.* Edited by David
        V. Erdman. Commentary by Harold Bloom, 4th printing,
        revised. Garden City, N.Y.: Doubleday.

Borrego Pla, Maria del Carmen
1973   *Palenques de negros en Cartagena de Indias a fines del
        Siglo XVII.* No. 216. Seville: Escuela de Estudios His-
        pano-Americanos de Sevilla.

Bosman, William
1967   *A New and Accurate Description of the Coast of
        Guinea.* (Published, 1704.) New York: Barnes & Noble.

Bowser, Frederick P.
1974   *The African Slave in Colonial Peru.* Stanford: Stanford
        University Press.

Briceño, Manuel
1878   *La revolución 1876–1877: recuerdos para la historia.*
        Vol. 1. Bogotá: Imprenta Nueva.

Brinton, Daniel G.
1968   *The Myths of the New World.* Reprint of 3rd edition,
        1896. New York: Haskall House Publishers.

Buechler, Hans C., and Buechler, J. M.
1971   *The Bolivian Aymara.* New York: Holt, Rinehart, and Winston.

Burtt, Edwin Arthur
1954   *The Metaphysical Foundations of Modern Science.* Garden City, N.Y.: Doubleday, Anchor Books.

Cardenal, Ernesto
1973   The Economy of Tahuantinsuyu. In *Homage to the American Indians,* translated by Monique and Carlos Altschul, pp. 35–43. Baltimore: Johns Hopkins University Press.

Carrasco, Pedro
1957   Tarascan Folk Religion. In *Synoptic Studies of Mexican Culture.* Middle American Research Institute, Publication No. 17, pp. 1–63. New Orleans: Tulane University Press.

Castro Pozo, H.
1924   *Nuestra comunidad indígena.* Lima: Editorial El Lucero.

Chandler, David Lee
1972   Health and Slavery: A Study of Health Conditions among Negro Slaves in the Vice-Royalty of New Granada and its Associated Slave Trade, 1600–1810. Ph.D. dissertation, Tulane University.

Chardon, Carlos E.
1930   *Reconocimiento agropecuario del Valle del Cauca.* San Juan, Puerto Rico.

Chayanov, A. V.
1966   *The Theory of Peasant Economy.* Edited by D. Thorner, B. Kerblay, and R. E. F. Smith. Homewood, Ill.: Irwin.

Cobo, Bernabé
1890–95 *Historia del nuevo mundo.* (Published, 1653.) 4 vols. Seville: Imprenta de E. Rasco.

Codazzi, Augustin
1959   *Jeografía física i politica de las provincias de la Nueva Granada; provincias de Cordoba, Popayán, Pasto, y Tuquerres i segunda parte, informes.* Bogotá: Banco de la Republica.

Cornblit, O.
1970   Society and Mass Rebellion in Eighteenth-Century Peru
        and Bolivia. In *Latin American Affairs*, edited by R. Carr,
        pp. 9–14. St. Anthony's Papers, No. 22, London: Oxford
        University Press.

Correa, Gustavo
1960   El espíritu del mal en Guatemala. In *Nativism and Syn-
        cretism*. Middle American Research Institute, Publica-
        tion No. 19, pp. 41–103. New Orleans: Tulane Univer-
        sity Press.

Costas Arguedas, José Felipe
1961   *Diccionario del folklore Boliviano*. 2 vols. Sucre, Bolivia:
        Universidad Mayor de San Francisco Xavier de Chu-
        quisaca.

CSF (Community Systems Foundation)
1975   Community Experiments in the Reduction of Mal-
        nourishment in Colombia: First Year Progress Report
        (June 30, 1974–June 30, 1975). Mimeographed. Ann Ar-
        bor: Comunity Systems Foundation.

Demetz, Peter
1978   Introduction to *Walter Benjamin. Reflections: Essays,
        Aphorisms, Autobiographical Writings*. Edited by Peter
        Demetz. New York: Harcourt Brace Jovanovich.

Dix, Robert
1967   *Colombia: The Political Dimensions of Change*. New
        Haven: Yale University Press.

Douglas Mary
1966   *Purity and Danger*. Harmondsworth: Penguin Books.

Dumont, Louis
1977   *From Mandeville to Marx: The Genesis and Triumph of
        Economic Ideology*. Chicago: University of Chicago
        Press.

Durnin, J. V., and Passmore, R.
1967   *Energy, Work, and Leisure*. London: Heineman Educa-
        tional Books.

Duviols, Pierre
1971   *La Lutte contre les religions autochtones dans le Pérou
        colonial*. Paris: Institut français d'Etudes andines.

Earls, John
1969   The Organization of Power in Quechua Mythology. *Journal of the Steward Anthropological Society* 1:63–82.

Eder, Phanor J.
1913   *Colombia.* New York: Charles Scribner's Sons.

1959   *El Fundador.* Bogotá: Antares.

Eliade, Mircea
1959   *Cosmos and History: The Myth of the Eternal Return.* New York: Harper and Row, Harper Torchbooks.

1971   *The Forge and the Crucible.* New York and Evanston: Harper and Row, Harper Torchbooks.

Estado del Cauca
1859   *Mensaje del gobernador del estado del Cauca a la legislatura de 1859.* Popayán, Colombia.

Estados Unidos de Colombia
1875   *Anuario estadístico de Colombia.* Bogotá: Medardo Rivas.

Evans-Pritchard, E. E.
1933   The Intellectualist (English) Interpretation of Magic. *Bulletin of the Faculty of Arts* (University of Egypt) 1:282–311.

1934   Lévy-Bruhl's Theory of Primitive Mentality. *Bulletin of the Faculty of Arts* (University of Egypt) 2:1–36.

1940   *The Nuer.* Oxford: Oxford University Press.

1965   *Theories of Primitive Religion.* Oxford: Oxford University Press.

Fals Borda, Orlando
1969   *Subversion and Social Change in Colombia.* New York: Columbia University Press.

Fanon, Frantz
1967   *The Wretched of the Earth.* Translated by C. Farrington. Harmondsworth: Penguin Books.

Fedesarrollo
1976   *Las industrias azucareras y panaleras en Colombia.* Bogotá: Editorial Presencia.

Forbes, David
1870   On the Aymara Indians of Bolivia and Peru. *The Journal of the Ethnological Society of London,* new series, 2:193–305.

Foster, George
1960–61 Interpersonal Relations in Peasant Society. *Human Organization* 19:174–78.

1965   Peasant Society and the Image of the Limited Good. *American Anthropologist* 67:293–315.

García, Evaristo
1898   *El platano en Colombia y particularmente en el Valle de Cauca.* Cali, Colombia: República de Colombia, Impr. de E. Palacios.

Garcilaso de la Vega
1966   *Royal Commentaries of the Incas and General History of Peru.* (Vol. 1 first published, 1609; vol. 2 first published, 1616–1617.) Translated by H. V. Livermore. Austin: University of Texas Press.

Genovese, Eugene D.
1974   *Roll, Jordan, Roll: The World the Slaves Made.* New York: Pantheon Books.

Gilhodes, Pierre
1970   Agrarian Struggles in Colombia. In *Agrarian Problems and Peasant Movements in Latin America,* edited by R. Stavenhagen, pp. 407–52. Garden City, N.Y.: Doubleday, Anchor Books.

Gilmer, Nancy Caldwell
1952   Huarochirí in the Seventeenth Century: The Persistence of Native Religion in Colonial Peru. M.A. thesis, Department of Anthropology, University of California.

Gilmore, Robert L.
1967   Nueva Granada's Socialist Mirage. *Hispanic America Historical Review* 36, no. 2:190–210.

Giménez Fernandez, Manuel
1947   *Las doctrinas populistas en la independencia de Hispano-América.* Seville: Escuela de Estudios Hispano-Americanos de Sevilla.

Gobernador del Cauca

1915   *Informe del gobernador del Cauca a la asamblea departmental.* Popayán, Colombia.

1919   *Informe del gobernador del Cauca a la asamblea departmental.* Popayán, Colombia.

1922   *Informe del gobernador del Cauca a la asamblea departmental.* Popayán, Colombia.

Hamilton, Colonel John Potter

1827   *Travels through the Interior Provinces of Colombia.* 2 vols. London: J. Murray.

Hanke, Lewis

1956   *The Imperial City of Potosí.* The Hague: Nijhoff.

Harrison, J. P.

1951   The Colombian Tobacco Industry from Government Monopoly to Free Trade: 1778–1876. Ph.D. dissertation, University of California.

1952   The Evolution of the Colombian Tobacco Trade to 1875. *Hispanic American Historical Review* 32:163–74.

Helguera, J. Leon

1971   Coconuco: datos y documentos para la historia de una gran hacienda caucana, 1832, 1842, y 1876. *Anuario colombiano de historia social y de la cultura* 5:189–203. Bogotá.

Helguera, J. Leon, and Lee López, Fray Alberto

1967   La exportación de esclavos en la Nueva Granada. *Archivos* 1:447–59. Bogotá.

Hernando Blamori, Clemente

1955   *La conquista de los españoles y el teatro indígena americano.* Tucumán, Argentina: Universidad National de Tucumán.

Herskovits, Melville J.

1958   *The Myth of the Negro Past.* Boston: Beacon Press.

Hesse, Mary

1963   *Models and Analogies in Science.* London and New York: Sheed and Ward.

Hill, Christopher
1969   *Reformation to Industrial Revolution.* 2nd ed. Harmondsworth: Penguin Books.

1975   *The World Turned Upside Down.* Harmondsworth: Penguin Books.

Holmer, Nils M., and Wassén, S. Henry
1953   The Complete Mu-Igala in Picture Writing: A Native Record of a Cuna Indian Medicine Song. *Etnologiska Studier* 21.

Holton, Isaac
1857   *New Granada: Twenty Months in the Andes.* New York: Harper and Brothers.

Hook, Sidney
1933   *Towards an Understanding of Karl Marx: A Revolutionary Interpretation.* London: Victor Gollancz.

Instituto de Parcelaciónes, Colonización, y Defensa Forestal
1950   *Informe del gerente, 1949–50.* Bogotá.

Isbell, Billie Jean
1974   Parentesco andino y reciprocidad. Kukaq: los que nos aman. In *Reciprocidad e intercambio en los andes peruanos,* edited by Giorgio Alberti and Enrique Mayer, pp. 110–52. Lima: Instituto de Estudios Peruanos.

Jacob, Margaret C.
1976   *The Newtonians and the English Revolution: 1689–1720.* Ithaca: Cornell University Press.

Jameson, Fredric
1971   *Marxism and Form.* Princeton: Princeton University Press.

Jaramillo Uribe, Jamie
1968   *Ensayos sobre historia social colombiana.* Bogotá: Biblioteca Universitaria de Cultura Colombiana.

Jayawardena, Chandra
1968   Ideology and Conflict in Lower Class Communities. *Comparative Studies in Society and History* 10:413–46.

Katz, Friederich
1972   *The Ancient American Civilizations.* Translated by K. M. Lois Simpson. New York: Praeger.

King, James Ferguson
1939   Negro Slavery in the Viceroyalty of New Granada. Ph.D.
         dissertation, University of California.

Klein, Herbert
1969   *Parties and Political Change in Bolivia: 1880–1952.*
         Cambridge: Cambridge University Press.

Knight, Rolf
1972   *Sugar Plantations and Labour Patterns in the Cauca
         Valley, Colombia.* Department of Anthropology, Univer-
         sity of Toronto Anthropological Series, No. 12.

Korsch, Karl
1971   Introduction to Capital. In *Three Essays on Marxism,* ed-
         ited by Karl Korsch, pp. 38–59. London: Pluto Press.

Kubler, George
1963   The Quechua in the Colonial World. In *Handbook of
         South American Indians,* edited by Julian Steward. Vol.
         2, pp. 331–410. New York: Cooper Square Publishers.

LaBarre, Weston
1948   *The Aymara Indians of the Lake Titicaca Plateau,
         Bolivia.* Memoir series, No. 68. Menasha, Wisconsin:
         American Anthropological Association.

LaFarge, Oliver
1947   *Santa Eulalia: The Religion of a Cuchumatan Town.*
         Chicago: University of Chicago Press.

Lea, Henry Charles
1908   *The Inquisition in the Spanish Dependencies.* New
         York: Macmillan.

Lévi-Strauss, Claude
1964   Reciprocity: The Essence of Social Life. In *The Family:
         Its Structure and Function,* edited by R. L. Coser. New
         York: St. Martin's Press.

1967a   *Structural Anthropology.* Garden City, N.Y.: Doubleday,
         Anchor Books.

1967b   *Scope of Anthropology.* London: Jonathan Cape.

Lockhart, James
1968   *Spanish Peru: 1532–1560.* Madison: University of
         Wisconsin Press.

Lombardi, J. V.
1971   *The Decline and Abolition of Negro Slavery in Vene-*
        zuela, 1820–1854. Westport, Conn.: Greenwood Publish-
        ing.

Lukács, Georg
1971   *History and Class Consciousness.* Translated by Rodney
        Livingstone. London: Merlin Press.

Madsen, William
1960   Christo-Paganism: A Study of Mexican Religious Syncre-
        tism. In *Nativism and Syncretism.* Middle America Re-
        search Institute, Publication No. 19, pp. 105–79. New
        Orleans: Tulane University Press.

1969   *The Virgin's Children: Life in an Aztec Village Today.*
        New York: Greenwood Press.

Malinowski, B.
1965   *Coral Gardens and Their Magic.* 2 vols. Bloomington: In-
        diana University Press.

Mancini, S.
1954   Tenencia y uso de la tierra por la industria azúcarera del
        Valle del Cauca. *Acta Agronomica* (Facultad de Agron-
        omía Palmira, Colombia) vol. 4, no. 1.

Marcuse, Herbert
1978   *The Aesthetic Dimension: Toward A Critique of Marx-*
        ist Aesthetics. Boston: Beacon Press.

Mariategui, José Carlos
1971   *Seven Interpretive Essays on Peruvian Reality.* Austin:
        University of Texas Press.

Marx, Karl
1967   *Capital: A Critique of Political Economy.* 3 vols. New
        York: International Publishers.

1973   *Grundrisse: Foundations of the Critique of Political*
        Economy. Translated by Martin Niclaus. Harmonds-
        worth: Penguin Books in association with New Left Re-
        view.

Marx, Karl, and Engels, F.
1970   *The German Ideology.* New York: International Pub-
        lishers.

Mauss, Marcel
1967   *The Gift.* Translated by Ian Cunnison. New York: Norton.

Medina, José Toribio
1889   *Historia del tribunal del santo oficio de la inquisición en Cartagena de las Indias.* Santiago, Chile: Imprenta Elzeviriana.

Meiklejohn, Norman
1968   The Observance of Negro Slave Legislation in Colonial Nueva Granada. Ph.D. dissertation, Columbia University.

Mercado, Ramon
1853   *Memorias sobre los acontecimientos del sur de la Nueva Granada durante la administración del 7 de marzo de 1849.* Bogotá: Imprenta Imparcial.

Métraux, Alfred
1934   Contribution au folk-lore Audin. *Journal de la Société des Americanistes de Paris* 26:67–102.

1969   *The History of the Incas.* New York: Schocken.

Michelet, Jules
1971   *Satanism and Witchcraft.* New York: Citadel Press.

Millones Santa Gadea, Luis
1964   Un movimiento nativista del Siglo XVI: el Taki Onqoy. *Revista peruana de cultura* 3:134–40.

Mishkin, Bernard
1963   The Contemporary Quechua. In *Handbook of South American Indians,* edited by Julian Steward. Vol. 2, pp. 411–70. New York: Cooper Square Publishers.

Molina de Cuzco, Cristóbal de
1943   *Relación de las fabulas y ritos de las Incas, 1573.* Los Pequeños Grandes Libros de Historia Americana. Series 1, vol. 4. Lima: D. Miranda.

Monast, J. E.
1969   *On les croyait chrétiens: les aymaras.* Paris: Les Editions du Cerf.

Monsalve, Diego
1927   *Colombian cafetera.* Barcelona: Artes Graficas.

Moore, Barrington, Jr.
1967   *Social Origins of Dictatorship and Democracy.* Boston:
        Beacon Press.

Morúa, Martin De
1946   *Historia del origin y geneologia real de los reyes Incas
        del Peru.* (Published, 1590.) Biblioteca Missional His-
        pánica. Madrid: C. Bermeto.

Mosquera, Tomas Cipriano de
1853   *Memoir on the Physical and Political Geography of New
        Granada.* New York: T. Dwight.

Murra, John
1956   The Economic Organization of the Inca State. Ph.D. dis-
        sertation, University of Chicago.

1968   An Aymara Kingdom in 1567. *Ethnohistory* 15:115–51.

Nachtigall, Horst
1966   Ofrendas de llamas en la vida ceremonial de los pastores
        de la puna de Moquegua (Peru) y de la puna de Atacama
        (Argentina) y consideraciónes historico-culturales sobre
        la ganaderia indígena. *Actas y Memorias* 36 Congreso In-
        ternacional de Americanistas, Seville, 1964.

Nash, June
1970   Mitos y costumbres en las minas nacionalizadas de
        Bolivia. *Estudios Andinos* 1, no. 3:69–82.

1972   The Devil in Bolivia's Nationalized Tin Mines. *Science
        and Society* 36, no. 2:221–33.

1976   Basilia. In *Dos mujeres indigenas.* June Nash and Man-
        uel María Rocca. Antropología Social Series, vol. 14, pp.
        1–130. Mexico, D.F.: Instituto Indigenísta Inter-
        americano.

Needham, Joseph
1956   *Science and Civilization in China.* Vol. 2, *History of Sci-
        entific Thought.* Cambridge: Cambridge University
        Press.

Neruda, Pablo
1974   *Toward the Splendid City: Hacia la ciudad espléndida.*
        Nobel Lecture. New York: Farrar, Strauss and Giroux.

248   *Bibliography*

Nuñez Del Prado, Oscar
1965   Aspects of Andean Native Life. In *Contemporary Cultures and Societies of Latin America*, edited by D. B. Heath and R. N. Adams, pp. 102–21. New York: Random House.

1968   Una cultura como respuesta de adaptación al medio Andino. *Actas y Memorias* 37 Congreso Internacional de Americanistas, Buenos Aires, 1966.

Nuñez Del Prado B., Juan Victor
1974   The Supernatural World of the Quechua of Southern Peru As Seen from the Community of Qotobama. In *Native South Americans*, edited by P. Lyon, pp. 238–50. Boston: Little, Brown.

Ollman, Bertell
1971   *Alienation: Marx's Concept of Man in Capitalist Society.* Cambridge: Cambridge University Press.

Ortega, Alfredo
1932   *Ferrocarriles Colombianos.* Vol. 3. Biblioteca De Historia Nacional, vol. 47. Bogotá: Imprenta Nacional.

Ortiz, Fernando
1921   Los cabildos Afro-Cubanos. *Revista Bimestre Cubana* 16:5–39.

Ossio A., Juan
1973   *Ideología mesiánica del mundo andino: antología de Juan Ossio A.* Colección Biblioteca de Antropología. Lima: Imprenta Prado Pastor.

Otero, Gustavo Adolfo
1951   *La piedra mágica.* Mexico, D.F.: Instituto Indigenista Interamericano.

Palau, E.
1889   *Memoria sobre el cultivo del cacao, del café, y del té.* Bogotá.

Palmer, Colin
1975   Religion and Magic in Mexican Slave Society. In Stanley L. Engerman and Eugene Genovese, *Race and Slavery in the Western Hemisphere: Quantitative Studies*, pp. 311–28. Princeton: Princeton University Press.

Palomino Flores, S.
1970   El sistema de oposiciónes in la comunidad Sarahua. Tesis
        Bachiller, Ciencias Antropologicas, Universidad Nacio-
        nal de San Cristobal de Huamanga, Ayacucho, Peru.

Paredes, M. Rigoberto
1920   *Mitos, supersticiónes y supervivencias populares de
        Bolivia.* La Paz: Arno Hermanos.

Parsons, James
1968   *Antioqueño Colonization in Western Colombia.* 2nd edi-
        tion, revised. Berkeley and Los Angeles: University of
        California Press.

Patiño, Hernando
1975   La lucha por la democracía y la nueva cultura en el seno
        de las facultades de agronomía e instituticiónes académi-
        cas similares. In *La tierra para él que la trabaja.* Bogotá:
        Asociación Colombiana de Ingenieros Agronomos, Edi-
        torial Punto y Coma.

Pavy, David
1967   The Negro in Western Colombia. Ph.D. dissertation,
        Tulane University.

Pérez, Felipe
1862   *Jeografía física i política del estado del Cauca.* Bogotá:
        Imprenta de la Nación.

Phelan, John Leddy
1967   *The Kingdom of Quito.* Madison: University of Wiscon-
        sin Press.

Polanyi, Karl
1957   *The Great Transformation.* Boston: Beacon Press.

Pons, François de
1806   *A Voyage to the Eastern Part of Terra Firma or the Span-
        ish Main in South America during the Years 1801, 1802,
        1803 and 1804.* Vol. 1. New York: I. Riley.

Posada, Eduardo, and Restrepo Canal, Carlos
1933   *La esclavitud en Colombia, y leyes de manumisión.*
        Bogotá: Imprenta nacional.

Price, Thomas J., Jr.
1955   Saints and Spirits: A Study of Differential Acculturation

in Colombian Negro Communities. Ph.D. dissertation, Northwestern University.

Quispe M., Ulpiano
1968   La Herranza de Choque-Huarcaya y Huancasancos. Tesis Bachiller, Universidad Nacional de San Cristobal de Huamanga, Ayacucho, Peru.

Radin, Paul
1957   *Primitive Man as a Philosopher.* New York: Dover.

Reichel-Dolmatoff, Gerardo
1961   Anthropomorphic Figurines from Colombia: Their Magic and Art. In *Essays in Pre-Colombian Art and Archaeology,* edited by Samuel K. Lothrop, pp. 229–41, 493–95. Cambridge: Harvard University Press.

Rippy, J. Fred
1931   *The Capitalists and Colombia.* New York: Vanguard.

Robbins, Lionel
1935   *An Essay on the Nature and Significance of Economic Science.* 2nd ed. London: Macmillan.

Rojas, Juan, and Nash, June
1976   *He agotado mi vida en la mina: una historia de vida.* Buenos Aires: Ediciónes Nueva Visión.

Roll, Eric
1973   *A History of Economic Theory.* London: Faber and Faber.

Rothlisberger, Ernst
1963   *El Dorado.* Bogotá: Publicaciónes del Banco de la Republica.

Rowe, John
1957   The Incas under Spanish Colonial Institutions. *Hispanic American Historical Review* 37, no. 2: 155–99.

1960   The Origins of Creator Worship amongst the Incas. In *Culture and History: Essays in Honour of Paul Radin,* edited by Stanley Diamond, pp. 408–29. New York: Columbia University Press.

1963   Inca Culture at the Time of the Spanish Conquest. In *Handbook óf Southern American Indians,* edited by Julian Steward. Vol. 2, pp. 183–330. New York: Cooper Square Publishers.

Rudwin, Maximilian
1959   *The Devil in Legend and Literature.* La Salle, Illinois: Open Court.

Ruskin, John
1925   *The Stones of Venice.* 3 vols. London: George Allen and Unwin.

Safford, Frank
1965   Foreign and National Enterprise in Nineteenth Century Colombia. *Business History Review* 39:503–26.

1972   Social Aspects of Politics in Nineteenth Century Spanish America: New Granada, 1825–1850. *Journal of Social History* 5:344–70.

Sahlins, Marshall
1972   *Stone Age Economics.* Chicago: Aldine Atherton.

Sandoval, Alonso de, S. J.
1956   *De Instauranda aethiopum salute: el mundo de la esclavitud negra en America.* (Published, 1627.) Bogotá: Empresa Nacional de Publicaciones.

Schenck, Freidrich von
1953   *Viajes por Antioquia en el año de 1880.* Bogotá: Archivo de la economía nacional.

Schmidt, Alfred
1971   *The Concept of Nature in Marx.* London: New Left Books.

Sébillot, Paul
1894   *Les Traveaux publics et les mines dans les superstitions de tous les pays.* Paris: J. Rothschild.

Sender, Ramón J.
1961   *Seven Red Sundays.* New York: Macmillan, Collier Books.

Sendoya, Mariano
n.d.   *Toribio: Puerto Tejada.* Popayán, Colombia: Editorial del Departamento.

Sharon, Douglas
1972   The San Pedro Cactus in Peruvian Folk Healing. In *Flesh of the Gods,* edited by Peter T. Furst. New York: Praeger.

Sharp, William Frederick
1970   Forsaken But for Gold: An Economic Study of Slavery
          and Mining in the Colombian Choco, 1680–1810. Ph.D.
          dissertation, University of North Carolina. (Published as
          *Slavery on the Spanish Frontier: The Colombian Chocó,
          1680–1810.* Norman: University of Oklahoma Press,
          1976.)

Shaw, Carey, Jr.
1941   Church and State in Colombia As Observed by Amer-
          ican Diplomats, 1834–1906. *Hispanic American Histor-
          ical Review* 21:577–613.

Siegel, Morris
1941   Religion in Western Guatemala: A Product of Accultura-
          tion. *American Anthropologist* 43, no. 1:62–76.

Smith, Adam
1967   The History of Astronomy. In *The Early Writings of
          Adam Smith,* edited by J. Ralph Lindgren, pp. 53–108.
          New York: A. M. Kelley.

Spalding, Karen
1967   Indian Rural Society in Colonial Peru: The Example of
          Huarochirí. Ph.D. dissertation, University of California.

Spurr, G. B.; Barac-Nieto, M.; and Maksud, M. G.
1975   Energy Expenditure Cutting Sugar Cane. *Journal of Ap-
          plied Physiology* 39:990–96.

Stein, William
1961   *Hualcan: Life in the Highlands of Peru.* Ithaca: Cornell
          University Press.

Stocking, George W., Jr.
1968   *Race, Culture, and Evolution: Essays in the History of
          Anthropology.* New York: Free Press.

Tambiah, S. J.
1973   Form and Meaning of Magical Acts: A Point of View. In
          Modes of Thought, edited by Robin Horton and Ruth
          Finnegan, pp. 199–229. London: Faber and Faber.

Tawney, R. H.
1958   Foreword to *The Protestant Ethic and the Spirit of Cap-
          italism,* by Max Weber. Translated by Talcott Parsons,
          pp. 1(a)–11. New York: Charles Scribner's Sons.

Tejado Fernandez, Manuel
1954   *Aspectos de la vida social en Cartagena de Indias du-
        rante el seiscientos.* No. 87. Seville: Escuela de Etudios
        Hispano-Americanos de Sevilla.

Thompson, Donald
1960   Maya Paganism and Christianity. In *Nativism and Syn-
        cretism.* Middle American Research Institute, Publica-
        tion No. 19, pp. 1–35. New Orleans: Tulane University
        Press.

Thompson, E. P.
1967   Time, Work-Discipline, and Industrial Capitalism. *Past
        and Present* 38:56–97.

Thompson, J. Eric
1970   *Maya History and Religion.* Norman: University of
        Oklahoma Press.

Thorndike, Lee
1936   Magic, Witchcraft, Astrology, and Alchemy. In *The
        Cambridge Medieval History.* Planned by J. B. Bury. Vol.
        8, pp. 660–87. New York: Macmillan.

Trimborn, Herman
1969   South Central America and the Andean Civilizations.
        In *Pre-Colombian American Religions,* edited by W.
        Krickberg et al., pp. 83–146. Translated by Stanley
        Davis. New York: Holt, Rinehart and Winston.

Tschopik, Harry, Jr.
1968   Magía en Chucuito: los Aymara del Peru. Translated by
        Ávalos de Matos (from the English edition, 1951, The
        Aymara of Chucuito, Peru, vol. 1, Magic. Anthropologi-
        cal Papers of the American Museum of Natural History,
        vol. 44, part 2). Ediciónes Especial, no. 50. Mexico, D.F.:
        Instituto Indígenista Interamericano.

Tschudi, Johann J. von
1852   *Travels in Peru during the Years 1838–1842.* Translated
        by T. Ross. New York: George P. Putnam.

Turner, Victor
1967   *The Forest of Symbols.* Ithaca: Cornell University Press.

Valcarcel, Luis E.
1967   *Etnohistoria del Peru antiguo.* Lima: Universidad Nacio-
          nal Mayor de San Marcos.

Vázquez de Espinosa, Antonio
1948   *Compendium and Description of the West Indies.* Trans-
          lated by Charles Upson Clark. Washington, D.C.:
          Smithsonian Institute.

Vico, Giambattista
1970   *The New Science of Giambattista Vico.* Translated by
          T. J. Bergin and M. H. Fisch from 3rd ed., revised and
          abridged. Ithaca: Cornell University Press.

Vogt, Evon
1969   *Zinacantan: A Maya Community in the Highlands of
          Chiapas.* Cambridge: Harvard University Press.

Wachtel, Nathan
1977   *The Vision of the Vanquished: The Spanish Conquest of
          Peru through Indian Eyes, 1530–1570.* New York: Barnes
          and Noble.

Wassén, S. Henry
1940   An Analogy between a South American and Oceanic
          Myth Motif, and Negro Influence in Darien. *Etnologiska
          Studier* 10:69–79.

Watts, Alan W.
1968   *Myth and Ritual in Christianity.* Boston: Beacon Press.

Weber, Max
1927   *General Economic History.* Translated by Frank H.
          Knight. New York: Greenberg.

1958   *The Protestant Ethic and the Spirit of Capitalism.* Trans-
          lated by Talcott Parsons. New York: Charles Scribner's
          Sons.

Webster, Steven
1972   The Social Organization of a Native Andean Com-
          munity. Ph.D. dissertation, University of Washington,
          Seattle.

West, Robert Cooper
1952   *Colonial Placer Mining in Western Colombia.* Louisiana
          State University Social Science Series, no. 2. Baton
          Rouge, Louisiana: Louisiana State University Press.

White, Robert Blake
1884   Notes on the Aboriginal Races of the Northwestern
        Provinces of South America. *Journal of the An-*
        thropological Institute of Great Britain and Ireland
        13:240–55.

Whitehead, Alfred North
1967   *Adventures of Ideas.* New York: The Free Press.

Williams, Raymond
1973   *The Country and the City.* New York: Oxford University
        Press.

Wisdom, Charles
1940   *The Chorti Indians of Guatemala.* Chicago: University
        of Chicago Press.

Wolf, Eric
1955   Types of Latin American Peasantry: A Preliminary Dis-
        cussion. *American Anthropologist* 57:452–71.

1958   The Virgin of Guadalupe: A Mexican National Symbol.
        American Journal of Folklore 71:34–39.

Wood, G. P.
1962   *Supply and Demand of Cacao in Colombia.* Mim-
        eographed. Bogotá: Universidad Nacional de Colombia,
        Facultad de Agronomía.

Wray, Joseph, and Aguirre, Alfredo
1969   Protein-Calorie Malnutrition in Candelaria: 1. Preva-
        lence, Social and Demographic Causal Factors. *Journal of*
        Tropical Pediatrics 15:76–98.

Zuidema, R. T.
1964   *The Ceque System of Cuzco: The Social Organization of*
        the Capital of the Inca. Leiden: E. J. Brill.

1968   A Visit to God. *Bidragen Tot De Tall, Land en Volken-*
        kunde 124:23–39.

Index